To Beth
Blessings!
In His Love,
Charles Allard
Romans 15:5.6 NIV.

ENCOURAGEMENT FOR THE DAY

Messages of Inspiration and Challenge

CHARLES ALLARD

WESTBOW
PRESS®
A DIVISION OF THOMAS NELSON
& ZONDERVAN

WestBow Press books may be ordered through booksellers or by contacting:

WestBow Press
A Division of Thomas Nelson & Zondervan
1663 Liberty Drive
Bloomington, IN 47403
www.westbowpress.com
844-714-3454

Interior Image Credit: Natalie B. Culler

ISBN: 978-1-6642-6228-7 (sc)
ISBN: 978-1-6642-6229-4 (hc)
ISBN: 978-1-6642-6227-0 (e)

Library of Congress Control Number: 2022905864

Print information available on the last page.

WestBow Press rev. date: 04/11/2022

This book is dedicated to my wife,

Gloria Little Allard,

whose daily devotional life
and commitment to God
has been an inspiration and
encouragement to me throughout
our sixty-three years of marriage.
She is my strongest supporter,
faithful companion,
the wind under my wings,
my steadfast confidant,
trustworthy critic, and
soul mate

PREFACE

I know of no greater need in our world today than encouragement. Everyone needs encouragement. I am grateful for all the people who have encouraged me throughout my life. Without encouragement, I'm not sure where I would be today. That is why the title of this devotional guide is *Encouragement for the Day: Messages of Inspiration and Challenge.*

This guide to a daily encounter with God grew out of twelve years of "Minute Messages" broadcast at random over Eastern NC radio stations WRHT–FM, Morehead City; WMBL–AM, Beaufort; and WBCZ–FM, Greenville, from 1988 to 2000, during and after the years I served as pastor of First Baptist Church, Morehead City, North Carolina from 1982 to 1994.

In those broadcast years, listeners urged me to put the "Minute Messages" into book form, but pastoral responsibilities and other interests took priority. Retirement and the Covid pandemic of 2020–21 have given me time to make this project a reality. My dear friend Dr. George Braswell, retired professor of world religions at Southeastern Baptist Theological Seminary and Campbell University Divinity School, has provided invaluable suggestions, critique, and encouragement. My daughter, Anita Culler, and grandson, Nathan Culler, were especially helpful in reviewing the manuscript and dealing with computer issues. Natalie Culler, my granddaughter, used her art skills to draw the "Prayer Hands." My wife, Gloria, has spent hours reviewing and correcting errors in my manuscript. My children, their spouses, and members of churches I have pastored have urged me to put these messages into print. For all their encouragement, I am deeply grateful.

This devotional guide has been a labor of love. I have grown stronger in my relationship with God through the discipline of putting these messages into book form and reflecting upon them in the process. Each message has a relevant scripture followed by a prayer. All scriptural quotations are from the New International Version.

As an appendix to the daily devotions, you will find a guide for the "Celebration of Advent at Home." While many churches celebrate Advent at Christmas, during public worship, there are additional blessings to celebrating Advent in the privacy of your home with family and friends. You are encouraged to prepare an Advent wreath and weekly light the candles representing hope, peace, joy, love, and Christ. Family members and friends are encouraged to participate in the readings, scripture, and prayer, and share thoughts on each subject.

Much of the material in this devotional guide has been collected over the sixty-one years of my ministry, either as a pastor or missionary. While every attempt has been made to give proper credit where credit is due, I am aware of my inability to identify every source or author mentioned. In no way have I purposely attempted to claim credit for someone else's work. My sincere apologies to anyone I have failed to identify. I am indebted to all those who have impacted my life by their friendship, sermons, teachings, writings, and conversations. I also recognize that when it comes to sharing the gospel, the message is more important than the messenger.

My purpose in compiling these devotional messages is to bring encouragement, inspiration, and challenge to all who desire to grow in their relationship with the Lord. It is my prayer that these messages will enrich your daily encounter with God, enhance your spiritual growth and encourage you to reach others for Christ. To God be the glory!

In His love,
Charles Allard

ACKNOWLEDGMENTS

Scripture quotations taken from the Holy Bible, New International Version (NIV). Copyright © 1973, 1978, 1984, 2011 by Biblica, Inc. © Used by permission. All rights reserved worldwide.

JANUARY 1

PRIORITIES

As a new year begins, we are not promised tomorrow. The Bible says, "Why, you do not even know what will happen tomorrow … If anyone, then, knows the good they ought to do and doesn't do it, it is sin for them" (James 4:14, 17).

Doing today what you know is right is the best way to live. The past is history. The new year is an opportunity. We are here on earth only once. We get it right in this life, or we don't get it right at all. We live by time, deadlines, and schedules. From birth to death, we are all on a countdown for eternity.

Our challenge is to live with purpose and meaning and make the best of our allotted time. Living for Christ and living in Him is the most important thing we can do each day.

Determine today to make every moment count for Christ. Devote yourself to worship, Bible study, prayer, fellowship with God's people, serving others, and witnessing for Christ. God's Word says, "But seek first His Kingdom and His righteousness." If we obey, we will not be preoccupied with ourselves. We will not have to worry about how we will make it in life because the promise from God is "all these things, (earthly needs such as food, drink, clothes, etc.) will be given to you as well" (Matthew 6:33).

God's Word: I was young and now I am old, yet I have never seen the righteous forsaken or their children begging bread (Psalm 37:25).

Prayer: Father, as I begin the new year, help me to use my time wisely and to know that by serving others, I am serving You. Amen.

JANUARY 2

HAPPINESS

Happiness is a state of well-being and contentment. If you ask a sick person to define happiness, he or she would say health. If you ask the ambitious, they will say wealth or power. The overworked man would say rest. The scholar would define happiness as knowledge.

What the dictionary does not tell us about happiness, life does. Happiness is not a goal but a journey toward a goal. It is not in having but in striving. Happiness is not idleness but usefulness. Happiness is a mountain to climb, a river to cross, a disease to conquer, a fear to overcome, being useful, a problem to solve, and work to finish.

We human beings are rarely content with the goal of our striving or the coveted object we thought we just had to have. We are happier when we are working to attain our goal than when we achieve it. Be happy—savor the journey!

God's Word: Whoever gives heed to instruction prospers, and blessed is the one who trusts in the Lord (Proverbs 16:20).

Prayer: Father, teach me to enjoy the journey of life as You direct my paths. Amen.

JANUARY 3

PURPOSE

Emily Dickinson is reported to have lived as a recluse in Amherst, Massachusetts. Her solitary life with all its limited opportunities did not, however, leave her with a cold heart. In her famous poem "If I Can Stop One Heart from Breaking," she spoke of helping at least one person with a broken heart or easing someone's pain or even helping a poor robin return to its nest. Her poem suggests that to avoid living in vain, we must meet a need.

It is essential to examine the purpose of your life. Life is too short to squander it. What contribution will you make to the welfare of humankind? It is a terrible thing to live in vain or have a feeling of uselessness. The truth is you can contribute to the good of society. You can make a difference in someone's life for good. Jesus Christ can put meaning into your life. Christ strengthens us and enables us to live with purpose.

God's Word: For to me, to live is Christ and to die is gain (Philippians 1:21).

Prayer: Father, help me to know the purpose for which I was born. Help me to be helpful to You and bring glory and honor to Your name. Amen.

JANUARY 4

LESSONS FROM A SPIDER

Hiding in a cave, discouraged and defeated, Robert Bruce of Scotland watched a tiny spider weave her web between two rocks. Attaching the web to one rock, the spider was having difficulty reaching the rock on the other side. Bruce watched intently as time after time the spider failed to reach the other rock. Each time she would swing, she would come short of her goal. Bruce started talking to the spider, giving her words of encouragement. He so identified with her efforts that he convinced himself to fight again if the spider would try one more time and succeed. The spider did try again, and this time she made it to the other side. So challenged, Robert Bruce took his men back to the battle, freed Scotland from the enemy, and became its king.

If you have suffered defeat or failure and are tempted to give up, remember the spider that inspired Robert Bruce. Try one more time.

God's Word: So we fix our eyes not on what is seen, but on what is unseen, since what is seen is temporary, but what is unseen is eternal (2 Corinthians 4:18).

Prayer: Father, when I am weak, You are strong. Help me to surrender my weaknesses to You and live in your strength. Amen.

JANUARY 5

GLORY TO GOD

An Austrian composer named Franz Joseph Hayden wrote 104 symphonies, fifty-two piano sonatas, eighty-three string quartets, thirty-eight trios, and many more inspiring pieces of music. Hayden was deeply religious, loved by everyone, and known for his great sense of humor and joy for living.

Hayden credited his cheerful music to his thoughts of God, which filled him with such joy that the music just leaped from his pen. Little wonder that "Papa Hayden," as he was affectionately called, dedicated his music "to the Glory of God." If a man like Hayden could dedicate his music to the glory of God, why can't we dedicate our lives to His glory? When you think of all that God has done for you, does your heart not fill with joy?

God's Word: Praise the Lord, my soul; all my inmost being, praise his holy name (Psalm 103:1).

Prayer: Father, let my life, my thoughts, and the work I do bring glory and honor to You. Amen.

JANUARY 6

HEARING GOD SPEAK

God can speak to us through a clap of thunder, the roar of a tornado, or through the winds and waves of a hurricane. He can speak to us any way He chooses, even in a still, small voice. The prophet Elijah discovered that God was not in the wind, the earthquake, or the fire but in the sound of a gentle blowing.

If you are looking for God to speak to you through some traumatic experience like the burning bush of Moses or the bright light that blinded Saul on the Damascus Road or in some other spectacular manner, you might be looking in the wrong place. Try being still. Try being quiet. As hard as it may be, don't speak, just listen!

God's Word: He says, "Be still and know that I am God; I will be exalted among the nations, I will be exalted in the earth" (Psalm 46:10).

Prayer: Father, there is so much noise in my life—so many distractions. Help me to practice being quiet and still. Help me to listen so that I can hear You speak. Amen.

JANUARY 7

OPPORTUNITY LOST

There is a fable of a businessman fishing in a lake. He caught a strange fish, one he had never seen before. Suddenly, the fish spoke to the man. "Please throw me back in the lake, and I'll grant you three wishes." The businessman considered the request and replied, "Make it five, and we've got a deal." "I can grant only three," gasped the fish. "Four and a half," the man suggested. "Three," the fish replied faintly. "Okay, we'll compromise on four wishes," the businessman conceded. The fish did not respond. It lay dead on the bottom of the boat."

Greed has caused many a person to lose a choice opportunity. Some people are never satisfied with what life offers. In the desire for more, they end up with nothing. Guard your heart against greed. Greed can leave you empty-handed.

God's Word: Then he said to them, "Watch out! Be on your guard against all kinds of greed; life does not consist in an abundance of possessions" (Luke 12:15).

Prayer: Father, help me understand that it is not what I possess that gives satisfaction and meaning to my life but who possesses me. Help me to find my fulfillment in You and not in things. Amen.

JANUARY 8

ON BEING RELIGIOUS

Being religious does not make you spiritual, nor does it automatically mean that you have a close relationship with God. You can be so caught up in religious practices and rituals that you don't even hear God or experience God. You can be so involved in church activities that you neglect prayer and Bible study. You can do religious things and still fail to have a daily walk with God.

Be careful that your religious fervor does not rob you of fellowship and intimacy with God. Be careful that your practice of religion does not become a substitute for a love relationship with the heavenly Father. How you relate to God is far more important than what you do for God.

God's Word: For if you live according to the flesh, you will die; but if by the Spirit you put to death the misdeeds of the body, you will live. For those who are led by the Spirit of God are the children of God (Romans 8:13–14).

Prayer: Father, help me to understand that how I relate to You is more important than how I worship. Teach me to recognize that practicing rituals is not the same as having my heart and mind fixed on You. Amen.

JANUARY 9

PATIENCE

Patience seems to be an unsought virtue in the world today. We belong to the "instant generation," and we want things now. Some even consider patience to be a weakness—a passive, uncomplaining acceptance of trying circumstances.

The biblical concept of patience stands in contrast to modern understanding. Biblical patience is active, not passive. It enables a person to stand fast and persevere under the most difficult and trying circumstances. Remember the patience of Job. He complained to God and even protested his calamities. He argued with his friends. There was nothing passive about Job. Yet, in all his difficulties, he never lost faith in God. He even rejected his wife's advice to "curse God and die" (Job 2:9). Job proved the truth of "hanging in there," knowing that God is in charge.

God's Word: I know that my redeemer lives, and that in the end he will stand on the earth. And after my skin has been destroyed, yet in my flesh I will see God (Job 19:25–26).

Prayer: Father, help me to trust You in the circumstances in which I live, knowing that You are in charge, and You are molding and shaping me into the person You want me to be. Amen.

JANUARY 10

SOMEONE TO LISTEN

Have you ever longed for someone to listen to how you feel? You may be lonely today because you have just been faced with bad news about your health or you've lost your job, or things are not going well at home. Perhaps, you and your spouse have had a disagreement, or your children may be trying your patience or living a lifestyle that is contrary to your standards.

In the middle of your dilemma, you feel like you are going to explode if you don't have someone who will listen. If at this moment you can't find a friend, a pastor, or a counselor to hear you out, find a quiet place and pour your heart out to God. He will listen. Read His Word and, let Him speak to your heart. We have a friend in Jesus to whom we can carry everything in prayer.

God's Word: Call to me and I will answer you and tell you great and unsearchable things you do not know (Jeremiah 33:3).

Prayer: Father, in my hour of loneliness, help me to know that You are my help and strength, my refuge in times of trouble. Amen.

JANUARY 11

SHOW ME A SERMON

Conversations with your children on the way to church or even during the week may reveal more about your relationship with God than what you do. The example you set with your life may say more about your true relationship with God than anything you say with your lips.

In the language of a past generation, you may talk the talk without walking the walk. What your family and neighbors need most from you is a devout example rather than a devout word. People may or may not be impressed by what you say, but they will never forget what you do. The old saying that "I'd rather see a sermon than hear one any day," is still true. Don't preach sermons with your lips; preach sermons with your life.

God's Word: May these words of my mouth and this meditation of my heart be pleasing in your sight, Lord, my Rock and my redeemer (Psalm 19:14).

Prayer: Father, help my words and my actions bring honor to Your name. Amen.

JANUARY 12

A LIFE WORTH IMITATING

I heard a child say, "I want to grow up and be just like my daddy." You could see the father swelling with pride, and rightly so. The highest respect and the greatest compliment that a child can give a parent is a desire to be just like him or her.

The desire of a child to imitate his parents is especially noble if that parent leads a godly life and is teaching the child by example the importance of walking in obedience with God. Is it so in your family? Do your children have such great love and admiration for you that they want to imitate your life and faith?

God's Word: In everything set them an example by doing what is good. In your teaching show integrity, seriousness and soundness of speech that cannot be condemned, so that those who oppose you may be ashamed because they have nothing bad to say about us (Titus 2:7).

Prayer: Father, help me to be an example to my children in speech, conduct, love, faith, and purity. Amen.

JANUARY 13

MEDITATION

Meditation is at the very heart of a relationship with God. The psalmist said, "May my meditation be pleasing to Him, as I rejoice in the Lord" (Psalm 104:34). If you desire a relationship with God, you must find time for meditation. Meditation is pleasing to the Lord, who invites you to fellowship with Him. When we concentrate on Him, our meditation becomes sweet.

As parents delight in holding their children close, so God delights in having us close to Him. As a loving parent never tires of relating to their children, God never becomes weary of our company. David—psalmist, and king of Israel—found happiness in the Lord. Have you made that discovery?

God's Word: I have hidden your word in my heart that I might not sin against you (Psalm 119:11).

Prayer: Father, may I know the sweetness of time spent with You. Amen.

JANUARY 14

COUNT YOUR BLESSINGS

In the business world, January is often dedicated to taking an inventory of profits and losses. It is a good business practice to know the status of how things are going and what changes need to be put into place.

How long has it been since you sat down and counted your many blessings? We take so much for granted and all too often grumble about the way things are or complain about what we don't have. Part of our misery is brought upon ourselves because we fail to appreciate what we do have.

Take time to list the things that are right in your life. List all the blessings that you can think of, and you may find that your attitude greatly improves. Most of us have far more blessings than we deserve. Instead of complaining or grumbling today–give thanks!

God's Word: Let us come before him with thanksgiving and extol him with music and song (Psalm 95:2).

Prayer: Father, hear my prayer for the many blessings that You have given me. Fill my heart with joy and gladness for what I have and what You mean to me. Amen.

JANUARY 15

PEACEMAKERS

A pair of Canadian geese inhabited a small Island on a large pond where they raised their young. One summer, only one of seven eggs hatched, and the young hatchling died the next day. The second pair of geese chose the same island to raise their young. All eight of their hatchlings survived. Since geese fiercely defend their young against intruders, the first occupants of the island were not happy with the arrival of a new family. The first day was an all-out war.

The farmer who owned the pond watched the drama play out. He was amazed on the second day when he looked out on his pond and saw eight baby geese swimming peacefully with one set of parents leading the hatchlings and the second set of parents bringing up the rear. If wild geese can find a way to peace, why can't human beings?

God's Word: Make every effort to live in peace with everyone and to be holy; without holiness no one will see the Lord. See to it that no one falls short of the grace of God and that no bitter root grows up to cause trouble and defile many (Hebrews 12:14).

Prayer: Father, help me to be a peacemaker by following Jesus the Prince of Peace. Amen.

JANUARY 16

THROWING ROCKS

In the Academy Award-winning movie *Forrest Gump*, Jennie returns to the farmhouse of her youth after years of living with drugs, immorality and being used up. Her downhill life is attributed to her abusive, alcoholic father, who sexually molested her. Venting her pent-up anger, Jennie begins to throw rocks at the house until she falls to the ground in tears. Forrest Gump then says, "Sometimes there aren't enough rocks to throw."

Throwing rocks at one's past will not remove the pain. Only God's love and forgiveness can change our lives for the better and enable us to move forward to a more productive life. Rather than cursing an unchangeable past, ask God for strength to make the best of the rest of your life.

God's Word: Forgetting what is behind and straining toward what is ahead, I press on toward the goal to win the prize for which God has called me heavenward in Christ Jesus (Philippians 3:13).
Prayer: Father, give me the wisdom to put the past behind me and the strength to press forward toward a future guided by You. Amen.

JANUARY 17

MEMORIES

Today you are building memories. Will they be bitter or sweet? How will you look back on this day? Be careful what you say today. Be careful what you do. Be careful of the thoughts that fill your mind. Be careful how you treat your family or how you treat those with whom you work.

When you look back on this day, will you feel that you wasted your time, or will you see today as fulfilled–a day of accomplishment–a turning point in your life–a day of pleasant memories?

Nobody has the power to make your day more than you. When Jesus taught that the kingdom of God is within you, He was teaching about the power we have for good. Make the most of today. Determine to make this day pleasant for those with whom you have contact. Determine to accomplish something worthwhile, lend a helping hand, and give a word of encouragement.

When you go to bed tonight, won't it be wonderful to say, "This day is worth remembering."

God's Word: Let us rejoice today and be glad (Psalm 118:24).

Prayer: Father, thank You for this day that You have given me. Help me to honor You and be a blessing to others so that it will be a day worth remembering. Amen.

JANUARY 18

SMELL THE ROSES

While visiting a friend in the hospital, a nurse entered the room on her routine check. Completing her duties, she commented on the beautiful roses that the patient had received. She went around to the other side of the bed so that she could smell them. As she was leaving the room, I said, "It's so nice to see someone stop to smell the roses." She laughed and left the room.

When was the last time in a busy day that you stopped to smell the roses or admired the flowers of the field, or gazed at a beautiful sunset? When have you stopped to hear the birds sing or to say a prayer of thanksgiving?

All around us, there is so much to appreciate, yet we take so little time to be grateful. Stop! Take a deep breath! Relax! Find something around you to appreciate. An attitude of gratitude will do wonders for your soul.

God's Word: When I consider your heavens, the work of your fingers, the moon and the stars, which you have set in place, what is mankind that you are mindful of them, human beings that you care for them (Psalm 8:3)?

Prayer: Father, help me never to be too busy to appreciate the beauty of Your creation. Refresh my soul on the thought of your presence and how much You love me. Amen.

JANUARY 19

SELF-EVALUATION

Pause for a moment and take a deep spiritual inventory of your life. It could be very helpful. It could also be painful. Whether you will do it depends upon whether you want to improve your life. Here are a few questions to consider: Do you fail to be true even to your accepted standards? What about deceiving yourself in the face of temptation, thinking that you can handle it? How about your failures to apply the same standards of conduct to yourself that you demand of others? Do you find it easier to be complacent about the wrongs that do not touch your life while being oversensitive to the wrongs that do? Do you find yourself with a hard heart toward your neighbor's faults and a readiness to make allowances for your own? How about your slowness to see the good in others and to see the evil in your own life?

Honesty with yourself in answering these questions can lead you to a better life. Once we acknowledge our need for change and improvement, the next step is to repent of the evil in which we are prone to engage. With acknowledgment of your sins, repentance, and asking God's forgiveness and direction, you can experience a transformation of life that will set you free of the burden that has weighed you down.

God's Word: Create in me a pure heart, O God, and renew a steadfast spirit within me. Do not cast me from your presence or take your Holy Spirit from me. Restore to me the joy of your salvation and grant me a willing spirit to sustain me. Then I will teach transgressors your ways, so that sinners will turn back to you (Psalm 51:10).

Prayer: Father, help me to acknowledge, confess and repent of my sins. Forgive me and guide me in the path that You would have me follow. Amen.

JANUARY 20

LIGHT AND FREEDOM

As a guest was leaving our home one evening, my wife started to close the door when a little sparrow zoomed past her and flew into our den. After repeated tries to catch the little fellow, who just kept flying from room to room, we finally realized the futility of our efforts.

We could imagine the fear and panic that was going on in the breast of this delicate creature of God. In exhaustion, the little bird found a perch on our bookshelf. Then, we decided to cut out all the lights in the house, open the front door and cut on the porch light. Within seconds the sparrow spotted the light and the way to freedom.

The Bible teaches that we are living in the darkness of sin. Jesus Christ, seeing our hopeless condition, opened the door of light and freedom for us by dying on the cross to save us from our sins. The light and freedom that Christ provides are for all who will leave the darkness and follow His light.

God's Word: For God, who said, "Let light shine out of darkness," made his light shine in our hearts to give us the light of the knowledge of God's glory displayed in the face of Christ (2 Corinthians 4:6).

Prayer: Father, enable me to recognize the darkness in which I am living and see the light and freedom that I am offered by Your Son, Jesus Christ. Amen.

JANUARY 21

SMORGASBORD

As a youth growing up in Wilmington, North Carolina, I remember how exciting it was when The Ark, a popular restaurant on the Cape Fear River waterfront, came up with the idea of a smorgasbord. The word itself sounded strange and even a little funny, but once you understood what it meant, you delighted in the opportunity to participate. Today, you don't often hear that word, but you do hear the word "buffet" and "all you can eat."

Whether you call it "smorgasbord," "buffet," or "all you can eat," we know it as a restaurant with a wide variety of choices on the menu. Some even boast about the number of choices.

In a sense, life is a smorgasbord or buffet. You can have anything on the menu, but not everything is good for you. At the center of life is choice. Your challenge is to choose wisely.

God's Word: "I have a right to do anything," you say—but not everything is beneficial. "I have a right to do anything," but I will not be mastered by anything … Do you not know that your bodies are temples of the Holy Spirit, who is in you, whom you have received from God? (1 Corinthians 6:12, 19).

Prayer: Father, the choices I make in life are the difference between good and evil. Give me wisdom and discernment to choose good. Amen.

JANUARY 22

ATTITUDE

We are living in what some call "the information era" or "the digital age." We are bombarded day and night with the news. Rather than getting just the facts, we get commentary, opinions, philosophies, and predictions. Have you noticed how many news reports end on a negative note? The internet makes it easier for lies, misinformation, rumors, and conspiracies to spread. Maintaining a positive attitude in the world we live in is a challenge.

Is the world a better place because you are in it? Each one of us has the potential to make it so. We improve the world by having a positive attitude, by being helpful and sensitive to the needs of others, by listening to the heartbreak of another person, and by having the mind of Christ.

We improve the world through acts of kindness, generosity, and love. Every time you meet a need, dry a tear, live with honor and integrity, and tell the truth, you make a difference in someone's life, and you make the world a better place.

God's Word: The King will reply, "Truly I tell you, whatever you did for one of the least of these brothers and sisters of mine, you did for me" (Matthew 25:40).

Prayer: Father, help me to understand that life is not about me but about serving You and helping others. Amen.

JANUARY 23

WHAT MATTERS

A bumper sticker on the back of a Jaguar caught my attention, "How does it feel to want?" As I thought about all the implications of that bumper sticker, I was reminded that God does not give us material possession to flaunt, to make us arrogant, or to feel superior to others who have a tougher economic road in life. We are to be good stewards of what God gives us. We are to use our possessions to bring honor to Him.

The bumper sticker shouted arrogance. It displayed ingratitude and self-centeredness. Material possessions are, at best, temporary. What we have today can be taken away or destroyed tomorrow. There is no security in things of this world.

God's Word teaches that life does not consist of what we possess but of what possesses us. It makes no difference to God whether we drive a Jaguar or a broken-down Chevrolet. It is not what we have that makes a difference to God but rather what we do with what we have. When all is said and done, only that which cannot be taken away matters for eternity.

God's Word: The Lord detests all the proud of heart. Be sure of this: They will not go unpunished (Proverbs 16:5).

Prayer: Father, give me discernment between what is temporary and what is eternal and help me to live with a grateful heart. Amen.

JANUARY 24

WHAT COUNTS IS ON THE INSIDE

How do you measure yourself? Do you look at your height *and* weight, your dress or shirt size? Do you look at your job, your bank account, the size of your house, or the cars you drive? What is the standard by which you measure your life?

Tony Campolo tells about a friend of his who encountered a little girl carrying a huge paper cone of cotton candy. When he asked her how she could eat all of it, she quickly responded that she was bigger on the inside than on the outside. God is looking for people who are bigger on the inside than on the outside. If you want a true measure of yourself, look inside—at your heart, your attitudes, your care, and your concern for others. Want a true measure of yourself? Look at your heart!

God's Word: But the Lord said to Samuel, "'Do not consider his appearance or his height for I have rejected him. The Lord does not look at the things people look at. People look at the outward appearance, but the Lord looks at the heart" (1 Samuel 16:7).

Prayer: Father, as I evaluate my life, help me to look on the inside as You do. Amen.

JANUARY 25

ON TIME

God always does things "on time." When Jesus came into the world, the Bible says, it was "the fullness of time." When Jesus died on the cross, it was right on time with God's plan. Three days later, He arose from the grave, right on time, just as He had said. No one can improve on God's timing.

In 1966, we put our house up for sale in Boone, North Carolina, and returned to the mission field in Brazil. The house did not sell, and we were forced to rent because we did not have the money to pay the mortgage. We wondered why our house did not sell when we were doing what we felt God called us to do. We prayed for the sale, but all we got was silence.

More than a year passed before we received a letter in the mail from our real estate agent with the good news of an offer to buy. A few years later, health issues caused us to return to the States. You can imagine our delight when we bought a new house within a week of the time permitted by the IRS to reinvest our funds without paying capital gains taxes. God's timing was perfect. When you ask God to do something, trust Him to do it right on time.

God's Word: For there is a proper time and procedure for every matter, though a person may be weighed down by misery (Ecclesiastes 8:6).

Prayer: Father, teach me to wait upon You for answers to my prayers. Amen.

JANUARY 26

LEARNING VS. DOING

A young girl was giving her mother a difficult time over an act of disobedience. In trying to correct her daughter, the mother reminded her of a recent assignment she had been given to learn the Ten Commandments. "Don't you remember that one of the Ten Commandments is to honor your father and mother?" the mother asked. The daughter responded, "Mom, you just have to learn it; you don't have to do it."

Unfortunately, too many people have the same attitude. What a tragedy! You can know all the Bible verses you care to memorize, but unless you put those verses into practice, you will never experience the benefit that truth affords. There is an enormous difference between knowing about the Bible and knowing the Bible. There is also a great difference between knowing about God and doing what He says.

Learning Bible verses without living in obedience to God may increase your knowledge, but it will not win God's approval. The only way to please God is to live by faith in obedience to Him

God's Word: Anyone who loves me will obey my teaching (John 14:23).

Prayer: Father, help me not just to memorize scripture but to apply its truth to my life. Amen.

JANUARY 27

KNOW WHERE YOU ARE GOING

Scientists have given a great deal of study to what they call "the processional caterpillar." The processional caterpillars are so named because they are experts in following their leader.

Scientists have taken groups of processional caterpillars and put them in a circle so that they follow one another around and around. These creatures will keep going around in a circle until they die. They don't stop. They just keep following the lead caterpillar.

People are sometimes like processional caterpillars, following a leader until they are destroyed in the process. If you are a follower, be a smart one. Don't follow a leader who is going to destroy you. Truly smart people are those who follow Jesus Christ, who will never lead you down the wrong road. Christ will lead you to life, joy, and peace.

God's Word: Jesus answered, "I am the way and the truth and the life. No one comes to the Father except through me" (John 14:6).

Prayer: Father, give me the wisdom to follow leaders who will not take me down the road to destruction. Amen.

JANUARY 28

RESPONSIBILITY

Are you one of those people who never seem to catch up on your work, and the list of things you need to do gets longer and longer? If so, before you know it, you're depressed in the face of overwhelming circumstances.

If you find yourself in that situation, you might want to ask, "What if I had absolutely nothing to do? What if no one needed me? What if I woke up in the morning and had no place to go and no responsibility? Without responsibility and a sense of usefulness, life would be the pits. Instead of lamenting over how much you must do, breathe a prayer of thanksgiving that you are important enough to have something to do, someplace to go, and someone to help.

The secret of a fulfilled life is in being useful to others and feeling that you are needed. Instead of complaining about responsibility, thank God that you can be responsible.

God's Word: Whatever you do, work at it with all your heart, as working for the Lord, not for human masters, since you know that you will receive an inheritance from the Lord as a reward. It is the Lord Christ you are serving (Colossians 3:23–24).

Prayer: Father, let me be thankful for the responsibilities that are mine. Give me the strength to work with joy, knowing that I am useful. Amen.

JANUARY 29

GROWTH

The growth of a child from infancy to adulthood is an amazing process filled with awesome responsibilities for parents who desire the very best for their children. In the same way that we as human beings are concerned about the overall development of our children, God is concerned about our growth and development. The Bible says that "Jesus grew in wisdom and stature and in favor of God and men" (Luke 2:52). In other words, Jesus grew intellectually, physically, spiritually, and socially. He was, in every sense of the word, a well-rounded person.

What greater goal can we set for ourselves than to imitate Jesus in our growth and development? The good news is that if we will surrender our lives to Christ and follow his example, He gives us the power to grow in all aspects of life.

God's Word: For this reason, since the day we heard about you, we have not stopped praying for you. We continually ask God to fill you with the knowledge of his will through all the wisdom and understanding that the Spirit gives, so that you may live a life worthy of the Lord and please him in every way: bearing fruit in every good work, growing in the knowledge of God, being strengthened with all power according to his glorious might so that you may have great endurance and patience, and giving joyful thanks to the Father, who has qualified you to share in the inheritance of his holy people in the kingdom of light (Colossians 1:9–10).

Prayer: Father, help me to grow in all aspects of life and bring honor to Your name. Amen.

JANUARY 30

HOME CLIMATE

What is the temperature in your home? This question is not about the thermostat on the wall but the emotional climate within your family. Is it cold inside with little communication? Is it hot because of constant conflict and heated arguments? Is your home lukewarm with little interest in what other family members are doing? Or is your home warm and comfortable because there is an atmosphere of love, acceptance, courtesy, and consideration?

Your home has a climate index created by the quality of relationships that exist when family members are together and even when they are not. If the climate center of your home is out of order, Jesus Christ is the repairman that you need. Get in touch with Christ before your family freezes to death or burns up!

God's Word: My people will live in peaceful dwelling places, in secure homes, in undisturbed places of rest (Isaiah 32:18).

Prayer: Father, help me to do all I can to maintain a climate of love and security in my home. Amen.

JANUARY 31

GOD'S CARE

A little girl was at home alone for a short period. When her parents returned, they were convinced that they would find her badly frightened. "I wasn't afraid," she said. "When you are here, God expects you to take care of me, but when you are gone, He does it all by himself."

Isn't it wonderful that children have such simple faith? Isn't it wonderful that we have a loving God who can take care of us? Confidence in God is essential if we are to have security and live without fear. Jesus said, "unless you change and become like little children, you will never enter the kingdom of heaven" (Matthew 18:3).

If you are an adult, perhaps the time has come for you to drop the false sense of security you have built up in material things and trust God, who can take care of you all by Himself.

God's Word: "Because he loves me," says the Lord, "I will rescue him; I will protect him, for he acknowledges my name. He will call on me, and I will answer him; I will be with him in trouble, I will deliver him and honor him. With long life I will satisfy him and show him my salvation (Psalm 91:14–15).

Prayer: Father, I acknowledge You as my refuge and strength. Give me childlike faith to trust You. Amen.

FEBRUARY 1

DIRECTIONS

Mount Corcovado is in the heart of Rio de Janeiro. At 2,329 feet, this granite peak located in the Tijuca Forest National Park is famous around the world for its iconic statue of Christ the Redeemer. The one-hundred-foot-tall statue with its panoramic view of surrounding mountains, beaches, forest, the Guanabara Bay, and the Atlantic Ocean is a photographic wonder greeting all who arrive by air, sea, or land.

The statue of Christ is more than a decoration to the Cariocas of Brazil; it is a trustworthy guide to anyone who is lost or seeking direction. Brazilians and tourists from around the world have come to trust the statue to get their bearings. The monument of Christ faces east with arms outstretched over the city. The right arm points south, the left arm points north, and the back faces due west, providing a reliable compass to all who seek guidance.

As human beings, we all need to be pointed in the right direction. We need a compass to point the way. As the statue of Christ the Redeemer gives guidance to the bewildered traveler in Rio de Janeiro, Christ, the Son of God, is the compass for the entire world.

God's Word: As Jesus walked beside the Sea of Galilee, he saw Simon and his brother Andrew casting a net into the lake, for they were fishermen "Come, follow me," Jesus said, "and I will send you out to fish for people." At once they left their nets and followed him (Mark 1:16–18).

Prayer: Father, help me to hear Your call and follow without hesitation. Amen.

FEBRUARY 2

FINANCIAL INTEGRITY

Second Samuel 24 records the story of King David, who was told by the prophet Gad to erect an altar on the threshing floor of Araunah. When David approached Araunah and told him that he had come to purchase the threshing floor to build an altar to God, Araunah offered the king not only the floor but the oxen and wood for the sacrifice. But David replied, "No, I insist on paying you for it. I will not sacrifice to the Lord my God burnt offerings that cost me nothing" (2 Samuel 24:24).

What is your attitude about giving to God? Each of us receives so much from the Lord. All too often, we take it for granted. How often do we stop to think about the bountiful gifts that come from the hand of God along with his abundant mercy? Yet, we give so little back to him. We are more prone to spend more on pet food than we are willing to give to God. We may even generously tip a waiter in a restaurant more than we put in the offering plate at church on Sunday.

David modeled financial integrity. He would not give an offering to God that cost him nothing. How about you?

God's Word: "Bring the whole tithe into the storehouse, that there may be food in my house. Test me in this," says the Lord Almighty, "and see if I will not throw open the floodgates of heaven and pour out so much blessing that there will not be room enough to store it" (Malachi 3:10).

Prayer: Father, help me to follow the example of David and demonstrate financial integrity in my offerings to You. Amen.

FEBRUARY 3

ENCOURAGEMENT

Opera singer Luciano Pavarotti might have missed his calling had it not been for a few people who made a difference in his life. As a little boy, his grandmother held him in her lap and told him that he would be great. He began as a young man teaching elementary school and sang only occasionally. His father recognized his gift and encouraged him to devote more time to singing. A voice teacher recognized his potential and devoted time to help him develop his God-given talent.

The turning point in someone's life may be a word of encouragement from you. Make a point to be an encourager. Every person needs a voice of encouragement, helping them and inspiring them to live up to their potential. Find someone who needs a word of encouragement today and make a difference in his or her life.

God's Word: Therefore encourage one another and build each other up, just as in fact you are doing (1 Thessalonians 5:11).

Prayer: Father, help me to be an encourager to others so that I can make a difference in their lives. Amen.

FEBRUARY 4

SHARK OR DOLPHIN

Sharks and dolphins are known to travel in schools but are not known to be companions in their travels. There is a notable difference in their behavior. For example, if a fellow shark is wounded and bleeding, other sharks will attack and devour the victim. In contrast, if a dolphin is injured or wounded, fellow dolphins will come to his aid, help him to the surface for a breath and even bring him food.

When it comes to your fellow human, are you a shark or a dolphin? Are you the kind of person who attacks and devours the down and out, or are you the kind that comes to their aid? Humans seem to have an abundance of animosity and a shortage of compassion.

Let this be a day when you show love, compassion, and understanding to those who are hurt, wounded, and in need. There is a saying that goes like this: "See a need and meet it. Find a wound and heal it." Put it into practice and experience the joy that it brings.

God's Word: Be kind and compassionate to one another, forgiving each other, just as in Christ God forgave you (Ephesians 4:32).

Prayer: Father, as you have been kind and compassionate to me, help me to be kind and compassionate to others. Amen.

FEBRUARY 5

THE WRONG ROAD

William Barclay tells the story of a dying man who was very troubled. With careful encouragement from a friend, the dying man finally confessed a sin that had worried him all his life. As a young man, he grew up at a crossroads. Feeling mischievous one day, he decided to twist the road signs around. The only problem was that he never corrected his prank. On his death bed, his principal worry was how many travelers he had sent down the wrong road.

You may never have deliberately twisted a road sign, but your life is a guide to many people, including some you may never personally know. Because of your example, how many people are traveling the right road or wrong road?

God's Word: Be very careful, then, how you live—not as unwise but as wise, making the most of every opportunity, because the days are evil (Ephesians 5:15).

Prayer: Father, help me to walk the path that You taught us so that those who follow me will not be led down the wrong road. Amen.

FEBRUARY 6

CHURCH OFFERINGS

During our days as missionaries to Brazil, it was a common practice in many interior churches to post the monthly contributions of church members on a prominent bulletin board near the entrance of the church. Each church member's name was listed with the amount of contribution given for the current month. Those who had not contributed to the church were not permitted to vote in the monthly business meeting. It was an accepted practice.

It is doubtful that such a practice would be well accepted in the United States. Giving to the church is considered a "private matter" between the giver and God. But the truth be known, those who are disciplined and faithful in giving their tithe and offering to the church are not inclined to be ashamed or threatened if someone knows about their gift. It has been my observation that those who give little or nothing to the church do not want anyone to know how stingy they are. Those who withhold their generosity from God would not want anyone to discover that a secretary gave more than her wealthy boss and that the man who rode around in an expensive automobile gave less than the widow who was sending her son through college on her pension.

If you would be embarrassed by having people know what you give to the church, why don't you give so that there would be no need to be ashamed? Isn't it strange that people's knowledge of our giving habits embarrasses us while God's knowledge does not?

God's Word: A tithe of everything from the land, whether grain from the soil or fruit from the trees, belongs to the Lord; it is holy to the Lord (Leviticus 27:30).

Prayer: Father, do not let me be embarrassed when I make my offering to You. Let me give cheerfully, generously, without shame, and with a heart of love and gratitude for Your mercy and grace. Amen.

FEBRUARY 7

TEMPTATION

Temptation varies from person to person and affects every human being. What tempts one person may not tempt another. For some, the temptation may be overeating; for another, it may be to cheat, lie, steal, or commit adultery. Still others may be tempted by alcohol or drugs. No one is exempt from temptation.

The battle against temptation is not won at the moment it occurs but before the enticement. A young man traveling in a foreign country was tempted to spend the night with a prostitute. His first thought was, who would know? He was thousands of miles from home, where no one knew him. As his temptation intensified, he remembered his marriage vows, his children, and his witness as a Christian. Realizing who he was and whose he was and the impact that it would have on his wife and children, he fled the temptation with the thought that "God will know!" Reinforced by prior commitments, he avoided the pitfall of adultery.

You cannot stop temptation from coming your way, but the choice to yield or to flee is yours alone. Never think for one moment that no one will ever know. God will always know, and the Bible says, "your sin will find you out" (Numbers 32:23).

God's Word: For God will bring every deed into judgment, including every hidden thing, whether it is good or evil (Ecclesiastes 12:14).

Prayer: Father, keep me from yielding to temptation and from ever thinking that if I sin, no one will ever know. Help me to avoid temptation by remembering before the temptation comes that You will always know what I do. Amen.

FEBRUARY 8

OUR GREATEST TEACHERS

If you have ever had someone tell you exactly what they think of you, you might have come away angry. The more you brood on what he or she said, the more your anger will turn to resentment or even hatred. You may never want to see that person again or have anything else to do with him or her. But stop just a moment and reflect upon what was said. Did what he or she said about you contain even a kernel of truth? Did the person even give you a hint of what you ought to change in your life? If so, count it a blessing that he or she had the courage to "tell you off."

Put your ego aside. Look at the hard, cold facts and start working on the area of your life that needs attention. The enemy who tells you the truth may be better for you than the friend who never disagrees with you. Wake up! Pay attention! Think about it! The person you are tempted to hate may turn out to be your greatest teacher.

God's Word: Consider it pure joy, my brothers and sisters, whenever you face trials of many kinds, because you know that the testing of your faith produces perseverance. Let perseverance finish its work so that you may be mature and complete, not lacking anything (James 1:2–4).

Prayer: Father, when I am wounded by the words of someone who tells me off, give me the grace to hear what was said and to recognize the changes that are needed in my life. Rather than hate him or her, enable me to love, pray for, and learn from the detractor. Amen.

FEBRUARY 9

GET TO THE SOURCE

Claudius Galenus, who lived in Rome in 163 AD, was a world-renowned physician at the age of forty. The doctor's wisdom is illustrated in the case of a prominent Roman scholar named Eudemus. Eudemus suffered from a paralysis of his right hand and sought the services of Dr. Galenus. The doctor took a careful history of his patient and discovered that his injury had occurred when he was thrown from a chariot, and his neck was injured when he hit a stone. Rather than treat the patient's hand, Dr. Galenus began to massage the nerves in Eudemus's neck. Within days, he had full usage of his hand, and the Roman Senate declared Dr. Galenus the "Prince of Physicians."

Treating the source of our illness rather than the symptoms is the key to good medicine. It is also the key to spiritual happiness. Unless we deal with the sin that is the source of our problem, treating the symptoms is useless.

God's Word: Above all else, guard your heart, for everything you do flows from it (Proverbs 4:23).

Prayer: Father, create in me a pure heart, and renew a steadfast spirit within me. Amen.

FEBRUARY 10

APPRECIATE WHAT YOU HAVE

One afternoon, I watched a horse straining his neck to reach a bit of grass outside his split-rail fence. Normally, I would not have paid much attention to his effort if the pasture in which he was confined had not been full of the same variety of grass that he was trying so desperately to reach. I was reminded of the saying, "the grass is always greener on the other side of the fence."

Obviously, horses are not much different from people in this respect. We never seem to be satisfied with what we have. We always imagine how happy we would be if we had our neighbor's job, house, salary, or beach cottage. In our discontent, we are like the horse surrounded by green, juicy grass straining outside our possibilities to eat on the other side of the fence.

Stop straining for something you want when you don't take advantage of what you have. Take a good look at your garage, attic, or rented storage bin and things you haven't used in years. Count your blessings. Live with appreciation and gratitude. Think of others who might greatly benefit from your abundance. Appreciate what you have.

God's Word: But godliness with contentment is great gain (1 Timothy 6:6).

Prayer: Father, help me to be thankful and content with what I have. Help me to use what I have in a way that is pleasing to You. Amen.

FEBRUARY 11

ORDINARY PEOPLE

Unknown, unrecognized, and obscure may be the way you feel about yourself sometimes. Here is a word of encouragement for you. It's hard to find a more obscure person in the Old Testament than Hur. Yet, without this humble servant of God, Israel could have lost a strategic battle to the Amalekites, and one of the world's greatest leaders would have been ridiculed to shame.

Read the story in Exodus 17. During the battle, as long as Moses held up his hands, Israel prevailed. When he lowered his hands, the enemy pushed back. Moses's arms grew weary to the extent that Aaron, the well-known spokesman for Moses and Hur, the unknown, unrecognized, and obscure assistant, held up the hands of the prophet.

Unknown, unrecognized, obscure, ordinary people, more often than given credit, make the difference between success and failure. Success is not a matter of being well known or famous but rather a matter of faithfulness to the task. God does not call us to notoriety or fame but rather to being faithful.

God's Word: Whoever can be trusted with very little can also be trusted with much (Luke 16:10).

Prayer: Father, help me to keep my eyes focused on You, not looking for recognition in what I do, but rather just being faithful. Amen.

FEBRUARY 12

THANKS

Have you ever thanked God for what you don't have? Some of the things we don't have can be as great a blessing as things we do have.

I read the story of a lady who dreaded to take a trip with her two sisters because they were so wealthy, and she, being poor, felt like a country mouse. She joined them on the trip anyway. On the first night, the two wealthy sisters began to worry about where they might hide their diamond-encrusted watches. The sister who had a fifteen-year-old Timex watch placed her timepiece on the nightstand beside her bed and breathed a prayer of thanks because she didn't have to worry if her watch was stolen.

Try thanking God for things you don't have. Thank Him that you don't have an uncaring church, a feuding family, a home burned to the ground, flooded, or destroyed by a hurricane, a terminal disease, etc. What you don't have could be a greater blessing than what you do have.

God's Word: Do not be anxious about anything, but in every situation, by prayer and petition, with thanksgiving, present your request to God. And the peace of God, which transcends all understanding, will guard your hearts and your minds in Christ Jesus (Philippians 4:6–7).

Prayer: Father, help me to be grateful for what I don't have, even for unanswered prayer, knowing that every good gift and every perfect gift comes from You. Amen.

FEBRUARY 13

FEEDING OUR MINDS

If the sixty-second commercial by repeated viewing can sell us a product, then a sixty-minute soap opera or a pornographic movie can sell us a lifestyle. You have heard the expression "You are what you eat." If that is true, it is likewise true that what you feed your mind, what you think about the most, is an indication of what kind of person you are.

If that fact scares you, perhaps it is time to evaluate the subjects, books, television programs, movies, and literature you read. Studies indicate that our imaginations, learning patterns, and behaviors are directly influenced by how we feed our minds.

Our value system is formed without conscious awareness on our part of what is happening to us. If your lifestyle is leading you down the wrong road, perhaps you should examine your mental intake. It may be time for a change of direction.

God's Word: Finally, brothers and sisters, whatever is true, whatever is noble, whatever is right, whatever is pure, whatever is lovely, whatever is admirable—if anything is excellent or praiseworthy—think about such things (Philippians 4:8).

Prayer: Father, let my lifestyle be guided by values that build me up rather than tear me down. Amen.

FEBRUARY 14

GOD'S HELP

For as long as I can remember, I've heard people say, "God helps those who help themselves." Algernon Sidney, an English political theorist, is first credited with having made the statement in 1698. Benjamin Franklin used the saying in his *Poor Richard's Almanack* in 1736. It has since been widely quoted. On the surface, this philosophy sounds good. It even sounds biblical, but it is not.

Scripture teaches that God helps those who are quite unable to help themselves. If you *think* about it, that includes everyone. It does not matter how gifted a person you may be or whether or not you take everything you hear for granted, just because someone makes a statement doesn't mean that it is true. Search the scriptures for truth.

God's Word: Come to me, all you who are weary and burdened, and I will give you rest (Matthew 11:28).

Prayer: Father, help me to recognize my dependence upon You and to live by grace with the help of the Holy Spirit. Give me the wisdom to test the validity of things I hear by your Word. Amen.

FEBRUARY 15

USELESS PRAYER

Do you ever feel that your prayers never get past the ceiling? You try to think spiritual thoughts, but you are so entangled in your daily struggles that you find it frustrating to express yourself to God.

Uncle Claudius, in Shakespeare's *Hamlet*, murders his brother and then marries his brother's wife. Hamlet discovers the method by which his father was killed and puts on a play acting out the murder. He invites Claudius to attend. As Hamlet hoped, Claudius sees himself in the play, hurries out of the theater, and runs to the chapel. He kneels to pray and realizes that his words go up, but his thoughts don't. He confesses that prayer without confession and repentance goes nowhere.

If we genuinely want God's attention, we must approach him with repentant hearts. Once our sins have been confessed, God responds with forgiveness and cleansing. To rephrase Shakespeare, "Prayers without repentance never to heaven go."

God's Word: If we confess our sins, he is faithful and just and will forgive us our sins and purify us from all unrighteousness (1 John 1:9).

Prayer: Father, thank you for letting me know that You are more than willing to forgive my sins if I will confess them and repent. If I simply admit the truth about myself, I can be set free from the burden of my sin. Amen.

FEBRUARY 16

PRIORITIES

A traumatic situation such as the death of a loved one, or a life hanging in the balance, can quickly change one's priorities. Suddenly, making money, earning a living, meeting schedules, having parties, being entertained, or trying to impress someone pales in importance when faced with death or a threat to life.

Death, tragedy, or trauma gets our attention. Have you ever considered that these experiences could be the only thing that will make us examine our priorities? Life is more than getting and spending. It is more than position and power. It is more than entertainment and pleasure. God never intended for life to be sad, but he did intend for life to be serious.

Those who scoff at spiritual things have no reserve when tragedy or trauma occurs. Those who have laid up treasures in heaven have God's assurance that no matter what happens, the heavenly Father is with them in and through the trauma to the end and beyond.

God's Word: Store up for yourselves treasures in heaven, where moths and vermin do not destroy, and where thieves do not break in and steal (Matthew 6:20).

Prayer: Father, teach me the value of having my priorities in order by giving priority to spiritual things so that when trauma or tragedy comes to me, I will have spiritual reserves to call upon. Amen.

FEBRUARY 17

HEARING, SEEING, SPEAKING

If you can hear, see, and speak, you are indeed blessed. When was the last time you thanked the Lord for these precious gifts? Imagine not being able to hear the voice of your loved ones. Imagine not being able to see the beauty of nature around you. Imagine not being able to speak and share your feelings. Yet, I never cease to be amazed at how those who are deaf, blind, or mute not only cope with their handicap; they inspire us.

While you may be blessed with all your faculties, have you considered that you may be deaf to God's Word or blind to what He is trying to show you or mute in communicating with Him?

We must hear what God is saying to us. It is important that we see God at work in our lives. It is important that we communicate with God through prayer. Stop right now and thank God for the gifts of hearing, seeing, and speech, and use these gifts for His honor and glory.

God's Word: Do you have eyes but fail to see, and ears but fail to hear? And don't you remember? (Mark 8:18). Call to me and I will answer you and tell you great and unsearchable things you do not know (Jeremiah 33:3).

Prayer: Father, help me to use my eyes, ears, and voice to the best of my ability and always in ways that honor you. Amen.

FEBRUARY 18

WITNESS

A group of computer salesmen from Milwaukee attended a convention in Chicago, promising their wives that they would be home for dinner. Convention business delay caused them to reach the train station almost at the hour of departure. In their hurry, the men knocked over a table supporting a basket of apples. All the men raced for the train except one man, who, having feelings for the young boy whose apples they spilled everywhere, returned to gather up the fruit. He immediately noticed that the young apple salesman was blind. Picking up the apples, the salesman realized that several of the apples were bruised. He gave the boy a ten-dollar bill to cover the damaged apples and apologized for the accident by saying, "I hope it didn't spoil your day." As the computer salesman walked away, the blind boy called after him, "Are you Jesus?"

Missing the train was of little consequence in light of the witness that the salesman had given the blind boy.

God's Word: So in everything, do to others what you would have them do to you, for this sums up the Law and the Prophets (Matthew 7:12).

Prayer: Father, in my daily life, let others see Jesus in me. Amen.

FEBRUARY 19

LOOPHOLES

Have you observed that there always seems to be people who think they are an exception to the rules? They live as if the law doesn't apply to them. They are constantly on the search for loopholes that excuse them from complying.

It has always been interesting to me, and tragic, I may say, to find people who want God to make exceptions in their case. How many people spend their lives satisfying their egos, filling their bank accounts, using their time for self-gratification, and totally ignore God? Then, when illness, tragedy, or trauma suddenly overtakes them, they cry out to God for resolution.

If you are looking for loopholes in the way God responds to you, forget it. When we give an account of ourselves to God, it will be based on His standard and not ours. God's judgment comes without plea bargaining or loopholes. We can only plead guilty before God and lean on his grace.

God's Word: For we must all appear before the judgment seat of Christ, so that each of us may receive what is due us for the things done while in the body, whether good or bad (2 Corinthians 5:10).

Prayer: Father, help me to recognize that life is serious and that I am accountable to You for what I do. Help me to know that I must live by Your standards and not expect You to make exceptions for me when I am in trouble. Amen.

FEBRUARY 20

GOD IS AT WORK

God is at work in your life, whether you recognize it or not. Even if you are one who chooses not to go to church, or you haven't read your Bible in years, or you can't remember the last time you prayed. Where do you think that you get the oxygen that you breathe or the health and strength that enable you to make a living? Oxygen, strength, and a multitude of other gifts you enjoy daily come from God who is working in your life.

How can you know that God is working In your life? The Bible declares it: "that you may be children of your Father in heaven. He causes his sun to rise on the evil and the good, and sends rain on the righteous and the unrighteous" (Matthew 5:45).

How then can you receive the abundant blessings of God and still ignore Him or live as though He doesn't exist? Isn't it time that you stop your selfish, frantic pace of living and acknowledge the grace and goodness of God? Isn't it time for you to confess your sins and receive Him into your life? God has more blessings to bestow upon you than you can imagine if you will just yield to Him.

God's Word: Every good and perfect gift is from above, coming down from the Father of the heavenly lights, who does not change like shifting shadows (James 1:17).

Prayer: Father, You work in mysterious ways. In arrogance, I am guilty of being blind to what You do for me every day. Open my eyes to see You at work in me and forgive me for not recognizing Your marvelous grace. Amen.

FEBRUARY 21

A WORD FITLY SPOKEN

What if you were the only human being on the face of the earth? Can you imagine what a lonely existence that would be? Adam, the first man, had that experience. God recognized his loneliness and said, "It is not good for the man to be alone. I will make a helper suitable for him" (Genesis 2:18).

It is our relationship with other human beings that makes life enjoyable and worthwhile. A friend of mine has greatly impressed me with his appreciation of others through his ministry of encouragement. He makes it a practice to greet everyone he encounters during the day with a compliment. Those receiving the compliment are immediately lifted in spirit. If the truth were known, their entire day is made better because of praise.

If you are disturbed by all the criticism that you hear and that people offer one another, why not determine that you will make a difference in the lives of those you meet by offering a word of encouragement.

God's Word: Gracious words are a honeycomb, sweet to the soul and healing to the bones (Proverbs 16:24).

Prayer: Father, in a world filled with criticism, help me to lift the spirit of others with encouragement, praise, and compliments. Amen.

FEBRUARY 22

FAILURE OF FAITH

Have you ever experienced a failure of faith? Perhaps you're going through a dark period in your life at this very moment. If so, you probably feel that your faith is extremely weak and that God is far away. Failure of faith is more common than many are willing to admit. When Simon Peter tried to walk on water, he experienced a failure of faith and sank in the waves. Most of the disciples, at one time or another, experienced a failure of faith. And so do we.

As Jesus stretched out his hand to lift Simon Peter to safety, He will do the same for you and me. "Oh, you of little faith" is not just a word for Jesus's disciples; it is a word for us.

The Bible says that "consequently, faith comes from hearing the message, and the message is heard through the word about Christ" (Romans 10:17). Faith can be restored by tuning out the voices of the world and by tuning in the Word of God. God can turn our failure of faith into a dynamic experience when we focus on Him.

God's Word: Turn to me and be saved, all you ends of the earth; for I am God, and there is no other (Isaiah 45:22).

Prayer: Father, I am weak and vulnerable. Help my unbelief. Help me to look to You when my faith fails, as did Simon Peter, and be renewed. Amen.

FEBRUARY 23

PRAY AND TRUST GOD

Can you say with the psalmist, "The Lord has heard my cry for mercy" (Psalm 6:9)? When you pray, do you pray believing that God will answer? The Bible teaches that God desires a love relationship with us. That being true, we can have confidence that God wants us to talk to Him. Likewise, we must be willing to listen.

God answers prayers—all of them—but not always in the way we want Him to answer. Sometimes, when we pray, we really don't know what we are asking. At all times, we must pray and trust God with the answer. We must understand that God sees the whole picture, and we cannot. God has the wisdom to know how to answer our prayers even if we are not wise in what we ask. That is why we must pray and trust God.

Sometimes God speedily grants our request. At other times, he waits for the right moment to respond. And there are times when our requests are so ridiculous that God just remains silent. It is in those silent times that we must trust God. It is helpful to keep a written record of our requests to God. By writing down our request and putting a date to it, we can record when the prayer is answered. If God doesn't answer our prayer, it is because what we request is not good for us or the timing is not right. But we must pray and trust God who knows what is best.

God's Word: Be still before the LORD and wait patiently for him; do not fret when people succeed in their ways, when they carry out their wicked schemes (Psalm 37:7).

Prayer: Father, help me to pray believing and with patience trusting Your wisdom to respond in the way that is best for me. Amen.

FEBRUARY 24

NEVER IN A HURRY

The next time you find yourself in a hurry, which might be right now, take a moment to think about Jesus. There is no indication in the Bible that Jesus was ever in a hurry, not even when he received word of the death of his dear friend Lazarus. Yet, in every way, he was right on time. Jesus lived a busy life, but he was never too busy to meet a need and never irritated by an interruption.

Our hurried lifestyle does little to enhance our spiritual life and often robs us of ministry opportunities. Slow down, take a deep breath, take stock of the wastefulness of hurry and the anxiety and tension it creates. Our heavenly Father said, "Be still and know that I am God" (Psalm 46:10). A slower pace and even the pause of stillness will make your life more enjoyable, efficient, and effective.

God's Word: Desire without knowledge is not good—how much more will hasty feet miss the way (Proverbs 19:2).

Prayer: Father, slow me down that I may hear You and be alert to opportunities to minister to others. Slow me down so that I will appreciate Your blessings and accomplish Your will. Amen.

FEBRUARY 25

GOD WORKS FROM THE INSIDE

Dr. Wayne Beneck, a Pennsylvania pastor, tells the story of a six-year-old boy who was helping his mom with spring gardening. The mother was absorbed in her work while her son was exploring the miracle of growth. Suddenly, the boy picked up a daffodil bud, sat down, held the bud in his hands, studied it, and then tried to force it into bloom. The result, of course, was disappointing and a mess.

Frustrated, he asked, "Mommy, why is it that when I try to open the bud, it falls to pieces and dies? How does God open it up to a beautiful flower?" Before his mother could respond, a broad smile came upon the child's face as he exclaimed, "Oh, I know. God always works from the inside." The next time you try to force something to happen, remember God works from the inside.

God's Word: For it is God who works in you to will and to act in order to fulfill his good purpose (Philippians 2:13).

Prayer: Lord, let my outward actions reflect a heart devoted to You. Amen.

FEBRUARY 26

SHAPING TO FIT

A man who lost his wife, his home, and his job was trying desperately to hold on to the only thing he had left—his faith. As he stood watching workmen doing stonework on a church, he noticed a stone cutter chiseling a triangular piece of rock. "What are you going to do with that stone?" he asked. "Do you see that little opening way up there near the spire? Well, I'm shaping this down here so that it will fit up there." Tears filled the observer's eyes as he walked away. God had spoken to him through a stone cutter who didn't know the ordeal through which he was passing.

As you face sorrow, disappointment, grief, and loss, remember that God is shaping us down here so that we will fit up there. We can better face our experiences on earth when we understand that God is preparing us for eternity.

God's Word: And we know that in all things God works for the good of those who love him, who have been called according to his purpose (Romans 8:28).

Prayer: Father, in my trials and tribulations, remind me that You are molding and shaping me for eternity. Amen.

FEBRUARY 27

PRAISE THE LORD

Psalm 103 says, "Praise the Lord, my soul; all my inmost being, praise his holy name." When was the last time you just praised the Lord? We are so geared in our society to getting and receiving that most of us think of prayer as asking God for what we want and expecting to get it when we want it. We so often treat God as some grandfather in the sky who sits around heaven waiting to answer our requests. Or perhaps we think of heaven as a shipping station with God as the manager ready to fill our order.

Isn't it time for us to be alone with God without asking for anything? Don't you sense the need to just praise the Lord for what He has already done for you? Let this be a day of praise and worship to God; ask nothing all day long—just give Him praise and thanksgiving.

God's Word: Through Jesus, therefore, let us continually offer to God a sacrifice of praise—the fruit of lips that openly profess his name (Hebrews 13:15).

Prayer: Father, today, I praise You and thank You for all that You have done for me through Jesus Christ your Son. Let my lips and my life be an expression of praise and thanksgiving. Amen.

FEBRUARY 28

FRUIT BEARING

While living in Brazil as missionaries, we lived on a fruit farm. We grew a variety of fruit-bearing trees like cashew, bananas, orange, lemon, lime, and coconuts. It was an education in itself to have these delicious fruits at our disposal. We learned that it takes a lot of water for banana plants and twelve months to produce a stalk of bananas. Cashew is a fruit with the nut coming along as a bonus. Orange, lemon, and lime trees take three years to produce the first fruit. Coconut not only provides meat for a delicious cake, but its water can help you survive in a hot desert as well as help keep you healthy.

Fruits have their times and seasons. So it is with human beings. So it is with our spiritual growth. It takes time, sunshine, rain, and nutrients in the soil to produce delicious fruit. Spiritual growth and maturity come from good times and bad, from high moments and low moments. All are necessary to mold and shape us into fruitful servants.

In John 15, Jesus explained the process of spiritual growth and fruit-bearing. As a fruit cannot be produced apart from the vine, Christians cannot be fruitful apart from a relationship with Jesus Christ. Nothing compares to vine-ripe fruit. Likewise, nothing compares to our being attached to Christ.

God's Word: By their fruit you will recognize them. Do people pick grapes from thornbushes, or figs from thistles? Likewise every good tree bears good fruit, but a bad tree bears bad fruit. A good tree cannot bear bad fruit, and a bad tree cannot bear good fruit. Every tree that does not bear good fruit is cut down and thrown into the fire. Thus, by their fruit you will recognize them (Matthew 7:16–20).

Prayer: Father, keep me close to You so that I will bear good fruit and be useful to You. Amen.

FEBRUARY 29

LEAP DAY

Have you ever wished you had more time in a day? How about a whole extra day to catch up? You have it, at least, you have one day every four years. We call it Leap Year and the day Leap Day. Leap Year and Leap Day are necessary because the Earth orbits the sun in approximately 365.25 days. That .25 creates the need for a Leap Year every four years. If the extra day added to February, which normally has only 28 days, was not added, over time and without correction, our calendar year would drift away from the solar year and be off by a day every four years. If we did not add a day to our calendar every four years, instead of February coming in the winter season, it would be a summer month in the Northern Hemisphere.

Never complain that you don't have enough time when every four years you are given the bonus of a full day. The truth is that we all have the same amount of time. It is our use of time that makes the difference in our productivity. What discipline do you need in your life to make your life more productive?

God's Word: A sluggard's appetite is never filled, but the desires of the diligent are fully satisfied (Proverbs 13:4).

Prayer: Father, teach me to be disciplined in the use of my time so that I can lead a productive life. Teach me how to balance my time between work, play, and rest so that I will not grow weary in well-doing. Amen.

MARCH 1

FOULED UP

A young navy pilot was engaged in maneuvers. The admiral had demanded absolute radio silence. However, the young pilot mistakenly turned on his radio and was heard to mutter, "Boy, am I fouled up!" The admiral grabbed the mike, ordered all channels to be opened, and said, "Will the pilot who broke the radio silence identify himself immediately!" A long silence ensued before a small voice was heard over the airwaves, "I'm fouled up but not that fouled up!"

Putting yourself in that navy pilot's position, you probably would not have identified yourself either. Perhaps you wouldn't have even responded at all. When we foul up, God knows it because nothing is hidden from Him. The good news is that God does not need us to identify ourselves. God knows our sins. He just wants us to recognize them and confess them. What are you waiting for?

God's Word: Then I acknowledged my sin to you and did not cover up my iniquity. I said, "I will confess my transgressions to the Lord." And you forgave the guilt of my sin (Psalm 32:5).

Prayer: Father, I know that you are aware of my failures. You know when I foul up. But Lord, help me to recognize and acknowledge my sins, confess them, and lean on Your mercy and grace for forgiveness. Amen.

MARCH 2

SUCCESSFUL PEOPLE

Studies show that successful people have positive attitudes. Because of their positive attitudes, they enjoy what they do. An old veteran employed by the city to polish the cannon at the civic center each day retired. Someone asked him what he was going to do with his leisure time. He said, "I'm going to buy a cannon and polish it every day."

Life is too short not to enjoy. Life should not be a drag on our emotions or dreaded. Find a job that challenges you, excites you, gives you fulfillment, and makes you want to get up in the morning. Life is too precious to waste. You only get one shot at it. Embrace the talents and abilities that God has given you. Develop them so that your work is a joy and pleasure rather than just a paycheck.

To be successful, give God the best that you have. Make Him the priority of your life. Serve others with joy as a testimony of your devotion to God. Never be satisfied with mediocrity.

God's Word: Do not conform to the pattern of this world, but be transformed by the renewing of your mind. Then you will be able to test and approve what God's will is—his good, pleasing and perfect will (Romans 12:2).

Prayer: Father, help me to keep my mind focused on You so that my attitude will be positive, and I can experience joy and fulfillment in what I do. Amen.

MARCH 3

OVERCOMING HATRED

Racism, racial hatred, and prejudice are among the greatest problems in the world. Ask yourself, "Am I a part of the problem or a part of the solution?" Do I really believe that all people were created by God? What if I had been born of a different culture or race? How would I want to be treated?

Is there any hope of overcoming this terrible evil? Nancy Hastings, in *Sojourners*, tells of Granny Lindsay, a ninety-year-old black lady who had been pushed around by racial prejudice all her life. A few years before she died, someone asked her how she had kept from being eaten up with anger and resentment. Her response was profound. "I never was much good at loving everybody. But I got pretty good at loving the someone who knew how to love them. And that was the beginning of healing."[1]

Loving God and allowing God's love to penetrate our lives until we can love others is the only solution.

God's Word: Anyone who claims to be in the light but hates a brother or sister is still in the darkness. Anyone who loves their brother and sister lives in the light, and there is nothing in them to make them stumble. But anyone who hates a brother or sister is in the darkness and walks around in the darkness. They do not know where they are going, because darkness has blinded them (1 John 2:9–11).

Prayer: Father, help me to walk in the light and to love my fellow man as You have loved me. Amen.

---

[1] *Sojourners*, Feb.-Mar, 1993, by Nancy Hastings Sehested, 35.

MARCH 4

KNOWING GOD

A little girl was puzzled, "What is God like?" She asked her mother, who told her to ask her father. Hopeful for an answer, she approached her father, saying, "Daddy, you know more than anyone in the whole world. Can you tell me what God is like?" Her father mumbled something from behind his daily paper, which left her frustrated and disappointed. Several days later, her parents found a piece of paper inscribed in a childish scrawl with these words, "I think if I had lived as long as my mother and father, I would know something about God." What about you? How would you respond if your child or anyone else asked you, "What is God like?"

The Bible, of course, takes first place among all books in helping us to understand more about God. J. I. Packer's book, *Knowing God*, has been an immense help to me in strengthening my relationship with God. Oswald Chambers's *My Utmost for His Highest* will enrich your spiritual life.

Isn't it time for you to get better acquainted with God, to whom you will give an account for how you have lived your life?

God's Word: This is what the Lord says: Let not the wise boast of their wisdom or the strong boast of their strength or the rich boast of their riches, but let the one who boasts about this: that they have the understanding to know me, that I am the Lord, who exercises kindness, justice and righteousness on earth (Jeremiah 9:23–24).

Prayer: Father, help me to know that the most important thing I can do as a parent is to introduce my children to God. Amen.

MARCH 5

THE GOOD OLE DAYS

People speak about "the good ole days" as if nothing is good about today. Admittedly, the world is filled with troubles, but so it has been ever since Adam and Eve sinned against God in the Garden of Eden.

People who live in the past forget that back then, scandals existed, wars raged, there was no indoor plumbing or air-conditioning, no microwaves, no weather warnings, no TV, cell phones or internet, or any of the conveniences we take for granted today. News, good and bad, moved slowly, and vaccines against dreadful diseases were unknown.

We so easily forget that the same God who held the future "in the good ole days" still holds it today. Whether you choose to live in the past or present is your choice, but it is God who makes the difference in how we face life. David, the poet-king, said, "My times are in your hands" (Psalm 31:15).

God's Word: God is our refuge and strength, an ever-present help in trouble. Therefore we will not fear, though the earth give way and the mountains fall into the heart of the sea (Psalm 46:1–2).

Prayer: Father, my time is in Your hands. Help me to recognize You as my refuge and strength. May my trust in You calm my fears. Amen.

MARCH 6

SLOW ME DOWN

We're in the first quarter of the new year, and you find yourself rushing around, filled with stress, and worried about how things are going to turn out. Your heart is pounding, and you long for a day of peace, quiet, and calm.

Think about what you are experiencing in this way: just as no one else can breathe for you, no one else can control the pace that you are living. It is up to you, but God can help. You need to quieten your mind so that you can think clearly. You need the still waters of which the psalmist speaks (Psalm 23:2). You long to experience the restoration of your soul. You need a night of restful sleep.

Today is the day for you to step back, stop your frantic activity, take a deep breath, and find a quiet place, if only for a brief time. Say to yourself, "Slow me down." Take a good look at what you are doing and set some priorities. Recognize that you cannot do everything, but you can do the most important things. Reduce the number of things that you are trying to do each day. Let God's Word and prayer be your priority. Then ask God to help you choose wisely and reasonably what needs to be done today. Give yourself minibreaks during the day—time to pause and look at a beautiful flower or plant, time to make a phone call to someone who is sick or lonely, time to look up into the heavens to see the splendor of God, or watch the birds or squirrels take care of their daily needs. For your health—mentally, physically, and spiritually—pray "slow me down, Lord.

God's Word: Be still before the Lord and wait patiently for him; do not fret when people succeed in their ways, when they carry out their wicked schemes (Psalm 37:7).

Prayer: Father, there is so much in life that I cannot control; help me to accept my limitations and learn to put things into Your hands. Let Your presence in my life slow me down and calm my pounding heart as I trust You to give me peace. Amen.

MARCH 7

CHAINS

The story is told of a blacksmith in medieval times who was taken prisoner. He was thrown into a dark and dirty dungeon. There he would remain, his arm and legs chained to a wall the rest of his days. In desperation, he examined the chains that bound him for some flaw that might make it possible to break the chain and escape. But immediately, he recognized that he was the one who had forged the chain. It was also he who had boasted for years that he could forge chains that no man could break.

Consider that we sometimes are forced to wear chains that we have made and cannot be easily broken. The only one who has the power to free us from the chain of our sins is Jesus Christ. Christ is the key to your freedom from the bondage of sin. Look to Him and be saved.

God's Word: When hard pressed, I cried to the Lord; he brought me into a spacious place (Psalm 118:5).

Prayer: Father, I confess that by my sins, I have brought trouble upon myself. I am helpless to break the chains that now bind me. I confess my sins and ask for Your mercy, grace, and forgiveness to free me from my bondage. Amen.

MARCH 8

VOICE OF ENCOURAGEMENT

A young man determined that he would sail around the world in a small boat. On the appointed day of departure, a large crowd gathered to see him off. Pessimism prevailed as people warned that the sun would broil him, he wouldn't have enough food, or that his boat could not withstand the waves of a storm. Some shouted, "You'll never make it." As the young man shoved off from the dock, one lone man began to wave and shout, "Bon voyage! You're really something! We're with you! We're proud of you! Good luck, brother!"

When you see someone making an honest effort to achieve something in life, are you a voice of pessimism and discouragement or a voice of hope and encouragement? In a world filled with pessimism, there is plenty of room for optimism. In a world determined to discourage and defeat him, apostle Paul placed his life in the hands of the One in whom all things are possible.

God's Word: I can do all things through Christ who strengthens me (Philippians 4:13).

Prayer: Father, help me to live in the power of Your strength and to understand that it is in Your strength that I can do what otherwise could not be done. Amen.

MARCH 9

INSPIRATION

A picture of my paternal grandfather, J. E. Allard, hangs above my desk. I look at his picture and remember what a wonderful man he was. He came to the United States from England as a young man and was in Oklahoma before the territory became a state. He learned to punch cattle, shoot guns, trade with Indians, and tame wild horses. He admitted that his early life was rough. Over the course of his life, he was a cowboy, a farmer, and a railroad man. When he turned his life over to Jesus Christ, he became a powerful preacher of the gospel. He raised five boys and a girl, all of whom became strong Christians. After his first wife died, he married again and had three more daughters.

My grandfather earned his living as chief draftsman of the Atlantic Coast Line Railroad in Wilmington, North Carolina. He pastored rural churches, my uncle said, that "no one else would pastor." He stayed in his last pastorate for thirteen years, retiring at the age of eighty-two. After retirement, he continued to attend church even when he lost most of his hearing. A deacon told him that they would understand if he didn't come to church anymore because of his hearing problem. My grandfather replied, "I don't want anyone to doubt whose side I'm on." My grandfather never gave up; he just wore out and went home to be with the Lord at the age of ninety-two.

He left our family an example and legacy of which we can be proud. As I look at his picture, I know that he can't see me, but he certainly does inspire me. If you have someone in your life who inspires you, thank God for him or her and live up to the challenge.

God's Word: Always set an example by doing good things. When you teach, be an example of moral purity and dignity. Speak an accurate message that cannot be condemned (Titus 2:6–8).

Prayer: Father, as people have inspired me, help me to live a life that will inspire others and honor Your name. Amen.

MARCH 10

RELIGION OR JESUS

Religion is not the answer to humankind's deepest need. Religion is humans searching for God or a power greater than themselves. The answer to our deepest problems cannot be found in religion but rather in Jesus Christ. Christianity is based on Jesus Christ, the Son of God, who came to this earth, died on the cross for our sins, and rose again, giving us a guarantee of eternal life. Christianity is God searching for humans.

Bad religion is one of the curses of the world. Bad religion and bad theology will lead you down the wrong road. The world doesn't need religion, although there is an abundance of it. The world needs Jesus. Jesus is the answer to those who walk in darkness. He is peace and hope. He is the Way, the Truth, and the Life. He is the one who gave himself as a sacrifice on our behalf. Jesus took the punishment that we deserve for our sins upon himself and died on the cross. Jesus, and only Jesus, can give us abundant life.

The popular thought that one religion is as good as another is a myth and misleading. The Bible does not promote religion. It centers on Christ and invites us to come to Him.

God's Word: For God was pleased to have all his fullness dwell in him, and through him to reconcile to himself all things, whether things on earth or things in heaven, by making peace through his blood, shed on the cross (Colossians 1:19).

Prayer: Father, thank you for sending Your Son into the world so that all who believe in Him might be saved and have eternal life. Amen.

MARCH 11

EMPATHY

Empathy is a much-needed virtue in today's world. Unless you have experienced the problem that others are having, it is difficult to understand their situation.

In the 1930s, Lamotte Cohn, general manager of what is now American Airlines, called all his managers to a meeting to discuss lost or displaced luggage. Lost luggage was the number one problem of the airline at that time, and all efforts to address the problem had failed. So Lamotte determined that he would get his manager's attention in a way that they would have empathy for distressed and inconvenienced passengers.

Cleverly, he called in the managers from all over the country to attend a meeting at company headquarters to resolve the lost baggage issue. What they didn't know was that on the day of their flight, he sent orders to all baggage handlers to make certain that all the manager's baggage was sent to the wrong destination.

Once the managers had experienced for themselves the frustration of lost baggage, the company greatly improved its efficiency in baggage handling. A personal loss causes us to be more sympathetic with others in the same situation. Find someone who is hurting in the way you have been hurt and lend a supporting hand.

God's Word: Praise be to the God and Father of our Lord Jesus Christ, the Father of compassion and the God of all comfort, who comforts us in all our troubles, so that we can comfort those in any trouble with the comfort we ourselves receive from God (2 Corinthians 1:3–4).

Prayer: Father, help me to grow in my empathy for the suffering of others and let my hurts enhance my ability to bring encouragement to my fellow humans. Amen.

MARCH 12

HITCHHIKER

As a young boy, I had three ways of getting around: walking, bicycling, or hitchhiking. I'll admit that the easiest alternative was hitchhiking, although it had its risks. It is also more dangerous today than when I was a youth. A hitchhiker is someone who goes along for the ride without paying for the gas or assuming any responsibility for insurance or car upkeep. If you pick up a hitchhiker and have an accident, you can be sued.

I have come to realize that there are hitchhikers in church. There are folk who come to the church saying, "I'll use your attractive building, enjoy your choir, and even listen to the sermon. I'll use your lights, heating system, restrooms, and air-conditioning and call upon the pastor or church staff if I have a need. But don't ask me to give money to the church or expect me to get involved in visitation or any of the ministries. I'll ride free but don't expect anything from me. And, if I get hurt, you will hear from me."

Are you a church hitchhiker? If so, it is clear that you have no understanding of Jesus, who loved the church and gave himself for it. You have no understanding of the truth that Jesus taught that "it is more blessed to give than to receive." The real joy in life, as in the church, is not in seeking a free ride but in pulling your own weight, being involved, serving, and being a part of the mission and ministry to which Jesus calls us. Discipleship has a cost.

God's Word: For even the Son of Man did not come to be served but to serve, and to give his life as a ransom for many (Mark 10:45).

Prayer: Father, let me know the joy of being a participant in Your kingdom work, serving with gladness, and not expecting anything in return. Amen.

MARCH 13

HEALTH

Doctors will tell you that exercise improves your mental abilities. Exercise can help you clear your mind and think better. Exercise strengthens your heart, reduces your stress level, improves your digestion, and helps you to have a restful night of sleep.

Exercise doesn't have to be excessive, expensive, or boring—walking will do. If you have a sedentary lifestyle, you can significantly increase your health by even a moderate change in lifestyle. Instead of lying down on the couch or raring back in your easy chair after a day of sitting in the office, get out in the fresh air and walk around the block. It is estimated that one year of a changed lifestyle can undo serious coronary disease damage.

When we recognize that our bodies are the temple of God, that should be incentive enough to keep His sanctuary healthy.

God's Word: Do you not know that your bodies are temples of the Holy Spirit, who is in you, whom you received from God? You are not your own; You were bought at a price. Therefore honor God with your bodies (1 Corinthians 6:19–20).

Prayer: Father, help me to respect and care for the body that You have given me so that I may serve You with strength and renewed energy. Amen.

MARCH 14

RETURNS

A retired minister took his grandson up into the mountains where he had been invited to preach in the absence of the pastor. When they passed the offering plate, the minister put in a crinkled dollar bill and the grandson put in twenty-five cents. At the close of the service, the church treasurer presented the guest preacher with the total love offering for the day, $1.25. Commenting to his grandfather as they left the church, the grandson said, "Grandpa, if we had put more into it, we would've gotten more out of it."

A basic principle of life is reaping what you sow. If you want joy, happiness, peace, and contentment in life, you must put those ingredients into it. To help us succeed in reaping a good return, God offers His Holy Spirit. Galatians 5:22–23 speaks of the fruits of the Spirit: love, joy, peace, forbearance, kindness, goodness, faithfulness gentleness, and self-control. When we allow the Holy Spirit to help us with our sowing, the joyful benefits of reaping will come in positive, fulfilling ways.

God's Word: Now he who supplies seed to the sower and bread for food will also supply and increase your store of seed and will enlarge the harvest of your righteousness. You will be enriched in every way so that you can be generous on every occasion and through us your generosity will result in thanksgiving to God (2 Corinthians 9:10–11).

Prayer: Father, help me to always be generous in every way as an expression of my gratitude for all that You do for me. Amen.

MARCH 15

RIGIDITY

It is possible to be so rigid in your religious convictions as to repel the very people you would like to influence. You can be so aggressive and overbearing in your witnessing that those you want to reach will avoid you. The scribes and Pharisees of Jesus's day were rigid, aggressive, and overbearing to the point that they were despised. An old saying is worth remembering: "It is possible to be so heavenly minded that you are of no earthly good."

In a forest after a big storm, plenty of broken oak limbs can be found lying on the ground. But you rarely find any branches from fir trees. Oak trees are big and strong, but they stand stiff, straight, and rigid. Because they are so inflexible, they crack and break. Fir trees, on the other hand, being very flexible, stand firm when the storm passes.

The flexibility of Jesus is seen in his empathy and understanding of the vulnerabilities of others. It is especially seen in his forgiving and loving nature toward sinners. Is it any wonder that Jesus's approach to people was more appealing than that of the scribes and Pharisees? Be careful in being so rigid in your convictions that you break the opportunity to be a fruitful witness.

God's Word: Jesus straightened up and asked her, "Woman, where are they? Has no one condemned you?" "No one, sir," she said. "Then neither do I condemn you," Jesus declared. "Go now and leave your life of sin" (John 8:10–11).
Prayer: Father, in my zeal to witness for You, help me to show empathy and compassion to those I am trying to influence. Amen.

MARCH 16

INTERRUPTIONS

If you have ever been interrupted right in the middle of something particularly important, you know how frustrating and irritating that can be. Interruptions can sometimes cause you to lose your train of thought or miss a deadline. They can also make you angry. What if you have planned an entire year for a special vacation, and sickness or death interrupts your plans, and everything must be canceled or delayed? The truth is that interruptions are a part of life. How you deal with an interruption is a test of your character.

A study of scripture shows that Jesus was often interrupted. On one occasion, he was speaking to a crowd of people inside a home when a sick man was let down through the roof by concerned friends who wanted Jesus to heal their friend. On another day, a sick woman sought the help of Jesus by reaching out and touching His garment while he was walking in a crowd of people. Jesus used His interruptions as a time to minister. When He was interrupted or inconvenienced, we never see Him frustrated, irritated, or angry. We see, in Him, empathy and compassion. Responding with compassion to an interruption was more important to Jesus than His schedule.

We can all learn from Jesus's example. The next time you are interrupted by the telephone, a casual visitor, sickness, death, or someone's pressing need, accept it as an opportunity to demonstrate compassion and love.

God's Word: (abbreviated) As Jesus and his disciples, together with a large crowd, were leaving the city, a blind man, Bartimaeus, was sitting by the roadside begging … he began to shout, "Jesus, Son of David, have mercy on me!"… Jesus stopped and said, "call him." So they called to the blind man,… he jumped to his feet and came to Jesus (Mark 10:46–52).

Prayer: Father, help me never to be so involved in my work or schedule that I fail to respond with love when I am interrupted. Amen.

MARCH 17

OVERLOOKED

We have eyes, but we do not always see. We have ears but do not always hear. The truth is that we can be both spiritually blind and spiritually deaf. It is certainly true that we often fail to see or hear what God is doing. There is the story of a church that received into their fellowship and baptized three nine-year-old boys. After the church was forced to close its doors, the only record for that year was a negative comment from the pastor that said, "It has not been a good year for our church. We have lost 27 members. Three joined the church and they were only children"[2]

Both pastor and church members failed to see what God did in that church in the year described as not being good. Those three boys who joined the church grew up. Dick White became a dedicated missionary. Bert Newman became a theological professor in Africa, and Dr. Tony Campolo became a Christian professor, sociologist, popular speaker, and one of the best-selling Christian authors in America.

God uses events and people to accomplish His work even when those who have eyes to see, don't.

God's Word: But blessed are your eyes because they see and your ears because they hear (Matthew 13:16).

Prayer: Father, help me to be alert to what You are doing around me and teach me to look for what You are doing. Amen.

---

[2] Marlene LeFever, "Only Children," *The Advocate*, September 1992, 13.

MARCH 18

EMERGENCY

In the cartoon, rather than call an expert, Dagwood proceeds to fix a leaking faucet by bringing three sizes of wrenches. When the small ones don't work, he uses the larger one, only to break the pipe, sending water rushing all over the kitchen while Blondie runs to call the plumber.

Dagwood's dilemma may be a reminder of the times you have tried to fix something only to make matters worse. It is a shame that we get ourselves into deep trouble before calling upon God. Trying to fix things ourselves, when we know full well that we are incapable of doing so, is foolish. Yet, we all must admit that God is often our last resource when He should be our first.

Jesus taught us that we have only to ask, and we will receive. We have only to knock, and the door will be opened. We have only to seek, and we will find. When God makes things so simple, why do we complicate them? The next time something goes wrong in your life, call God first.

God's Word: May the Lord answer you when you are in distress; may the name of the God of Jacob protect you. May he send you help from the sanctuary and grant you support from Zion. May he remember all your sacrifices and accept your burnt offerings (Psalm 20:1–2).

Prayer: Father, be my first responder because I seek You first and rely on Your wisdom. Give me discernment in making decisions and keep me from foolishness. Amen.

MARCH 19

WORDS

Watching the news on TV, hearing it over the radio, or reading the newspapers of current events on the local and national scene, the impact of words comes vividly to mind. How we speak, the tone of our voice, the choice of vocabulary, all say something about who we are. Words can heal and encourage, or they can depress and destroy. Words can change lives or wreck them. Words are tools of comfort or instruments of warfare.

It is important to take note of how we speak and what we say. It is a bitter pill to have to eat our own words. Recognizing that the tongue is a fire, "a world of evil among the parts of the body" (James 3:6), we should take note of what we say and how we say it. In other words, it is wise to think before we speak and measure the impact of what we say.

Let your words today be helpful and not hurtful, encouraging and not discouraging, uplifting and not degrading. When it comes to expressing ourselves, we need help. The Bible says "No human being can tame the tongue. It is a restless evil, full of deadly poison" (James 3:8). It's a good idea to think before we speak. It's a better idea to ask God to help us say things the right way.

God's Word: May these words of my mouth and this meditation of my heart be pleasing in your sight, Lord, my Rock and my Redeemer (Psalm 19:14).

Prayer: Father, let me guard my lips and the words of my mouth so that I will not offend others or dishonor you. Amen.

MARCH 20

CREATIVITY

How we see our world has everything to do with attitude. There is so much beauty to see if we will only look. There is so much music to enjoy if we will only listen. There are so many people to appreciate if we will only take the time. There is also so much to explore and imagine if we will only allow ourselves to be creative.

An art teacher was instructing her elementary school class to draw a flower. All the students set to work drawing ordinary representations of flowers. The teacher went around the room admiring their work and then stopped to look at one picture that did not look like the rest. She looked at the nonconformist student and said, "Flowers don't have smiles." Little Walt Disney looked right at her and answered, "Mine do."[3]

Someone expressed the creativity of God by saying, "Lovely flowers are the smiles of God's goodness." Walt Disney saw it that way. Do you? The next time you are given an assignment, use your creativity!

God's Word: A happy heart makes the face cheerful (Psalm 15:13).

Prayer: Father, open my eyes to see the joy and beauty that is all around me, the good that is in others, and the smiles that nature gives. Amen.

---

[3] A Creative Approach to Living," Rick Fowler, EdD, *Christian Psychology for Today*, vol. 7, no. 2, 28–29.

MARCH 21

AN ANCHOR

Everyone knows about Niagara Falls, but perhaps fewer people know that the Niagara River itself is a violent, tempestuous body of water that spills over the falls at thirty-two feet per second hitting the base of the falls with 280 tons of force on the American side and 2,509 tons on the Canadian side. The falls produce four million kilowatts of electricity, which is shared by both countries.

A tourist noticed an upstream sign on the Niagara River that asked daredevil boaters, "Do you have an anchor?" A few feet beyond that sign was another that asked, "Do you know how to use it?"

In life's tempestuous rush to a climatic end, those two questions are relevant and deserve an answer. The Bible teaches that Jesus is an anchor for the soul. Do you have Him in your life? And are you living for Him?

God's Word: I know whom I have believed, and am convinced that he is able to guard what I have entrusted to him until that day (2 Timothy 1:12).

Prayer: Father, Thank You for Jesus, who is my Savior, my Lord, my anchor. Amen.

MARCH 22

GOALPOSTS

After hearing life compared to an athletic contest, a young man asked the speaker, "How are we going to play the game of life when we don't know where the goalposts are?" The Bible is our guide to knowing the goalposts, and God is the one who established them. Apostle Paul wrote about goalposts when he said, "Whatever is true, whatever is noble, whatever is right, whatever is pure, whatever is lovely, whatever is admirable—if anything is excellent or praiseworthy—think about such things" (Philippians 4:8).

When you see greatness, admire it. When you witness majestic qualities of character, honor them. When you see dedication, desire it for yourself. When you see perseverance, imitate it. Just as an athlete improves his skills by playing with the best, you can improve your life by pursuing excellence. Excellence is the goalpost that God has established. The Holy Spirit is the one who enables us to be our best and pursue excellence.

God's Word: Have the same mindset as Christ Jesus (Philippians 2:5).

Prayer: Father, help me keep my mind on Jesus Christ so that my life will be pleasing to You. Amen.

MARCH 23

WISDOM

Wisdom is something we can all use in abundance. Hear and ponder the words of James, the brother of Jesus.

"Who is wise and understanding among you? Let them show it by their good life, by deeds done in the humility that comes from wisdom. But if you harbor bitter envy and selfish ambition in your hearts, do not boast about it or deny the truth. Such "wisdom" does not come down from heaven but is earthly, unspiritual, demonic. For where you have envy and selfish ambition, there you find disorder and every evil practice. But the wisdom that comes from heaven is first of all pure; then peace-loving, considerate, submissive, full of mercy and good fruit, impartial and sincere. Peacemakers who sow in peace reap a harvest of righteousness" (James 3:13–18).

Make certain that the wisdom you follow is not of this world but from God, who knows more about us and the world we live in than we will know in a lifetime.

God's Word: How much better to get wisdom than gold, to get insight rather than silver (Proverbs 16:16).

Prayer: Father, give me the desire to always seek Your wisdom before I make decisions. Help me to distinguish between the wisdom that You so freely offer and the wisdom of this world. Amen.

MARCH 24

PICKING UP THE PIECES

We all owe a debt of gratitude to individuals and business firms that adopt a highway or road and spend hours picking up trash that thoughtless people throw out of their cars every day. Have you ever wondered how any one of us would get around in this world if someone didn't pick up the trash?

Hats off to people who care. A special thanks to those who love life and nature enough to protect the rest of us from the dangers and diseases of garbage and trash. A salute to those who are dedicated to making our world a cleaner place to live.

Wouldn't it be wonderful if every person cared enough to make our world more beautiful and healthier? The next time you are tempted to throw trash out of your car or truck, *don't*! God placed us on this earth to cultivate the soil and to keep it—not trash it.

God's Word: The Lord God took the man and put him in the Garden of Eden to work it and take care of it (Genesis 2:15).

Prayer: Father, help me to so appreciate this world that you have made that I will do everything within my power to care for it and protect it. Amen.

MARCH 25

BROKEN THINGS

The world is filled with broken things. Look at any junkyard or visit any repair shop. It is not just things that break—people break, health fails, marriages dissolve, homes break, hearts break, relationships shatter, dreams demolish.

The good news is that Jesus Christ understands brokenness. He was broken for us. Because humans broke their relationship with God, our heavenly Father sent His Son to restore our brokenness by dying on the cross and rising again to assure us that we can be whole again and secure for all eternity.

Only the cross could demonstrate the tragedy of brokenness and personal sin. Only the cross could confirm God's love and desire to restore our soul.

God's Word: We all, like sheep, have gone astray, each of us has turned to our own way; and the Lord has laid on him the iniquity of us all (Isaiah 53:6).

Prayer: Father, thank You for healing my brokenness. Thank You for giving to me Your great salvation so rich and free. Amen.

MARCH 26

LEARNING NEW THINGS

The myth has passed down from generation to generation that "you can't teach an old dog new tricks." It's not true. It's just a myth. It's a lie. It's a put-down of seniors. It's a negative attitude and totally false.

The truth is that we never get too old to learn something new. Regardless of our age we can keep our brain functioning by taking up a new hobby or by working on challenging projects. Learning new things, even in our senior years, stimulates and enhances our brainpower.

In the same light, no one is too old to receive Jesus Christ as Lord and Savior. No one is too old to recognize personal sin or to ask for God's forgiveness. We are never too old to enhance our relationship with God. If we can learn new things mentally, we can also learn new things spiritually.

God's Word: I will instruct you and teach you in the way you should go; I will counsel you with my loving eye on you (Psalm 32:8).

Prayer: Father, I thank You that You don't put an age limit on learning and growing in our knowledge of You. Amen.

MARCH 27

GOD'S PLAN

The George Washington Bridge is an imposing double-decked suspension bridge spanning the Hudson River between New Jersey and New York. Towering six hundred feet high with a main span of thirty-five-hundred feet, each of the four supporting cables is a yard thick and consists of nearly twenty-seven thousand wires—enough wire to circle the earth four times at the Equator. This magnificent bridge began as a dream. The dream became a design on paper with every detail examined and reexamined before any actual work was begun.

Every great accomplishment begins with a vision or dream; then comes the plan, and finally the execution of the plan. So it was with God's purpose for the world and your life and mine. God has a plan for you and me. Ask Him, and He will reveal His plan for you.

God's Word: For we are his workmanship, created in Christ Jesus for good works, which God prepared beforehand, that we should walk in them (Ephesians 2:10).

Prayer: Father, help me to know Your plan for my life and to be faithful in carrying it out. Amen.

MARCH 28

THE VICTORY

Are you one of those individuals who starts a project but just never seems to finish it? You are not alone. Your numbers are legion. Perhaps you can be inspired by a lesson we can all learn from baseball as the season gets underway.

In baseball, victory is determined not by hits but by runs. The player who gets to third base doesn't get credit for three-quarters of a run. The satisfaction in baseball is crossing home plate. Fulfillment in life means completing the task.

Apostle Paul said, "I have fought the good fight, I have finished the race, I have kept the faith" (2 Timothy 4:7). Victory doesn't come with a good start; it comes at the finish line.

God's Word: Now finish the work, so that your eager willingness to do it may be matched by your completion of it according to your means (2 Corinthians 8:11).

Prayer: Father, help me to finish well the things that I enthusiastically start so that I will know the joy of fulfilling the task. Amen.

MARCH 29

JUST SHOW

In the early 1990s, financial woes forced Great Britain to cut back on the ceremonial changing of the guard at Buckingham Palace. For the most part, Palace Guards had become more show than actual security. Tradition overtook function and the cost of the guards overtook practicality.

The Christian life is not intended to be more show than service. Christians are not actors pretending to be like Jesus but rather true disciples living out the faith that Jesus taught. In Christian living, tradition should never overtake function. The Bible speaks of counting the cost before claiming to be a Christian.

The Christian life is to be lived with purpose, conviction, and in a way that honors Christ in word and deed. Jesus warned those who followed Him not to fall into the trap of showmanship. He warned against giving offerings, praying, and fasting just to be seen by men. Just "show" does not gain our Lord's approval. Those who do the right things for the wrong reasons have no reward in heaven.

God's Word: Be careful not to practice your righteousness in front of others to be seen by them. If you do, you will have no reward from your Father in heaven (Matthew 6:1–4).

Prayer: Father, help me to be genuine in serving You. Keep my heart and motives focused on pleasing You rather than impressing others. Amen.

MARCH 30

DON'T LOSE HEART

Job is more than just a book in the Bible. It is the story of a man who suffered great loss including family, friends, and possessions. You might say he lost everything he had, yet he refused to take his wife's advice to "curse God and die" (Job 2:9). In one of his low moments, Job said, "Yet when I hoped for good, evil came; when I looked for light, then came darkness" (Job 30:26). Job was, without a doubt, the classic sufferer of the Old Testament. In your suffering, you can find a companion in Job. It is helpful to know that you are not alone.

I once counseled a young lady who had given up on doing good for others. She said, "It seems like every time I stick my neck out to help someone, I get slapped in the face." Such experiences are certainly discouraging, and we are not exempt from having them.

Let us not forget that despite great suffering, grief, and disappointment, Job never lost his faith. He said, "Though he slay me, yet will I hope in him; I will surely defend my ways to his face. Indeed, this will turn out for my deliverance, for no godless person would dare come before him" (Job 13:15–16)!

Don't lose heart in times of difficulty. Let Job be your mentor and companion in keeping the faith.

God's Word: Let us not become weary in doing good, for at the proper time we will reap a harvest if we do not give up. Therefore, as we have opportunity, let us do good to all people, especially to those who belong to the family of believers (Galatians 6:9–10).

Prayer: Father, in the face of my suffering and difficulties, help me, like Job, to keep my faith. Amen.

MARCH 31

AWARENESS OF GOD

Scientists tell us that the earth rotates at one thousand miles per hour, and we are traveling around the sun at thirty-six thousand miles per hour without sensing the movement of our planet.

Just as we are unaware of the speed with which our earth moves through space, we are often unaware of the work of God. Just because we do not perceive something to be happening does not in any way mean that nothing is going on.

Much about life that you and I take for granted is just another manifestation of the grace and glory of God. Take a moment to thank God for all that he does even when we are unaware of it.

God's Word: For it is God who works in you to will and to act in order to fulfill his good purpose (Philippians 2:13).

Prayer: Father, help me to appreciate and give thanks for all that You do even when I am unaware that You are at work. Amen.

APRIL 1

RESPONDING TO AN ENEMY

The adage is "An eye for an eye and a tooth for a tooth." In other words, if someone wrongs you, get them back. Some even think you should hit back twice as hard. A little boy asked to quote the Golden Rule replied, "Do one unto others before they do one unto you." That is not what Jesus taught, but sadly it is how many people think and react.

Scripture gives clear instructions on how we are to respond to an enemy. We are to pray for our enemies, love them, do good to them, and bless them. Abraham Lincoln suggested that we work at eliminating our enemies by making them our friends. That is a great thought but sometimes difficult to achieve. The prophets Isaiah and Jeremiah demonstrated another approach. Rather than intensifying their efforts against their enemies, they deepened their relationship with God. Perhaps that is one reason Isaiah said, "You will keep in perfect peace those whose minds are steadfast, because they trust in you" (Isaiah 26:3).

The closer we are to God, the more Christlike we will be to our enemies. Soft answers and kind gestures can do a great deal to dispel violence. But in all situations of adversity, moving closer to God is wise and constructive.

God's Word: But I tell you, love your enemies and pray for those who persecute you, that you may be children of your Father in heaven (Matthew 5:44–45).

Prayer: Father, when it comes to responding with love, kindness, and goodwill to my enemies, I know that without Your Holy Spirit working in me, I cannot do it. So, keep me close to You so that my response to my enemies will bring honor to Your name. Amen.

APRIL 2

INVESTMENT OF YOUR LIFE

In what way are you investing your life and energy? It is important to know. Life is precious, time is short, and eternity awaits us.

Don't live selfishly. Don't spend your life accumulating more and more of what can be taken from you. Don't get caught up in the fever to possess, to accumulate, and to horde. Clean out your attic, garage, and closet and give to those who can benefit from your abundance. If you devote your life to that which is temporary, you end up with nothing.

Every material possession can be taken away from you in an instant. Invest your time and energy in bringing hope and encouragement to others. Seek to touch the life of another human being because what you engrave on the heart is immortal, and your investment will last for eternity.

Above the triple doorway of the Milan Cathedral are three inscriptions: "All that which pleases is but for a moment." All that which troubles us is but for a moment." "That only is important which is eternal."

God's Word: What do workers gain from their toil? I have seen the burden God has laid on the human race. He has made everything beautiful in its time. He has also set eternity in the human heart (Ecclesiastes 3:9–11).

Prayer: Father, teach me to invest my time and energy in that which is eternal rather than the temporary things of this earth. Amen.

APRIL 3

THE WORD OF GOD

Newspaper columnist Lewis Grizzard, writes about meeting a man named Otis "Smokey" Bailey who believed that everyone should have at least one Bible. So, he spent considerable time passing out Bibles to strangers in Atlanta, Georgia. Smokey believed that God's Word sets you free, and without it, you are prey to the devil.

The Bible is not a book of magic that will make your troubles go away. It is the Word of God that will help you through your trouble. When Jesus was tempted by Satan in the wilderness, He used the Word of God as his defense. Committing scripture to memory, as Jesus did, gives us a powerful weapon when temptation comes or when we need encouragement and guidance. Jesus modeled the power of scripture in the face of evil.

God's Word: Your word is a lamp for my feet, a light on my path. I have taken an oath and confirmed it. That I will follow your righteous laws (Psalm 119:105).

Prayer: Father, help me to keep your word on my mind and in my heart so that my testimony will point people to Christ. Amen.

APRIL 4

GOD'S WARMTH

Having trouble getting in touch with God? Do you feel that He is a long way off and unreachable? Perhaps you should take a good look at your schedule. It could be that you are too busy, too preoccupied, too distracted to sense God's presence. Pull back, take a good long walk on the beach or in the woods, around the block, or wherever you can be alone and find solitude. There is something about the peace and calm of nature that brings us closer to God.

If you sleep next to someone or sit down beside someone, and then they move, for a time, you can still feel the warmth where they were. If you are attentive, you can also sense the warmth of God's presence. When you are tuned in, you can walk into a house and sense that your loved one is absent or present. In the same way, we are aware of God's presence or absence. God gives us that sensory perception. If God seems to be far away from you, guess who moved?

God's Word: Submit yourselves, then, to God. Resist the devil, and he will flee from you. Come near to God and he will come near to you. Wash your hands, you sinners, and purify your hearts, you double-minded. Grieve, mourn and wail. Change your laughter to mourning and your joy to gloom. Humble yourselves before the Lord, and he will lift you up (James 4:7–10).

Prayer: Father, You have promised to be with me always. If I feel that You are far from me, help me to see that it is my sins that have separated us. Help me to come to You in repentance and feel the warmth of Your love and forgiveness. Amen.

APRIL 5

WHEN TO OPEN AND SHUT THE DOOR

We know from daily experience when to open a door and when to shut a door. Doors are both figuratively and literally prominent in the Bible. After Noah and his family were safely inside the ark, "Then the Lord shut him in" (Genesis 7:16). After Christ's death and absence from the disciples and before they experienced new power and courage at Pentecost, they "were together with the doors locked for fear of the Jewish leaders" (John 20:19). The five foolish virgins who went for extra oil found on their return that the door to the marriage feast was shut (Matthew 25:10). Jesus said, "I am the gate; whoever enters through me will be saved" (John 10:9). In Revelation 3:20, Jesus said, "Here I am! I stand at the door and knock."

We should always open the door to Jesus, but we should shut the door to Satan. We should open the door to the present and opportunities to serve the Lord, but we should shut the door to the past. Apostle Paul said, "I press on to take hold of that for which Christ Jesus took hold of me" (Philippians 3:12). Then he said, "But one thing I do: Forgetting what is behind" (Philippians 3:13).

We should open the door to conversation with God and shut the door to anything that interferes with our fellowship with Him. The instructions in Matthew 6:6 are clear: "When you pray, go into your room, close the door and pray to your Father, who is unseen. Then your Father, who sees what is done in secret, will reward you."

God's Word: These are the words of him who is holy and true, who holds the key of David. What he opens no one can shut and what he shuts no one can open (Revelation 3:8).

Prayer: Father, give me the wisdom to know when to shut a door and when to open it. Keep me from evil but draw me to that which honors you. Amen.

APRIL 6

EMERGENCY PRAYERS

They agreed that they needed to pray together before leaving the trench, but all three men were in the heat of battle in the war against Iraq. Three American soldiers found themselves in the same trench mixed with emotions but mostly just afraid. Unfamiliar with spiritual matters, one soldier pulled a crucifix from his pocket, a gift from his sister before being deployed. They stared at each other for a moment when two other soldiers joined them. One of the new arrivals was a chaplain. "Man, one of the soldiers said, "Are we glad to see you!" Holding up the crucifix he asked, "How do you work one of these things."

It is sad indeed when we face an emergency or even death and don't know how to pray. It is sad to think about God only in an emergency hoping that He will get us out of trouble.

Faith that is cultivated daily keeps us from pushing the panic button in times of trouble. If we, as the Bible instructs, pray without ceasing, we are building a relationship with God in such a way that we don't have to worry about how to pray when an emergency arises.

God's Word: The Lord is far from the wicked but he hears the prayer of the righteous (Proverbs 15:29).

Prayer: Father, help me to keep my relationship with You up-to-date so that when trouble comes, I can pray with confidence that You will hear my prayer. Amen.

APRIL 7

MY BODY

Stop! Look! Listen! You may be old enough to remember these words of warning on cross beams at a railroad track. These words are not only appropriate in warning travelers of the danger of an oncoming train, but they apply also to the way we treat our bodies. Most people are not abused by others; they abuse themselves.

People who overeat, consume alcoholic beverages, use drugs, disregard proper hygiene, overextend themselves, fail to get proper rest or get regular medical checkups, suffer the consequences of their abuse and neglect. If you are one of the self-abusers of whom I speak, isn't it time for you to *stop*, *look*, and *listen* to what you are doing to your body? When you are abusing your body, believe me, your body will let you know it. Self-abusers can rarely help themselves. They need professional attention. If you are in the trap of self-abuse, acknowledge your problem. Help is available if you will seek it. It is a decision you must make yourself. There is a better way to live, but you must want it.

God's Word: Do you not know that your bodies are temples of the Holy Spirit, who is in you, whom you have received from God? You are not your own; you were bought at a price. Therefore honor God with your bodies (1 Corinthians 6:19–20).

Prayer: Father, help me to present my body to You as a living sacrifice. Cleanse me from my sin; help me in my helplessness to lean upon You. Amen.

APRIL 8

STYROFOAM

Have you noticed that we live in a Styrofoam society? So many things that we order today come packaged in Styrofoam. Why? Because Styrofoam provides great protection and insulation. Styrofoam is a remarkable material composed of zillions of tiny foam particles pressed together. But you may have noticed that if these particles separate, they fly away in every direction and stick to almost everything. If the particles are together, they are useful. Separated, they are a mess.

The church is a lot like Styrofoam. When God's people are bonded together in the church, they experience a sense of protection and purpose. Together, Christians can face and endure almost anything. Detached from the church body, like separated Styrofoam, it is easier to stick to almost anything. Separated from the body of Christ, a believer is vulnerable to temptation and the attacks of Satan.

The world has far too many people who are blown about by every conceivable influence and wind of doctrine. It is vitally important to be bonded together in the Word of God and the family of God.

God's Word: Let us hold unswervingly to the hope we profess, for he who promised is faithful. And let us consider how we may spur one another on toward love and good deeds, not giving up meeting together, as some are in the habit of doing, but encouraging one another—and all the more as you see the Day approaching (Hebrews 10:23–25).

Prayer: Father, help me to see the value of belonging to the body of Christ knowing that apart from Christ and separated from His church, I am weak and vulnerable. Amen.

APRIL 9

ONE THING AT A TIME

There is a fable about a clock that was bought in a store and placed on the shelf in a large farmhouse. Almost at once, it began to worry about all the work it had to do. It had to give 120 ticks a minute, 7,200 ticks an hour, 172,800 ticks every day, 63,072,000 ticks a year. Just thinking about it strained the clock's nervous system, and it passed out from the stress of it all.

When the clock came to itself, it reasoned that it only had to make one tick at a time. With this new insight came renewed courage, and the clock started to tick again. For twenty-five years everyone on the farm lived by the clock's faithful tick.

If you are overwhelmed with responsibility and stressed to the point of giving up, just remember the clock. Live one tick at a time. In other words, do one thing at a time. Give yourself praise for what you accomplish and don't stress out about what you don't accomplish. Faithfully doing one task at a time will, over a day, a month, or years produce fabulous results. The only demand that God places upon us is faithfulness. Be faithful. Stick to the task one tick at a time, and you will be amazed at how fulfilling life can be.

God's Word: Therefore do not worry about tomorrow, for tomorrow will worry about itself. Each day has enough trouble of its own (Matthew 6:34).

Prayer: Father, help me to understand that You do not require me to do the impossible but to be faithful in what I do. Calm my stress and give me Your peace. Amen.

APRIL 10

JUST HANG LOOSE

The motto of Hawaii, our beautiful island state, is "just hang loose." It's a reminder to all who live there and to tourists that this is a place to cool it. Living the scheduled, regimented life that most of us do on the mainland, it is refreshing to know that there is a place on earth that is not in a rush.

David, king of Israel, said of the Lord, "He leads me beside quiet waters, he refreshes my soul" (Psalm 23:2). Jesus, our Lord spoke to His disciples in this way: "Do not worry about your life" (Matthew 6:25), and "Peace I leave with you; my peace I give you" (John 14:27). When pressed by the crowds, Jesus invited His disciples to come away to a quiet place. Jesus never got in a hurry, never stressed out or freaked out with anxiety because He kept in constant contact with the heavenly Father and did only what the Father instructed Him to do. Jesus modeled serenity, calm, and peace.

For this reason, Peter said, "Cast all your anxiety on him because he cares for you" (1 Peter 5:7). In Hawaiian lingo, with Jesus, you can "just hang loose."

God's Word: Be still, and know that I am God (Psalm 46:10).

Prayer: Father, let me experience the serenity, calm, and peace that only You can offer. Help me to truly cast my anxiety and stress upon You. Amen.

APRIL 11

A SACRIFICE OF LOVE

Following an evangelistic crusade in Lima, Peru, in 1988, a group of young people from the church that had hosted us visited our hotel the day before we were to return to the United States. They came to say goodbye and to thank us for our ministry. The mother of our interpreter sent some hot tortillas she had made for our lunch. After eating this delicious treat, we discovered that to include meat in the tortillas, the mother had killed her only hen. Her daughter said, "because she loves you."

In a world in which so many look out for themselves, an expression of this magnitude is a powerful testimony of sacrificial love. Our expenditure in going to Peru was nothing in comparison to this mother's gift. It was like the widow's mite. She gave the best that she had. She gave a gift that cost her dearly. We were all so emotional over the gift that our pitiful words of appreciation seemed totally inadequate.

How long has it been since you sacrificed something of value to express your love to someone or to God?

God's Word: And do not forget to do good and to share with others, for with such sacrifices God is pleased (Hebrews 13:16).

Prayer: Father, thank you for the generosity of the dear mother in Peru who made a personal sacrifice to express her love to us. And thank you for Jesus, who made a personal sacrifice to save us from our sins and to give us eternal life. Amen.

APRIL 12,

OLD THINGS HAVE PASSED AWAY

Flying home from Brazil for furlough after four intense years of service and being away from family and friends in the United States, it suddenly dawned on me that many of the things I needed in Brazil would no longer be needed in the States. For example, the Portuguese language, my Portuguese Bible and hymn book, Brazilian customs such as clapping at the door rather than knocking or ringing the doorbell, and always walking a visitor to the sidewalk after a visit or taking someone to a requested designation rather than pointing the way. I would no longer be stopping at the bakery at the bottom of the hill for a fresh, hot loaf of bread for dinner.

Customs, lifestyles, and language would all be changed in a matter of hours as I moved from one country to another. So it is when we receive Christ and are transformed by His saving grace. Once we receive Christ into our lives, old things pass away; behold all things become new. The old sinful life is transformed into a new life with Christ. Instead of a worldly mind, having the mind of Christ becomes my focus. The Bible that sat on the table, collecting dust, in Christ becomes a living Word for me. Being born again, old things pass away; behold all things become new.

God's Word: So from now on we regard no one from a worldly point of view. Though we once regarded Christ in this way, we do so no longer. Therefore, if anyone is in Christ, the new creation has come: The old has gone, the new is here (2 Corinthians 5:16–17)!

Prayer: Father, thank You for saving my soul and giving me a new life in Christ. Help me to leave the past behind with all its old sinful ways for a walk in newness of life with Christ. Amen.

APRIL 13

DIGGING YOUR OWN GRAVE

A modern-day Houdini decided to have himself buried in a clear plexiglass box. Instead of dirt, he ordered concrete to be poured over his homemade casket. But he failed to calculate the weight of the concrete. The plexiglass gave way before the workers had finished pouring.

With the help of a backhoe, rescuers dug an adjacent hole, chipped away frantically at the rapidly hardening concrete, and finally reached the entrapped magician with an oxygen mask. Their effort was too late. He was dead.

The magician had counted on the plexiglass to protect his life. By his miscalculation, he dug his own grave. If you are building your security on your calculations and material things such as stocks, bonds, insurance policies, money in the bank, and other things of this world, you may be sealing your eternal doom.

God's Word: There is a way that appears to be right, but in the end it leads to death (Proverbs 14:12).

Prayer: Father, give me discernment to distinguish between the temporal and the eternal by trusting You rather than following my instincts. Amen.

APRIL 14

DECISIONS

If you haven't learned the lesson by now, sooner or later, life will teach you that if you do not make your own choices, someone else will make them for you. Parents generally make choices for their children. But as a child matures into adolescence and then adulthood, hopefully, they have learned that blessings or serious consequences rest upon choices that are made.

God has given us the ability and the responsibility to make our own decisions. When we give an account to him personally, it will not matter what someone else wanted us to do. Every individual faces the decision on what to do with Jesus Christ. He is the Savior of the World through his death on the cross and His glorious resurrection. He bids all who will believe in Him to confess their sins, repent, and surrender their lives to Him. In doing so, He offers forgiveness for our sins and eternal life. You, and you alone, must decide what you will do with Jesus. If you have not already done so, will you receive Him into your life right now? Failure to choose Christ is a decision.

God's Word: For God so loved the world that he gave his one and only Son, that whoever believes in him shall not perish but have eternal life. Whoever believes in him is not condemned, but whoever does not believe stands condemned already because they have not believed in the name of God's one and only Son (John 3:16,18).

Prayer: Father, help me to understand that life is filled with decisions and that deciding to follow You should be at the top of the list. My commitment to follow You will influence all the other decisions that I make in life. Amen.

APRIL 15

THE IRS

Do you need to be reminded that today is income tax day? Probably not! George Albert, a former employee of the IRS in New York, suggested among other things that you may need help with a tax audit if your situation is complicated or weak, if you are nervous or anxious, or if you can't prepare your case.

These same conditions apply when it comes to facing God for the sins that we have committed. The fortunate thing for all of us is that we have the Holy Spirit who interprets the feelings of our hearts and who intercedes for us. The Holy Spirit not only convicts us of our sins, but He also teaches us, comforts us, and guides us in the right direction. He is our constant companion and helper.

You may never face an IRS audit, but you will most certainly face an audit better known as judgment day. Be prepared! Invite the Holy Spirit into your life today if you have not already done so. When He comes in, He will bring forgiveness, cleansing, salvation, and peace. With Him as your advocate, you won't have to worry about the audit.

God's Word: In the same way, the Spirit helps us in our weakness. We do not know what we ought to pray for, but the Spirit himself intercedes for us through wordless groans. And he who searches our hearts knows the mind of the Spirit, because the Spirit intercedes for God's people by the will of God (Romans 8:26–27).

Prayer: Father, thank You for Your daily presence in my life through the Holy Spirit. Thank You that He intercedes for me and gives me peace, Amen.

APRIL 16

MATURITY

Imagine yourself as an adult going into a local restaurant and asking the waitress to bring you a bottle of milk and a few jars of baby food. For one reason or another, you might drink milk or eat baby food at home, but you would be embarrassed to do so in public. Yet, there are professing Christians who are identified in scripture as spiritual babies.

A spiritual baby is still dealing with the elementary teachings of scripture. A spiritual baby majors on minor and insignificant aspects of life rather than the deeper truths of God's Word. If you are still struggling with the basics of the Christian life such as confessing your sins, repenting, baptism, the resurrection, eternal life, and judgment, you are a spiritual baby. If you must be constantly told how to live the Christian life, you have not grown in your knowledge of God or obedience to Him. If Bible study, prayer, worship, ministry, or giving your tithes and offerings to God's work is not part of your lifestyle, you have failed to grow up in Christ.

The sixth chapter of Hebrews addresses this problem and urges us to move beyond the elementary teachings about Christ and move forward to maturity. Second Peter 3:18 admonishes us to "grow in the grace and knowledge of our Lord and Savior Jesus Christ."

God's Word: So then, just as you received Christ Jesus as Lord, continue to live your lives in him, rooted and built up in him, strengthened in the faith as you were taught, and overflowing with thankfulness (Colossians 2:6–7).

Prayer: Father, help me to grow in my relationship with You and mature in my faith so that I can be of service to You and others. Amen.

APRIL 17

COMPLAINING

It is said that Ida Eisenhower, the mother of Dwight D. Eisenhower, played cards with her sons. During a family game, young Dwight was dealt what he considered to be a bad hand. He complained about it, and his mother wisely told him that they were only playing a game. She explained that he was at home surrounded by love, but one day he would grow up, and in a tough world he would be dealt many bad hands. She questioned Dwight on what he would do then. Would he complain? She told him that by playing the hand that you are dealt in life with courage, you would be successful beyond your dreams.

If you feel that life has handed you a bad deal, remember that playing out the hand courageously can bring success. Jesus never promised us that life would be easy. He taught just the opposite. In real life, we have the Holy Spirit to help us deal with our difficulties. Complaining only adds misery to our lives. Doing the best that you can under the circumstances and facing the challenge of overcoming a bad hand not only gives you confidence but also enhances your success.

God's Word: I am not saying this because I am in need, for I have learned to be content whatever the circumstances. I know what it is to be in need, and I know what it is to have plenty. I have learned the secret of being content in any and every situation, whether well fed or hungry, whether living in plenty or in want (Philippians 4:11–12).

Prayer: Father, when I am dealt a bad hand, with the power of Your Holy Spirit, help me to accept the challenge before me without complaining. I know that You are with me and that by accepting the challenge, I will emerge a stronger person better equipped to serve You. Amen.

APRIL 18

FOCUS

In 1991, I was program chairperson of the North Carolina Baptist State Convention. From Monday evening until Wednesday noon, we concentrated on the business at hand in the Asheville Civic Center. During that time, I was virtually out of touch with news, weather, and world events. When I emerged from my responsibilities on Wednesday afternoon, I did not, in the least, feel deprived. I discovered that the task at hand had consumed my time and energy and that something very positive had taken place in my life.

Everyone needs a break from world news and the bombardment of media reports. Those who focus on the news, all the commentary, and hype, will find themselves in a negative and depressed state of mind.

It is good to focus your attention and priorities on constructive tasks and separate yourself from the world. So much of what you hear in the media is speculation and opinion and things that you have no control over and can do nothing about. Limit your daily access to news; immerse yourself in tasks that are productive and helpful to yourself and others. Take time to meditate and pray. Read good books, listen to beautiful music, and make a better world for yourself. In the end, you will have a more positive attitude, you will be of benefit to others, and you will rest better at night.

God's Word: Then because so many people were coming and going that they did not even have a chance to eat, he said to them, "Come with me by yourselves to a quiet place and get some rest" (Mark 6:31).

Prayer: Father, there is so much noise and distraction in the world. Help me to get away to a quiet place with You, regain my perspective, and find rest. Amen.

APRIL 19

HUGS

Take time daily to hug your spouse and your children and tell them that you love them. A daily hug and kiss can last a lifetime. Children who are accustomed to hugs have a greater chance of building solid, healthy relationships in their adult years. The love and security that a child experiences early in life give them more stability and confidence in later years. A child who has known love is more likely to pass it on to others.

A hug, kiss, and warm affection work even amid serious problems like divorce, alcoholism, and economic distress. A hug and kiss send a message of love, acceptance, security, and belonging. It adds to the emotional stability of children and adults and offers security in a turbulent world. Hugs and kisses will make everyone's day.

God's Word: Greet one another with a kiss of Love, Peace to all of you who are in Christ (1 Peter 5:14).

Prayer: Father, help us to love one another as You have taught us to love. Amen.

APRIL 20

EVIL

With billions of particles of pollen flying, it's little wonder that allergies abound at this time of year. If you are like me and subject to sneeze at any moment, you probably keep a box of Kleenex handy.

Have you ever wondered why people say, "Bless you" or "God bless you," when they hear you sneeze? Hundreds of years ago, people thought that when you sneezed your soul came out of your body, or an evil spirit would enter your body. As protection against the evil, they would say, "Bless you," or "God bless you."

Evil doesn't come or go with a sneeze. Yet, evil does abide in the human heart in the form of jealousy, anger, hatred, revenge, etc. A tissue or a simple "bless you" won't wipe away this kind of evil. But Jesus Christ, who has the power to cast out demons, can transform your life. Jesus can help you fight evil with good. He can fill your life with love, kindness, trust, and compassion.

The next time you sneeze, let it be a reminder that there are deeper problems of the heart that only God can cure.

God's Word: When evening came, many who were demon-possessed were brought to him, and he drove out the spirits with a word and healed all the sick (Matthew 8:16).

Prayer: Father, thank You that You have the power to drive evil out of me so that I can live for You. Amen.

APRIL 21

PATIENCE

Patience is one of the qualities that impressed me about my dad when I was a little boy. If he was fishing, he could sit right there even when the cork wasn't bobbing. He never seemed to be in a hurry, yet he accomplished a remarkable amount of work in a single day. He never appeared to be too tired to play with me after a hard day's work at the railroad. He was never too busy to read me a story or tell me Bible stories until I fell asleep. He was imaginative, creative, and could stay at a task for hours until it was completed to his satisfaction.

When I think of my dad. the virtue of patience—the ability to endure or to stand firm—comes to mind. Patience enables us to wait on God, to think things through, to keep our calm, and to make better decisions. Parents, be patient with your children; teach them patience by example. They'll remember it for a lifetime.

God's Word: Be completely humble and gentle; be patient, bearing with one another in love (Ephesians 4:2).

Prayer: Father, help me to be patient and loving toward my children and others as You are patient and loving to me. Amen.

APRIL 22

SERVING THE LORD

Serving the Lord is serious business. No half-hearted spirit will do. We must serve Him with our whole heart and a willing mind. Reluctance to serve the Lord is indicative of a serious spiritual problem.

Scripture teaches us that we serve the Lord with gladness, or we don't serve Him at all. We serve Him with all our hearts, with enthusiasm, love, and devotion, or our service is unacceptable. God not only sees our service; He knows the thoughts and attitudes behind it. David, king of Israel, gave his son Solomon solid counsel that is helpful to all who will ponder it and put it into practice.

God's Word: And you, my son Solomon, acknowledge the God of your father, and serve him with wholehearted devotion and with a willing mind, for the LORD searches every heart and understands every desire and every thought. If you seek him, he will be found by you; but if you forsake him, he will reject you forever (1 Chronicles 28:9).

Prayer: Father, help me to serve You with gladness and a willing heart and apply the counsel of David to my life. Amen.

APRIL 23

UPDATING

In a fast-changing world, there is a word that has become synonymous with progress and success. The word is *updating*. The media is constantly updating the news. To stay abreast of the latest technology, businesses, manufacturers, and professional people must constantly update their skills and knowledge as well as their computers. In a technological society, it doesn't take long to get behind if you neglect the updating process.

In the realm of spiritual matters, it is also a vital necessity to be up-to-date in our relationship with the Lord. It is important to frequently check yourself and take a spiritual inventory of your life. Are you up-to-date in your prayer life? How about in your worship of God? Are you up-to-date with your tithes and offerings? How about your service to others? Keeping an updated relationship with the Lord can make a difference in how we face life's unexpected troubles and tragedies. If it is important to keep up-to-date in the secular world, how much more important it is to keep up-to-date in your spiritual life.

God's Word: Therefore, my dear brothers and sisters, stand firm. Let nothing move you. Always give yourselves fully to the work of the Lord, because you know that your labor in the Lord is not in vain (1 Corinthians 15:58).

Prayer: Father, help me to be up-to-date in my relationship with You so that my life is a constant testimony of Your love and grace and a light to the paths of those who are influenced by my life. Amen.

APRIL 24

GROWTH

If you stop to compare your life now with where you were ten years ago, can you say that you have grown more mature, more confident, more understanding, more forgiving, more loving? Are you a better husband, a better wife, a better parent today than you were back then? Are you dealing with life's situations in the same way you handled them a decade ago?

Growing in knowledge, discernment, wisdom, and relationships is vital to our well-being. If you are discouraged about your lack of growth in maturity—mentally, socially, and spiritually—there is a word for you from Philippians 3:12–14: "Not that I have already obtained all this, or have already arrived at my goal, but I press on to take hold of that for which Christ Jesus took hold of me." You can improve. You can deal with life's situations in more mature ways, but you must make the effort. Only you can determine to press forward toward maturity. No one else can do it for you.

God's Word: For this very reason, make every effort to add to your faith goodness; and to goodness, knowledge; and to knowledge, self-control; and to self-control, perseverance; and to perseverance, godliness; and to godliness, mutual affection; and to mutual affection, love. For if you possess these qualities in increasing measure, they will keep you from being ineffective and unproductive in your knowledge of our Lord Jesus Christ (2 Peter 1:5–8).

Prayer: Father, help me to concentrate on growing in maturity in every aspect of my life so that I will be effective and productive as Your servant. Amen.

EVERYONE IS IMPORTANT

A major American corporation announced that it was moving its corporate offices across the country. During an interview with the press, the board's chairman was asked if he expected most employees to make the move. He responded by saying that most of the important employees would transfer, but secretaries and others would not.

When the secretaries read the chairman's comments in the newspaper the next day, they decided to act. They did all their regular duties, but throughout the day, they answered no phones. The turmoil not only shocked the executives but caused the board chairman to apologize for overlooking their importance.

In the kingdom of God, everyone is important. "God's love for the world is central to biblical teaching. God's love is inclusive, not exclusive. We don't have to act or demonstrate in any way to get God's attention. He proved on the cross that everyone is important.

God's Word: Are not two sparrows sold for a penny? Yet not one of them will fall to the ground outside your Father's care. And even the very hairs of your head are all numbered. So don't be afraid; you are worth more than many sparrows (Matthew10:29–31).

Prayer: Father, I thank You that You love everyone so much that You sent Your only Son, Jesus Christ, to die for the sins of every human being. Amen.

APRIL 26

THE PERSONAL TOUCH

Do not underestimate the power of your influence. A survey by the Alban Institute on church newcomers in twenty-two congregations of various denominations in Indianapolis, Philadelphia, and Atlanta asks people why they chose a certain church. Two percent had responded to an advertisement. Six percent had been invited by the pastor. Six percent were contacted through a church outreach program and 80 percent chose the church because of an invitation from a friend or family member.

The personal touch matters most. If you want people to come to your church, you must personally invite them. You can influence others. Use your influence to invite people to worship with you. They are more likely to respond if you ask them.

God's Word: Then the Master told his servant, "Go out to the roads and country lanes and compel them to come in, so that my house will be full" (Luke 14:23).

Pray: Father, help me to be a recruiter for You. Amen.

APRIL 27

WE DECIDE

There are many things over which we have no control or choice. We do not choose our birth, parents, country, our time in history, or how we are brought up. For the most part, we don't choose to die or how we will die. But we can choose how we live—whether with courage or as a coward, whether with honor or dishonor, whether with a purpose or aimlessly. We can choose what is important over what is trivial, what is significant to do or not do. We have the power to make our own decisions. No matter what we choose, we must understand that the choices we make determine the life we live. But in the end, we decide. We choose. But always, we are accountable to God.

God's Word: Since, then, you have been raised with Christ, set your hearts on things above, where Christ is, seated at the right hand of God (Colossians 3:1).

Prayer: Father, help my decisions and choices to be in keeping with Your will for my life. In Jesus's name, I pray. Amen.

APRIL 28

FINISHING WELL

Of the many things that we can say about the life and ministry of Jesus, perhaps the most notable is that He finished well. Throughout His thirty-three years of life on earth, Jesus knew His reason for being. He knew His purpose in life.

In the Garden of Gethsemane Jesus prayed, "Not my will but yours be done" (Luke 22:42). In this great emotional struggle, Jesus surrendered to the fulfillment of His mission. On the cross, He prayed for the forgiveness of those who crucified Him and experienced the abandonment of the heavenly Father as He cried out, "My God, my God, Why have you forsaken me?" (Matthew 27:46). Having fulfilled His mission, He cried out, "It is finished" (John 19:30).

By any means of examination, Jesus started well, continued well, and finished well. Our challenge for His glory and honor is to do the same.

God's Word: However, I consider my life worth nothing to me; my only aim is to finish the race and complete the task the Lord Jesus was given me—the task of testifying to the good news of God's grace (Acts 20:24).

Prayer: Father, help me to keep my eyes on Jesus so that I will fulfill the purpose for which I was created and finish well. Amen.

APRIL 29

HARD WORK

Work is not God's punishment for sin. Look closely at scripture, and you will discover that God gave Adam and Eve the responsibility of taking care of the Garden of Eden before they sinned against Him. Work is not punishment. Work is a means whereby we become co-laborers with God. Work enables us to be useful, productive, creative, and fulfilled. There is great satisfaction in completing a difficult assignment and doing it well. Work builds character, challenges us to give our best, and produces the sweet fruit of contentment.

Work brings out the best in us. Work brings great joy when we do it not for the praise of men or for the sole benefit of making a living but for the glory of God. With God as your partner, strive for excellence in your work. God deserves nothing less than our best.

God's Word: Whatever you do, work at it with all your heart, as working for the Lord, not for human masters, since you know that you will receive an inheritance from the Lord as a reward. It is the Lord Christ you are serving (Colossians 3:23).

Prayer: Father, let my work be pleasing to You and for Your glory. Amen.

APRIL 30

VISION

Millions of people visit the Blue Ridge Parkway each year and enjoy the majestic mountains, valleys, streams, forests, flowers, and wildlife. Had it not been for the vision and persistence of Colonel Joseph Hyde Pratt, head of the North Carolina Geological and Economic Survey in the early 1900s, the highway on the crest of the Blue Ridge might never have been built. Pratt drew up the plans for the scenic highway and promoted its construction because he wanted to promote economic growth and tourism. Thank God for people with vision who make our lives more enjoyable because they dare to dream unselfishly.

Had it not been for apostle Paul's vision of taking the gospel to the Gentiles, Christianity might not have survived the first century. The vision and foresight of hundreds, if not thousands, of Christians down through the ages has kept the gospel alive despite every effort to extinguish it. Give thanks to God for these faithful visionaries.

God's Word: Therefore, since we are surrounded by such a great cloud of witnesses, let us throw off everything that hinders and the sin that so easily entangles, and let us run with perseverance the race marked out for us, fixing our eyes on Jesus, the pioneer and perfecter of faith (Hebrews 12:1–3).

Prayer: Father, give me a vision for what You want me to accomplish in life and the perseverance to see it through. Amen.

MAY 1

MAY DAY

May Day is an ancient festival tradition celebrated around the world with different emphasis depending upon the country and culture. But it is also as American as baseball and apple pie. In the nineteenth century, May Day became a day to celebrate the worker and promote workers' rights with a push toward better labor conditions. For almost everyone, it is a celebration of the change of seasons moving from winter to summer, with May 1 being the midpoint between the two. It is a time to enjoy cake, make merry, dance, and sing.

The Bible is filled with stories of celebration and festivals such as the Feast of Tabernacles, the Feast of Harvest, Passover, Pentecost, the return of the prodigal son, the birth of Jesus, the resurrection, etc. Ecclesiastes 3:4 says that there is "a time to weep and a time to laugh, a time to mourn and a time to dance." Celebration is good for the soul. It relieves tension and stress; it takes you out of the doldrums of everyday tension and worries and lifts your spirit. Celebrating transports you to a world of joy, and who doesn't need joy in their life?

God's Word: Praise the LORD. Praise God in his sanctuary;
praise him in his mighty heavens. Praise him for his acts of power;
praise him for his surpassing greatness. Praise him with the sounding of the trumpet,
praise him with the harp and lyre, praise him with timbrel and dancing,
praise him with the strings and pipe, praise him with the clash of cymbals,
praise him with resounding cymbals. Let everything that has breath praise the Lord. Praise the Lord (Psalm 150:1–6).

Prayer: Father, help me to celebrate life with joy and always in ways that bring honor to Your name. Amen.

MAY 2

LISTEN

The key ingredient to building relationships is listening. A father who thought he was listening to his sons was told, "Dad, you listen, but you are always doing something else when we talk to you, and you always answer yes, no, or "I'll think about it." Disturbed by his son's remarks, the father determined from that point on he would listen. So, at mealtime, when his sons talked, he developed the habit of putting down his fork and giving them his undivided attention. The results were phenomenal. Over time, dinner conversation grew from ten to forty-five minutes. The father not only strengthened his relationship with his sons, but he also lost fifteen pounds over five weeks. But more importantly, he gained a deeper love, respect, and appreciation from his sons. And the sons learned that they had a father who listened.

Whether it is family or friends, put down the fork, stop doing what you are doing, shut out other distractions, and build relationships—*listen*!

God's Word: Consider carefully what you hear ... with the measure you use, it will be measured to you—and even more (Mark 4:24).

Prayer: Father, teach me the importance of listening to others, giving them my full attention, and being more concerned about building relationships than completing something on my agenda. Amen.

MAY 3

GIVING ACCOUNT

You may be one of those persons who does not go to church because you believe there are too many hypocrites there. You probably don't make the same judgment when you attend a club meeting or a ball game. But think for just a moment. Where can you go in this world and not find hypocrites?

God does not judge us based on the conduct of someone else. We are judged based on our conduct and our decisions. We will be judged on whether we have received Jesus Christ, His Son, into our lives. Individual responsibility and individual accountability are emphasized in scripture. We will never be judged based on what someone else does. We will be judged on what we do.

God's Word: So then, each of us will give an account of ourselves to God (Romans 14:12).

Prayer: Father, help me to accept responsibility for my sins and my accountability to You. Amen.

MAY 4

DELAYED MAIL

The night before we departed by ship to Brazil, my wife wrote a letter to her parents and put our Brazilian return address on it. One year later, we received that same unopened letter. The letter was stamped many times "address unknown." We looked at the original forwarding address. It was correct, readable, and without a logical explanation for not reaching its intended destination. Where it had traveled for a year, we will never know.

I heard of a letter that was returned to a young man in Canada in 1974. The letter was postmarked on March 28,1918. There was no logical explanation for the fifty-six-year delay.

If we are frustrated by delayed mail, can we imagine how God must feel? His correctly addressed message of love, forgiveness, salvation, and eternal life, sent to us through the Bible, has yet to be delivered to many lost souls. Through indifference, neglect, and disregard, the sender has not been recognized; the message remains undelivered and unread.

If you have an unused, unread Bible, I urge you to open it and read God's love letter. It is addressed to you. If you are a Christian, God has appointed you as His messenger to deliver His message of love to the world. Don't let God's delayed mail be your fault!

God's Word: Therefore go and make disciples of all nations (Matthew 28:19).

Prayer: Father, thank you for sending your message of love to me. Let there be no delay in receiving it and acting upon it. Amen.

MAY 5

CONSUMED BY SUCCESS

There is nothing wrong with being successful. However, being obsessed with success can lead to a downfall. Success-driven people fall into many temptations. They are tempted to take shortcuts. They are tempted to step on other people at any cost to achieve their goal. They are tempted to live by the motto, "The end justifies the means." They are tempted to be dishonest. They are tempted to use people to accomplish their goals. They are tempted to leave God out of their lives. In their love for money and compulsion to gain the world, successful people can and do lose their family and their soul.

If your primary goal in life is money and success, you will never find peace, and you will miss the purpose for which you were created. Consumed by success is a selfish road.
Ponder this thought: What good is it to come to the end of your life and discover that you have exhausted your energy and in essence thrown it away on something that can't last and something you can't take with you?

God's Word: What good is it for someone to gain the whole world, yet forfeit their soul?" (Matthew 16:26).

Prayer: Father, let my focus in life be on that which is eternal rather than on things that are temporal and can easily be taken away from me. Amen.

MAY 6

TOO BUSY

The "Veggie Tale" videos are a cartoon version of familiar Bible stories and a favorite of children and parents. In a presentation of "The Good Samaritan," one of the songs addresses the modern-day problem of busyness. It is possible that we become so busy and so wrapped up in what we are doing that we have no time to help others.

For that reason, you may need to take a step back and get a grip on what matters. If you are too busy to help a person in need or to play with your children or sit down to a meaningful conversation with your spouse, you are too busy. If you are too busy to spend time in Bible study, prayer, and worship, you are too busy.

Take a careful look at how you are spending your time and on what you are spending it. Perhaps you need to reexamine your priorities. Life is a terrible thing to waste on busyness.

God's Word: Therefore, since we have these promises, dear friends, let us purify ourselves from everything that contaminates body and spirit, perfecting holiness out of reverence for God (2 Corinthians 7:1).

Prayer: Father, help me to guard against busyness and to keep my focus on that which is genuinely important, constructive, and helpful to others. Amen.

MAY 7

SECRET SUFFERER

Are you one of those individuals who are afraid to let others into your life? You get sick or go through a difficult time but don't want anyone to know about it. You must go to the hospital, but you leave strict orders not to tell anyone. You are what some call "a private person" or a secret sufferer.

Whatever your reason for secrecy, give thought to Robert Fulghum's story from *All I Really Need to Know I Learned in Kindergarten*. He describes a doctor friend who had terminal cancer but refused to tell anyone, including members of his own family because he didn't want them to suffer with him. He died without others discovering his illness. But the truth came out. Some considered him brave, but his family and friends felt betrayed. They were angry because he didn't need them and didn't trust their strength, and it hurt that they didn't get to say "goodbye."

Being secret about your life and health grieves those who love you and want to pray for you and give their support. It is not bravery to be a secret sufferer. It's selfishness.

God's Word: Carry each other's burdens and in this way you will fulfill the law of Christ (Galatians 6:2).

Prayer: Father, help me to love and trust my family and friends in such a way that I will share my burdens with them and be embraced by their love and support. Amen.

MAY 8

WORRY

Is it worth dying for? That is a question asked by Dr. Robert Eliot in a book by that title. He speaks of the stressful price we pay for our worries. Each of us pays an emotional price for our predicaments, and according to Dr. Eliot, most of us overspend.

Is what you worry about worth dying for? Think about it! If not, perhaps you are overdoing it. Much of the worry and stress we put upon ourselves is not worth the emotional price we pay for letting it ruin our health and our lives. There is no burden so heavy that God is not willing, ready, and able to help us carry the load. If what upsets you is not worth dying for, step back, take a deep breath, inhale, exhale, and determine to release it into God's hands. Turn up the volume of your faith, and trust God. The Bible has good advice. Let God fight the battle for you.

God's Word: But those who hope in the Lord will renew their strength. They will soar on wings like eagles; they will run and not grow weary, they will walk and not be faint (Isaiah 40:31).

Prayer: Father, worry tears me down. Trust in You builds me up. Help me to turn my worries over to You and live by faith. Amen.

MAY 9

GOD'S LOVE

When Admiral Byrd was exploring the Arctic Ocean, he decided to measure the ocean's depth at a certain point. He commanded a crewman to let down the measuring line. When he had let down all the line without reaching the bottom he shouted, "It's deeper than that!" He tied on more line and let it down again. Again, he shouted, "Deeper than that!" Byrd then tied all the line they had on board and let it down again. Once more the crewman shouted, "It's deeper than that!" So it is with God's love. No matter how great our need, God's love is "deeper than that." His love and grace are greater than all our sins.

No matter what your sins may be, you can find forgiveness by simply confessing your sins to God and receiving His forgiveness. He offers you the gift of grace, mercy, and love. You don't deserve it. You can't buy it. You can't earn it. But you can accept it.

God's Word: For I am convinced that neither death nor life, neither angels nor demons, neither the present nor the future, nor any powers, neither height nor depth, nor anything else in all creation, will be able to separate us from the love of God that is in Christ Jesus our Lord (Romans 8:38–39).

Prayer: Father, thank You for Your unlimited love and the encouragement and strength that it gives me. Amen.

MAY 10

CATEGORIES

Four days into its maiden voyage from Southampton, England to New York, the Titanic struck a gigantic iceberg and sank in the wee hours of April 15,1912. You might have thought that the newspapers reporting the tragedy would have written about the categories of passengers aboard—millionaires, celebrities, people of moderate means, famous people, right down to maids, cooks, and deckhands. Yet, when the newspapers published the story of the tragedy, only two categories of people were noted—the lost and the saved. Tragedy had eliminated all other distinctions.

The world is filled with people who fall into all kinds of human categories. Some are internationally known, and others live obscure lives. On life's voyage toward eternity, it doesn't matter if you are rich or poor, healthy or sick; it isn't important whether you drive a Lexus or ride a bicycle. All such distinctions disappear, and the only list of importance is the lost and the saved. God offers you eternal salvation today. Don't neglect it. Nothing else in life is more important.

God's Word: Here I am! I stand at the door and knock. If anyone hears my voice and opens the door, I will come in and eat with that person and they with me (Revelation 3:20).

Prayer: Father, thank You for reaching out to me with Your love and the gift of salvation. Help me to acknowledge my sins, repent, and accept Your wondrous offer. Amen.

MAY 11

OVERCOMING

Some of the most inspiring people who have ever lived have had some handicap. Helen Keller was deaf and blind, yet she became an author, political activist, and lecturer. Stephen Hawking, diagnosed with ALS at age twenty-one and paralyzed from head to toe for over thirty years, became a world-famous theoretical physicist. Franklin Roosevelt, afflicted with polio, became a revered president of the United States and world leader. Andrea Bocelli, completely blind, has thrilled the world with his beautiful voice.

The list of handicapped people who have accomplished remarkable things is legion. They inspire us and challenge us to do the best we can with what we have. Rather than lament their condition and complain about their handicap, with a positive attitude they all turned their infirmity into a blessing. As we study their lives and marvel at their accomplishments, we are challenged to set aside our self-pity and put every ounce of our energy into making the best of the situation. Overcoming handicaps is not only self-gratifying; it is a blessing and a challenge to others.

God's Word: But he said to me, "My grace is sufficient for you, for my power is made perfect in weakness." Therefore I will boast all the more gladly about my weaknesses, so that Christ's power may rest in me (2 Corinthians 12:9).

Prayer: Father, give me the courage to overcome my handicaps and teach me how to turn them into blessings. Amen.

MAY 12

BURSTING BALLOONS

A mother bought a balloon craft kit for her little daughter complete with step-by-step instructions on creating everything from giraffes to dachshunds. Excited by the gift, the daughter failed to hear her mother repeatedly remind her about bedtime. Startled by her mother's angry shout, the little girl popped the balloon. Picking up the craft kit, the mother's eyes fell on the instruction sheet which read, "Twist and shape the figures gently to avoid popping." Disturbed by her harshness, the mother wrapped her arms around her daughter and asked for forgiveness.

Wrapped up in our agendas, we often pop the balloon of our children because we fail to be gentle in our twisting and shaping. Parents need to be reminded that the goal in bringing up children is to shape them—not break them.

God's Word: Fathers, do not exasperate your children, instead bring them up in the training and instruction of the Lord (Ephesians 6:4).

Prayer: Father, bringing up children in the love and admonition of the Lord is not an easy task. Please help me to mold and shape my children to be Your faithful servants with love, gentleness, and patience. Amen.

MAY 13

GETTING GOD'S ATTENTION

A friend, just back from a two-year overseas teaching experience, said that she had observed people ringing a bell when they entered their religious shrine. She was told that worshippers ring the bell to wake up their god and get his attention.

The Bible does not say anything about us having to wake God up. On the contrary, our problem is being awake to Him. We do not have to wake God up or clamor for his attention. The Bible teaches that God is always alert, always ready to hear from us, always waiting for our call.

The Bible teaches that God takes the initiative in seeking us. He told Noah how to save his family and the animals of the world from the flood. With Moses, He formed a nation of believers out of slaves and entered a covenant relationship with them. He sent prophets with messages of love and warning. Then, He sent His only Son to die for us on the cross. The bottom line is that we have God's attention. The question for us to answer is, "Does God have our attention?"

God's Word: "Am I only a God nearby," declares the Lord, "and not a God far away? Who can hide in secret places so that I cannot see them?" declares the Lord. "Do not I fill heaven and earth?" (Jeremiah 23:23–24).

Prayer: Father, thank You that You are always available to me. Help me to be available to You. Amen.

DEALING WITH PERSONAL SIN

A strange fact of human nature is that we often know when we are in the wrong. We know when we have not done our best—when our effort has only been mediocre. We know when we have come up short, and it makes us angry. The strangeness of it all is that we take our anger out on someone else or even God rather than being angry with ourselves.

Such conduct was first noted in the Garden of Eden when Cain brought a mediocre gift to God while his brother Abel brought God a gift of the best he had. God accepted Abel's gift but rejected Cain's offering. Cain was angry with himself for his failure, but he took his anger out on Abel and killed him.

Dealing with personal sins is difficult. We always want to blame someone else. Instead of admitting our own sins, repenting, and seeking God's forgiveness, we are prone to seek a scapegoat. Pride keeps us from admitting personal sins. In resenting our failure, we often hurt those we love and even take our frustration out on strangers.

The only solution to personal sins is confession, repentance, and asking God's forgiveness. Otherwise, personal sin will destroy us and bring harm to others in the process. What sins do you need to confess today?

God's Word: Whoever conceals their sins does not prosper, but the one who confesses and renounces them finds mercy (Proverbs 28:13).

Prayer: Father, help me to swallow my pride, confess my sins, repent, and receive your forgiveness. Amen.

MAY 15

SOUND ADVICE

Jonah Martin Edelman, in a preface to his mother's book *The Measure of Our Success*, speaks of a threefold legacy he received from his mother:

1. Don't feel entitled to anything you don't sweat and struggle for.
2. Never give up. You can make it no matter what comes. Nothing worth having is ever achieved without struggle.
3. Always remember that you are never alone. You are loved unconditionally. There is nothing you can ever say or do that can take away God's love.[4]

Parental advice doesn't get much better than that. Fortunate is the child who has a parent filled with such wisdom. And wise is the child who not only hears sound words of advice but puts them into practice.

God's Word: If any of you lacks wisdom, you should ask God, who gives generously to all without finding fault, and it will be given to you (James 1:5).

Prayer: Father, help me to recognize good counsel when I hear it, but more importantly, help me to apply good counsel to my daily life. Amen.

---

[4] Marian Wright Edelman, *"The Measure of Our Success: A Letter to My Children and Yours*, Kindle Books.

MAY 16

THE BIBLE

My home library is filled with hardbacks and paperbacks covering history, theology, novels, multiple translations of the Bible, commentaries, dictionaries, languages, cultures, and travel guides. Right before my eyes, I have a wealth of information, research material, inspiration, and knowledge at my disposal. Each book is a treasure in itself. Having a comprehensive library is one thing—using it is another.
No matter how valuable my books or how much information they contain, they are only helpful if I use them. Otherwise, they are mere decorations on bookshelves.

The same is true of the Bible. It is a library unto itself of knowledge, wisdom, spiritual guidance, and information. The Bible is, year after year, the number one best-selling publication in the world. It is also unparalleled in its understanding of human nature. But above all, the Bible is God's love letter to humanity. It tells of God's love, man's sin, God's redemption, forgiveness, eternal life, and how we can experience it.

But for all its value, the Bible is only helpful to those who read it and apply its truths to their lives. Unused, the Bible is no more than a decoration on the table or bookshelf.
Owning one Bible or multiple Bibles is one thing; using and applying its teachings to our lives is another. The value of an unused Bible is about the same as having no Bible at all. The value of a Bible read, studied, and applied is immeasurable.

God's Word: Your word is a lamp for my feet, a light on my path. I have taken an oath and confirmed it, that I will follow your righteous laws (Psalm 119:105–106).

Prayer: Father, thank You for Your written Word and Jesus Christ, the living Word. Help me to apply Your Word to my life so that I will honor You and be a faithful witness. Amen.

MAY 17

MONEY

1 Timothy 6:10 says: "For the love of money is a root of all kinds of evil. Some people, eager for money, have wandered from the faith and pierced themselves with many griefs."

Ponder the misconceptions that people have about money.

1. Money is the root of all evil.
2. God needs my money, or the church will fail.
3. Having enough money will make you happy.
4. If I had enough money, I could do a lot of good.
5. God doesn't want me to have money.
6. The church is not supposed to talk about money.
7. Money solves all our problems.
8. Having money is equal to being successful.

The biblical response to these misconceptions is worthy of our attention.

It is not money itself but the love of money that is the root of all evil (1 Timothy 6:10). You don't give money to God because He needs it but because you need to express your gratitude and demonstrate your love for him (Psalm 50:10). There will never be enough money to make you happy (Philippians 4:19). You can do a lot of good with the little you have. Jesus praised the widow's mite (Luke 21:1–4). God is the supplier of all that you have including money (James 1:17). Jesus talked more about money than any other subject (Matthew 6:21). You cannot serve God and money (Matthew 6:24). Success is having God in your life, not money in the bank (Proverbs 15:16).

God's Word: But seek first his kingdom and his righteousness, and all these things will be given to you as well (Matthew 6:33).

Prayer: Father, help me to keep my priorities focused on You and trust You to provide for all my needs. Amen.

MAY 18

PAUSES

Music composers build in pauses and rests to enhance the music and to allow the musician or singer time to catch a breath. God rested in the creation process, and He provided night and day so man could have time for both work and rest. To do good work, rest is essential for both animals and man.

A stressed-out life—living at breakneck speed and thinking that we are indispensable—is counterproductive. When the crowds pressed in on Jesus as they often did, Jesus recognized the need to take a break. He often took His disciples to a quiet place. We all need a rest, a break, a quiet place.

If you value your life and health, your family, the people with whom you work, and the quality of the work you do, give value also to rest. Rest will not only renew your energy but will also help you feel better about yourself. It will help others feel better about you.

God's Word: Come to me, all you who are weary and burdened, and I will give you rest. Take my yoke upon you and learn from me, for I am gentle and humble in heart, and you will find rest for your souls. For my yoke is easy and my burden is light (Matthew 11:28–30).

Prayer: Father, refresh my soul and my body so that I might be more useful to You. Amen.

MAY 19

HELP

At one time or another, everyone needs help. We are dependent souls although we try to convince ourselves and others of our independence. The psalmist said, "I lift up my eyes to the mountains—where does my help come from? My help comes from the Lord, the Maker of heaven and earth (Psalm 121:1–2).

Two powerful truths stand out in these verses. The first truth is that "I need help." The second truth is that "My help comes from the Lord." No one is as independent as he or she may think. We are interdependent upon each other as long as we live on this earth, and we are dependent upon God. While we cannot always count on other people to help us, we can always count on God. The psalmist knew this truth. Do you know it?

God's Word: May the Lord answer you when you are in distress; may the name of the God of Jacob protect you (Psalm 20:1).

Prayer: Father, daily I need Your help. Guide my paths, calm my fears, heal my wounds, guard my lips against evil, fill my heart with love, and create in me a pure heart. Amen.

MAY 20

DAY OF TROUBLE

Some days seem to be full of trouble. You may be having one of those troubled times today. A day of trouble is when nothing seems to go right, or everything seems to be breaking down, or there is trauma in your life. If you are experiencing a day of trouble, there is good news for you. Psalm 50:15 is an invitation from God which says, "Call on me in the day of trouble; I will deliver you, and you will honor me."

Peter Marshall, the late Senate chaplain, used to say that trouble is "God's tap on the shoulder." Our troubles are reminders of just how much we need God in our lives. Trouble points out our inadequacies to deal with life's problems alone. Regardless of the nature of our trouble, we have a loving heavenly Father who invites us to call upon Him.

If God is tapping you on the shoulder today, turn to Him and seek Him with all your heart. You don't have to face your troubles alone. God can help you. He will make your day.

God's Word: Hear my prayer, Lord; listen to my cry for mercy. When I am in distress, I call to you, because you answer me (Psalm 86:6).

Prayer: Father, I am weak and fragile. Today my troubles overwhelm me. I need Your help, Your presence, Your guidance. Give me strength in this day of trouble. Help me to face my problems in confidence that the Holy Spirit will guide me. Let my response to trouble enhance my witness to others. Amen.

MAY 21

A GOD-SIZED TASK

Henry Blackaby's challenging book, *Experiencing God*, reminds us that a God-sized task is one that only God can handle. He calls attention to Moses, who faced the Red Sea with the Egyptian Army pressing down upon him, and Joshua facing the rushing waters of the Jordan River. In both situations and many others, these men of God faced circumstances far beyond their ability to resolve.

You may be facing a situation today that is out of your control and beyond your ability to resolve. Face the fact that there are many difficulties in life for which we as human beings have no solution. What we face in such times is beyond doubt "A God-sized task."

Scripture is clear—God is the God of the impossible. He parted the Red Sea for Moses and held back the rushing waters of the Jordan River for Joshua. He has the power to do what you can't do. Follow the example of Moses and Joshua. Recognize your limitations. Recognize God as your deliverer. Release the problem into God's hands. Stand back and see what only God can do.

God's Word: I waited patiently for the Lord; he turned to me and heard my cry. He lifted me out of the slimy pit, out of the mud and mire; he set my feet on a rock and gave me a firm place to stand. He put a new song in my mouth, a hymn of praise to our God. Many will see and fear the Lord and put their trust in him (Psalm 40:1–3).

Prayer: Father, help me never to forget that with You nothing is impossible. Give me the wisdom to recognize a God-sized task and turn the problem over to You. Amen.

MAY 22

THE TRULY COMMITTED

Those who know me, know how I love to plan mission trips and take groups to far-off places to help others in the name of Jesus Christ and experience the joy of helping people know God. Those who have gone on these trips have given testimony of how their lives have been forever changed.

Every time I plan a new trip, numbers of people tell me with excitement, "I want to go." I'm sure they are sincere. But the real test comes when I ask for the deposit. On payday, the number of enthusiasts shrinks. Only the committed make the deposit.

The Bible tells us that "Not everyone who says to me, 'Lord, Lord,' will enter the kingdom of heaven, but only the one who does the will of my Father who is in heaven" (Matthew 7:21). Desiring to go on a trip or the desire to go to heaven is not just a simple matter of wanting to go. It's a matter of commitment, of making the deposit. We commit by surrendering our life to Jesus Christ and living for Him.

God's Word: Commit your work to the Lord, and your plans will be established (Proverbs 16:3).

Prayer: Father, help me to know the joy of full surrender to You, holding nothing back, but placing my life completely into Your hands. Amen.

MAY 23

THE MINISTRY OF SILENCE

While serving as pastor of a church in the mountains of North Carolina, I was called upon to minister to a family of a neighboring church whose two sons had been brutally murdered in a drug deal that went bad. There were no words that I could find that would console the family. The only thing I could do was to sit with them in silence. When Job lost everything he had, his three friends sat with him in silence for seven days and seven nights.

Encouragement to a grieving family does not require words. There is a ministry of silence that cannot be measured. I recall a story of a man's family who lost three sons. A visitor came and talked and talked, and when he left, they were happy to see him go. Another visitor came and sat silently for hours, listened, and briefly responded when asked a question. He said a simple prayer before leaving. The family was comforted. They wished he had stayed longer. Never worry about what you will say to those who grieve. Just be there.

God's Word: It is good to wait quietly for the salvation of the Lord (Lamentations 3:26).

Prayer: Father, in times of grief, help me to know when to be silent and when to speak. Let me experience the power of just being present. Amen.

MAY 24

REPENTANCE

Proverbs 6:16–19 lists seven things that are detestable to God:

- haughty eyes
- a lying tongue
- hands that shed innocent blood
- a heart that devises wicked schemes
- feet that are quick to rush into evil
- a false witness who pours out lies
- a person who stirs up conflict in the community

These seven sins are detestable to God. But do not overlook that all sin is detestable to God. All sins, not just seven, are subject to God's judgment and punishment. The Bible teaches that the punishment for sin—any sin—all sin, is death.

But there is good news. God is gracious, merciful, loving, and forgiving. Through God's Son, Jesus Christ, the punishment we deserve for our sins was placed upon Him. "God made him who had no sin to be sin for us, so that in him we might become the righteousness of God" (2 Corinthians 5:21). Because of our sins, we deserve God's wrath and judgment but instead, when we repent of our sins, confess Jesus Christ as Lord, and turn our lives over to him, God offers us forgiveness and eternal life. You can confess your sins right now, repent, and ask for God's forgiveness. You don't have to wait until Sunday; you can do it now.

God's Word: If we confess our sins, he is faithful and just and will forgive us our sins and purify us from all unrighteousness (1 John 1:9).

Prayer: Father, I confess that I am a sinner. I have sinned against You and my fellowman. Today, I repent and ask Your forgiveness, knowing that Jesus Christ died for my sins and offers me eternal life. Come into my heart and by the power of the Holy Spirit enable me to live my life for You. In Jesus's name, I pray. Amen.

MAY 25

ROOTS

My grandfather, Joseph Edward Allard, was born on this day in 1881. For twenty-five years (1925–50), he was pastor of Wells Chapel Baptist Church near Wallace, North Carolina. In 1992, I was invited to speak to the senior adults at Wells Chapel. I cannot adequately describe the emotions that welled up in me when they showed me the pulpit from which my grandfather preached and the pulpit Bible that he used all those years.

A self-taught man, my grandfather pastored churches until he was eighty-two years of age and went home to be with the Lord on August 11,1973, at the age of ninety-two. The motivating factor of his life was his love for the Lord, his love for people, and his passion to bring the two together.

As my grandfather passed his faith to my father, and my father passed his faith to me, I must pass it on to my children. That is God's plan for the continuation of the gospel down through the ages. We must all do our part to keep the faith alive. Thank God for Christian roots.

God's Word: These commandments that I give you today are to be on your hearts. Impress them on your children. Talk about them when you sit at home and when you walk along the road, when you lie down, and when you get up. Tie them as a symbol on your hands and bind them on your foreheads. Write them on the doorframes of your houses and on your gates (Deuteronomy 6:6–8).

Prayer: Father, I thank You for my spiritual heritage, and I pray that I will be faithful in passing my faith to my children as my parents and grandparents passed their faith to me. Amen.

MAY 26

PRESUMPTUOUS BRAGGING

Have you ever boasted that you would never do something only to find yourself doing it? The interesting thing about human nature is that too often, we think that we are better than others. The truth is, we are all sinners. Our attitude of superiority over others may be a clue to why gossip is so prevalent in everyday conversation. Our critical, judgmental attitude is often revealed in our presumptuous bragging.

Of all the disciples, most of us can more easily identify with Simon Peter, who once declared to Jesus, "Even if all fall away on account of you, I never will" (Matthew 26:33). Jesus answered, "this very night before the rooster crows, you will disown me three times" (Matthew 26:34).

Like Simon Peter, we have all been guilty of presumptuous bragging at one time or another. Peter failed his Master, and he failed himself. Who among us has not experienced the same failure? The positive side to this story is that Peter repented. He found forgiveness and became the rock of faith that held the church together in a time of fierce persecution. In Jesus, we can overcome our failures. We can be useful and victorious over our failures.

God's Word: Do not think of yourself more highly than you ought, but rather think of yourself with sober judgment, in accordance with the faith God has distributed to each of you (Romans 12:3).

Prayer: Father, guard my lips against presumptuous bragging and any feeling of superiority over others. Thank You, that like Simon Peter, I can find forgiveness and usefulness in service to You. Amen.

MAY 27

HOW DO YOU SAY GOODBYE?

An ABC News reporter asked a father who had lost his son in the Oklahoma bombing, "What was the last thing you said to your son? In tears, the father answered, "I love you." How do you say goodbye? We never know when we walk away from a loved one if we will ever see them again. Do you sometimes leave your loved ones in anger or with words of criticism? Do you leave them with animosity on your face or with love in your heart? Do you leave them agitated and out of sorts or do you leave them with a hug, a kiss, and the words, "I love you?"

Outside of our relationship with God, nothing is more important than our family relationships. Isn't it time that you pay attention to how you say "goodbye"?

God's Word: They all wept as they embraced him and kissed him. What grieved them most was his statement that they would never see his face again. Then they accompanied him to the ship (Acts 20:37–38).

Prayer: Father, help me to recognize the importance of saying goodbye and the lasting memory that it will leave on a loved one if I never come back. Amen.

MAY 28

SEARCHING AND FINDING

Young people sometimes say, "I don't know what I'm going to do with my life right now. I'm trying to find myself." Life for some is a constant search for purpose and meaning. Some find it and others wander in the desert for a lifetime.

I once read about two birds—a vulture and a hummingbird—that fly in the great western desert of the United States. The vulture searches for decaying carcasses, and the hummingbird searches for the nectar of the fragile desert flowers. The interesting thing is that both find that for which they are searching.

In your search for life's meaning, remember the vulture and the hummingbird. We are most likely to find that for which we are searching. If you are searching for life's meaning, you dare not neglect the Word of God where life's purpose and meaning are spelled out. Look at the natural gifts and talents that God has given you. Pursue them, develop them, and mold them into honoring and serving God, and you will find fulfillment.

God's Word: But seek first his kingdom and his righteousness, and all these things will be given to you as well (Matthew 6:33).

Prayer: Father, help me to seek You first, knowing that You will show me how to use the talents and gifts that You have given me to honor You. Amen.

MAY 29

LANGUAGE

A pastor was invited to eat lunch with one of his church families who had two rambunctious sons. Under their mother's watchful eye, the boys sat rigidly through the meal. Afterward, unable to contain themselves any longer, the boys began to chase each other through the house shouting vulgarities. Embarrassed, the mother apologized to the pastor and said, "I just don't understand where they get such language; they hardly ever leave the house."

What kind of language are your children hearing at home? Our tendency may be to look outside of the home and place blame on others for their bad language and conduct. But the real problem could be the home environment itself. Children do not practice what we preach, they imitate what they see.

God's Word: Start children off on the way they should go, and even when they are old they will not turn from it (Proverbs 22:6).

Prayer: Father, as a parent, help me to realize the importance and impact of the example I set for my children knowing that they are more than likely to model how I live than listen to what say. Amen.

MAY 30

THE COLD WAR

The term "cold war" is usually used to describe the estranged relationship between two countries. But "cold war" can also be the atmosphere within our home. Husbands, wives, and children can live in the same household and because of conflict pass each other like ships in the night. If you don't communicate with each other, you don't have a relationship. Busy lives and separate interests have brought many families into what Dr. Joyce Brothers calls a "quiet hell."

If cold war exists in your home, isn't it time that you work on restoring family relationships? Isn't it time to call for a family conference and have a good heart-to-heart talk about what is going on and how you are tearing each other apart? Only love can build a home and restore relationships. Happy homes are filled with love and a desire to help each other be the best that you can be under God's leadership.

God's Word: Submit to one another out of reverence for Christ (Ephesians 5:21).

Prayer: Father, help the relationships in our family to reflect the reverence and love that we have with You. Amen.

MAY 31

PARENTAL ACCOUNTABILITY

Pity the children whose parents don't want them and don't have time for them. Pity the children who never hear a kind word and never receive a word of encouragement. Pity the children who are rarely held, cuddled, or told "I love you." Pity the children who watch their single mothers and fathers bring adult friends into their home to spend the night. Pity the children who must help their mother or father who is so drugged or drunk that they don't know where they are. Pity the children whose parents tell them they wish they were never born or who say to them in a department store, "Break that, and I'll break you."

The Bible teaches us that children are to be loved, nurtured, and caressed. Children are to be taught, guided, and aimed in positive directions. God gives us children to teach us patience and understanding so that we can be godlike. God holds parents accountable for how they treat their children.

God's Word: Children are a heritage from the Lord, offspring a reward from him. Like arrows in the hands of a warrior are children born in one's youth. Blessed is the man whose quiver is full of them. They will not be put to shame when they contend with their opponents in court (Psalm 127:3–5).

Prayer: Father, thank You for the gift of children and the joy and laughter they bring to the home. Help me to be a loving, responsible parent, teaching my children to love and serve You. Amen.

JUNE 1

OUR FOCUS

Dr. Albert Schweitzer was a remarkable man, highly intellectual and multitalented. He was a theologian, accomplished organist, philosopher, writer, missionary, and doctor all rolled into one dedicated servant of God. He could have served in any place in the world and lived in the best situations that life has to offer, but he chose French Equatorial Africa and the Lambarene Hospital.

Dr. Schweitzer could have been a multimillionaire with the $33,000 Nobel Peace Prize money he received in 1952. But he used that money to build a hospital ward for the treatment of leprosy.

Those who knew him best recognized that Dr. Schweitzer set lofty standards for himself. He gave his life to those in need. Not too many people are so multitalented as Dr. Albert Schweitzer. But all of us can learn from his life of unselfish service. He is a powerful testimony to the truth that if our focus is on God with compassion for others, we will not have lived in vain.

God's Word: The King will reply, "Truly I tell you, whatever you did for one of the least of these brothers and sisters of mine, you did for me" (Matthew 25:40).

Prayer: Father, give me a compassionate heart and a desire to live for others and in the process honor you. Amen.

JUNE 2

NAIL HOLES

A father eager to guide his son in living a responsible life instructed him to drive a nail into a post every time he did something bad and to withdraw one nail each time he did something good. The son did as his father instructed. One day, as father and son were looking at the post and talking about good and bad things that the son had done, the father asked his son what lessons he had learned from driving nails and removing them from the post. The son replied, "I have learned that when you pull a nail out of the post for a good deed done, that the nail holes remain."

God can forgive sins, but the consequences of our sins continue throughout a lifetime and even longer. Think before you act.

God's Word: To him who is able to keep you from stumbling and to present you before his glorious presence without fault and with great joy—to the only God our Savior be glory, majesty, power, and authority, through Jesus Christ our Lord, before all ages, now and forevermore! Amen (Jude 1:24).

Prayer: Father, help me to understand the destructive power of sin and to repent knowing that I cannot erase the past but with You, I can have a glorious future. Amen.

JUNE 3

PRIORITIES

There is a simple way to understand your priorities in life. Just look at your finances. How you spend your money reflects the real you, not just who you think you are. Your financial statement is a running commentary of what is important to you. Take a serious look at your expenses over the past six to twelve months. It won't take you long to recognize your priorities.

Jesus said, "For where your treasure is, there your heart will be also" (Matthew 6:21). The things you spend money for reflects the focus of your life. What percentage of your spending reflects a relationship with God, spiritual things, giving to the poor, or meeting human needs? What percentage of your spending reflects selfishness and greed?

After reflection on your priorities, are you really who you want to be? Are you surprised at yourself, disappointed, ashamed, embarrassed? What are you going to do about it?

God's Word: Set your minds on things above, not on earthly things (Colossians 3:2).

Prayer: Father, help my priorities to be on things that are eternal and things that cannot be taken away from me rather than things of the earth that are temporary and fade away. Amen.

JUNE 4

ANGER

Anger is an emotion. On the one hand, it can be a powerful, destructive force. On the other hand, it can be channeled in constructive and healthy ways. A person who lives with an emotional short fuse is a danger to himself and others. Unresolved, pent-up anger, holding grudges, and allowing irritating issues to simmer can result in serious health issues. Persons with such anger need medical and psychological attention.

In and of itself, anger is not a sin. But anger can lead you into sin. If you find yourself gripped by anger, look for constructive, healthy ways to release it. It is healthy to be angry about evil, injustice, and things that are harmful and hurtful. Take your anger to the cross and ask God to help you, forgive you, and channel it toward positive results.

God's Word: In your anger do not sin: Do not let the sun go down while you are still angry, and do not give the devil a foothold (Ephesians 4:26–27).

Prayer: Father, guard my heart against anger so that I will not sin against my fellow human or You. Help me to channel my anger toward constructive and helpful ends. Amen.

JUNE 5

STRENGTH AND PEACE

As human beings, we are subject to the storms of life. Everyone has heartaches and tensions, pressures at work, and pressures at home. Some face terminal diseases while others cope with aging parents or wayward children or both at the same time. Life, at best, is a mixture of joys and sorrows, health and sickness, good days and bad. Those who know that their help comes from the Lord are blessed.

How encouraging it is to know that there is a God who gives strength and peace to those who are going through the storms of life. Whatever storm you face today, take it to the Lord in prayer. Nothing you experience is too great or too small for God's consideration. Find strength and peace through God's presence in your life, the comfort that He provides through the Holy Spirit, and the peace that He alone can give you.

God's Word: And my God will meet all your needs according to the riches of his glory in Christ Jesus (Philippians 4:19).

Prayer: Father, I give You thanks for Your presence in my life, for the comfort the Holy Spirit brings to me, and the peace I find in You. Amen.

JUNE 6

AVAILABILITY

Jo Ann Shelton, guest soloist during revival services at Snyder Memorial Baptist Church, Fayetteville, North Carolina, said, "God is not as interested in your ability as He is your availability."

In late summer or early fall, the Nominating Committee in most churches is busy trying to fill places of responsibility for the various ministries of the church. The difficulty in finding willing servants often leads to frustration, disappointment, and unfulfilled positions. The unavailability of far too many church members weakens the church and places an undue burden upon those who are willing to serve.

In the average church, far too many church members are pew warmers rather than active participants. There are always those in the pew who should be in the choir or teaching a Sunday school class or working with youth, children and even helping in the nursery or serving as an usher or greeter. Isn't it time that you get serious about your availability to God and leave your abilities up to Him?

God's Word: Commit your way to the Lord; trust in him and he will do this (Psalm 37:5).

Prayer: Father, I am tired of making excuses about my abilities and deceiving myself into thinking that I love You when I know in my heart that I have not made myself available to You. Forgive me. I surrender all to You. Amen.

JUNE 7

FREEDOM

Victor Frankl made a life-changing discovery as a prisoner in a Nazi Germany death camp. He called it "the last of the human freedoms." Having lost his parents, his brother, and his wife to death in the gas ovens of prison, Frankl himself suffered indecencies we shudder to repeat. Not knowing one minute to the next whether he would shovel the ashes of those who had died in the flames or become ashes himself, Frankl found himself naked and alone in a small room. In that humiliating condition, he discovered that while he could do nothing about his circumstances, he could do something significant about his response.

In the process, he gained freedom and a power that enabled him to comfort other prisoners and even minister to his Nazi captors. Frankl's discovery of "self-awareness power" changed his life and has since changed the lives of countless others.

It's not your circumstances but how you respond that sets you free or makes you a prisoner. That freedom is offered to us by our relationship with Jesus Christ.

God's Word: Now the Lord is the Spirit, and where the Spirit of the Lord is, there is freedom (2 Corinthians 3:17).

Prayer: Father, despite the circumstances in which I may find myself, help me to know and experience the freedom that I have in Jesus Christ. Amen.

JUNE 8

THE TONGUE

"The tongue is a small part of the body, but it makes great boasts. Consider what a great forest is set on fire by a small spark. The tongue also is a fire, a world of evil among the parts of the body. It corrupts the whole body, sets the whole course of one's life on fire, and is itself set on fire by hell" (James 3:5–6).

There is nothing that can get us into trouble faster than our tongue. Some people can't hold jobs or keep relationships because they cannot control their tongue. It is neither wise nor appropriate to say everything we think. Put your mind in gear before you put your mouth into motion. It can save you from heartache and regret.

God's Word: Those who consider themselves religious and yet do not keep a tight rein on their tongues deceive themselves, and their religion is worthless (James 1:26).

Prayer: Father, teach me to think before I speak and to acknowledge the destructive power of words ill-spoken. Amen.

JUNE 9

NO MORE SEA

For lovers of the sea, it might be quite disappointing to read, "Then I saw a new heaven and a new earth, for the first heaven and the first earth had passed away, and there was no longer any sea" (Revelation 21:1). You might ask, "How can it be Heaven without a sea?" A logical explanation might help you. Ancient peoples hated the sea. They saw it as hostile and threatening. They saw the sea swallow up and separate innocent people from their loved ones.

John's vision of heaven was written in the context of the times in which he lived. He saw things on earth as hostile, threatening, and to be feared. He saw heaven as a place where everything was new. He saw heaven as being in the eternal presence of God—a place of beauty, peace, joy, and no separation. Take comfort in this truth.

God's Word: Do not let your hearts be troubled. You believe in God; believe also in me. My Father's house has many rooms; if that were not so, would I have told you that I am going there to prepare a place for you? And if I go and prepare a place for you, I will come back and take you to be with me that you also may be where I am (John 14:1–3).

Prayer: Father, thank You for providing a place in heaven for me. Cast out my fears of death because in heaven all the threats of the earth are gone. Amen.

JUNE 10

WHAT IF?

We suffer useless anxiety if we are constantly asking "What if?" It's a miserable life to worry about what might happen. The "What If" mentality paralyzes our progress, robs us of joy, destroys creativity, and cramps our freedom. A wise man said, "Worry is interest paid on trouble before it is due." Worry never does anything but bring useless stress and sorrow.

Jesus taught us not to be anxious by reminding us that each day has enough trouble of its own. If God takes care of the birds and lilies of the field, He can certainly take care of you. Not even a sparrow falls without God's notice, and you are more valuable to God than a sparrow. So, take a deep breath, inhale, trust in God, and exhale your anxieties.

God's Word: You will keep in perfect peace those whose minds are steadfast, because they trust in you (Isaiah 26:3).

Prayer: Father, take away my anxiety and replace it with complete trust in You. Give me Your peace and the reassurance that You are with me all the way. Amen.

JUNE 11

SUBSTITUTES

It's interesting how some people handle their feelings. Feeling blue, some find solace in shopping and spending money. Feeling lonely, people turn on the radio, TV, or pick up their iPad or smartphone. Feeling empty, people eat ice cream, chocolate chip cookies, or snacks. Feeling upset, some wash clothes, clean the house, or mow their lawn. Feeling sad, they pick up a joke book or watch a comedy on TV. It's amazing how we try to satisfy our moods or feelings with things.

Loneliness, despondency, being bored, or feeling empty, worthless, or sad cannot be cured with material things. We do not have the power within ourselves to solve our deepest problems. But there is a God who can! There is no feeling that we can't take to God. There is nothing that we experience that He can't understand. There is nothing we face that does not concern Him. Don't wallow in your misery. Don't try to substitute material props for an intimate relationship with God. Leaving God out of your life will cause you to come up empty every time. Jesus said, "Apart from me you can do nothing" (John 15:5). Believe it and take your burden to the Lord.

God's Word: So do not fear for I am with you; do not be dismayed, for I am your God. I will strengthen you and help you; I will uphold you with my righteous right hand (Isaiah 41:10).

Prayer: Father, help me to understand that feelings are deceptive and that I am never alone because You have promised to be with me always. Amen.

JUNE 12

TRAGEDY

History records eight main factors in the fall of the Roman Empire: foreign invasions, economic troubles, overreliance on slave labor, overexpansion, military spending, government corruption, political instability, and the growth of Christianity. A reference to the Roman Empire in the book of Revelation says: "They did not repent of their murders nor of their sorceries nor of their immorality nor of their thefts" (Revelation 9:21).

The tragedy of the Roman Empire is that despite calamities, people refused to repent of their sins. In their refusal to repent, they remained hostile to God. The tragedy of tragedies is for people to experience the tribulations of life and reject God who alone can save them.

If there is any significant lesson to be learned from life, it should be that there is no security in nature, human flesh, material things, or world powers. The only genuine security that we can have is in the hands of a sovereign God. To ignore, disregard, deny, or reject Him in any way is utterly foolish and tragic. To reject God is to commit the only unpardonable sin.

God's Word: Therefore he is able to save completely those who come to God through him, because he always lives to intercede for them (Hebrews 7:25).

Prayer: Father, thank You for the security and peace that I have in my heart because I have surrendered my life to You. Thank You that nothing can separate me from Your love. Amen.

JUNE 13

WORD OF GOD

In Dorchester County, Maryland, two inmates discovered that a stiff cover on a Bible left in their cell was just the tool they needed to pry back the defective lock on their cell door. That door led to the fire escape, which led to their freedom. But freedom was short-lived.

True freedom, offered to us by God through His Son Jesus Christ, does not land us back in prison. Rather, the freedom that God offers delivers us from the power of sin. The proper use of the Bible moves us closer to God, to others, and away from the shackles of sin.

God's Word is not a book of magic, nor is it a fairy tale or a decoration piece for home or office. It is rather a living word to be applied in practical ways to our everyday lives. You may have many versions of the Bible on your bookshelves, but it is the message of the Bible living in our hearts that makes the difference.

God's Word: I have hidden your word in my heart that I might not sin against you (Psalm 119:11).

Prayer: Father, Your Word is not to be used for evil purposes but rather to guide me in doing the right thing. Help me to always use it correctly. Amen.

JUNE 14

MOTIVATION

The pew in a little congregational church in Brunswick, Maine, is a special attraction to visitors. A brass plate on the pew has this inscription:

> "It was while seated in this pew, listening to her husband preach that Harriett Beecher Stowe had the vision which led to Uncle Tom's Cabin."

Worship is powerful, inspiring, and life-changing. Harriet Beecher Stowe's worship experience resulted in a book that transformed America's attitude toward slavery. It is far more likely that a person will catch a vision of God in the experience of worship than anywhere else. It is not that God cannot speak to us in other surroundings, but it is a matter of our focused attention upon God. If you want a life-changing word from the Lord, you must be tuned in. Worship allows you to get on the right frequency. Make worship a priority in your life.

God's Word: Come, let us bow down in worship, let us kneel before the Lord our maker (Psalm 95:6).

Prayer: Father, help me to make worship a priority in my life so that I keep my focus on You and turn my ear to hear Your voice. Amen.

JUNE 15

PREPARATION

The Bible Club of New Hanover High in Wilmington, North Carolina, sponsored daily devotions at the United Methodist Church adjacent to the school property. We met each morning before classes began. It was my privilege to bring the devotional message. My messages were brief and to the point simply because of inexperience. I did not realize at the time that one day I would be doing daily telephone devotions, minute messages for radio broadcast, bringing brief devotions at noon luncheons in our church fellowship hall, or preaching to hundreds.

God has a unique way of preparing, shaping, and molding us for greater tasks. Each little thing that we do, as we grow and mature, is preparation for greater responsibility. Do not despise little tasks, especially those that require daily discipline and stretch you in the process. When someone asks you to take on the responsibility, before you say no, look back over your life and see if God has prepared you for this very hour. If so, accept the job with joy. Otherwise, you may miss your calling.

God's Word: For we are God's handiwork, created in Christ Jesus to do good works, which God prepared in advance for us to do (Ephesians 2:10).

Prayer: Father, help me to see the direction in which You are aiming my life and help me to be faithful in fulfilling the purpose for which I was born. Amen.

JUNE 16

GIFTS

Johann Sebastian Bach, the great musician, had a simple response to a compliment he received for his remarkable gift of playing the organ. He said, "There is nothing remarkable about it. All one has to do is hit the notes at the right time and the instrument plays itself." The true professional always makes it look easy.

Whether it is playing a musical instrument, acting in a drama, or playing a sport, those who do it best are often modest about their ability. Nevertheless, behind the seemingly effortless achievement are hours upon hours of hard work, discipline, sweat, and tears.

God may gift us in music, art, science, sports, etc., but it is up to each one of us to develop that gift. It has been wisely said that "What you are is God's gift to you. What you make of yourself is your gift to God." Whatever you do with the gift that God has given you, do it all for the glory of God.

God's Word: Each of you should use whatever gift you have received to serve others, as faithful stewards of God's grace in its various forms (1 Peter 4:10).

Prayer: Father, help me to wisely develop and use the gifts that You have given me to serve others and to glorify You. Amen.

JUNE 17

LAUGHTER

It's healthier to laugh. Scientists tell us that when you have a hearty laugh, you don't feel pain, meaning that something physiological takes place inside your body. That something is the brain's natural pain suppressants, which are stimulated by laughter.

If you find life depressing, stressful, and painful, you might spend some time reading comics or watching TV comedies or reading joke books. While the laughter they produce may give you temporary relief from pain, a better remedy is to get better acquainted with Jesus Christ.

Christ offers joy, hope, love, peace, and abundant life. God never intended life to be somber, sad, sulky, and downhearted. Joy is God's desire for you. You are better off when you get your joy from Him.

God's Word: Those who go out weeping carrying seed to sow, will return with songs of joy, carrying sheaves with them (Psalm 126:6).

Prayer: Father, help me to know the joy that is in Christ Jesus my Lord. Amen.

JUNE 18

FUTURE

"Check out your future." That's the catchy title of an article on how to win the retirement game. The article points out the importance of checking on retirement and disability benefits you and your survivors will receive from Social Security.

Checking out your future benefits with Social Security is a wise thing to do. But what about your future beyond retirement—after you die? You don't have to fill out forms or wait for a reply to know if you have eternal security. You can know that immediately by receiving Jesus Christ as your Lord and Savior.

Social Security benefits are important for this life alone. Eternal security gives you peace of mind now and for the future beyond this life. Check out your future!

God's Word: Whoever has the Son has life: whoever does not have the Son of God does not have life (1 John 5:12).

Prayer: Father, help me to understand that all the insurance policies in the world, including Social Security, cannot take the place of the assurance You offer me for eternity through Jesus Christ. Amen.

JUNE 19

TEARS

We don't know much about the emotions of a crocodile, but we do know that they shed tears. Unlike the tears of human beings that are usually produced by great sorrow or great joy, crocodiles shed tears for neither reason. Crocodile tears are nature's way of getting rid of excess salt from the water in which they live. The tears of a crocodile appear as sadness, but they have nothing at all to do with emotions.

People have been known to shed crocodile tears. That is, they appear to be sad when they are not, or they appear to be happy when they are not. Sometimes people act religious, usually on Sunday, but during the week, they are not religious at all.

Christianity is not acting; it is being. We are to love the Lord God with all our heart, mind, and soul. Pretending to be Christian will not give you peace or bring you forgiveness or security. Faith and trust in Jesus Christ must be real, or else it is no more than crocodile tears.

God's Word: My sheep listen to my voice; I know them, and they follow me. I give them eternal life, and they shall never perish; no one will snatch them out of my hand" (John 10:27–28).

Prayer: Father, thank You that my faith and trust in You is secure for all eternity. Amen.

JUNE 20

COME

Any loving parent can identify with the word "come." How many times have you said to your children, "come"? With that single word, you have called them away from danger, invited them to sit in your lap, asked them to ride or walk with you. With that single word, you have called them to the table to be fed and nourished, or you have called them to be tucked into bed. With that one word you have taken them to church or school or to places where they would develop socially, physically, mentally, or spiritually.

As a parent, if you can understand the importance of the word "come," as you guide the lives of your children, can you not also understand the importance of "come" when God calls? God's invitation for you to "come" is the most important of all calls. You can only give your children limited security, but God gives to those who come to him eternal security. Don't neglect God's call. Come to Him today.

God's Word: Come to me, all you who are weary and burdened, and I will give you rest. Take my yoke upon you and learn from me, for I am gentle and humble in heart, and you will find rest for your souls. For my yoke is easy and my burden is light (Matthew 11:28–30).

Prayer: Father, there are many calls for my attention. Help me to hear Your call above all others and know, that you are offering me security and peace that cannot be found elsewhere. Amen.

JUNE 21

EATING

Andy Rooney is credited with saying, "The two biggest sellers in any bookstore are the cookbooks and the diet books. The cookbooks tell you how to prepare the food, and the diet books tell you how not to eat any of it."

Americans are obsessed with eating. It is close to impossible to have a meeting where food is not involved. Is it any wonder that 41 percent of men and 51percent of women consider themselves overweight? What a difference it would make if we were more concerned with feeding our souls than we are with feeding our bodies; the world we live in might be a different place.

The next time you sit down for a meal or take a snack break, remember that you also have a soul that needs food. We feed our souls when we read and study the Bible, take time to pray, and listen to God. We feed our souls by reading books that point us to God and how we can enhance our spiritual life. We feed our souls when we make worship a priority in our daily lives. As someone has well said, "What value is there in feeding a dying body and starving a living soul?"

God's Word: Do not work for food that spoils, but for food that endures to eternal life, which the Son of Man will give you (John 6:27).

Prayer: Father, teach me the importance of feeding my soul on that which is eternal. Give me a hunger and thirst for You and Your Word. Amen.

JUNE 22

CONTENTMENT

How contented are you? If you find it difficult to appreciate what you have because you are focused on what you don't have, it may be time for you to reevaluate your life.

Instead of concentrating on what is missing in your life, be grateful for what you have. Solomon, in his wisdom, said, "Better what the eye sees than the roving of the appetite. This too is meaningless, a chasing after the wind" (Ecclesiastes 6:9). It is better to see, use, and enjoy what you have than to spend your time wanting more.

Life can truly be enjoyed if you get rid of the "I never have enough" mentality.

God's Word: Watch out! Be on your guard against all kinds of greed; life does not consist in an abundance of possessions (Luke 12:15).

Prayer: Father, give me a heart of gratitude and appreciation for the things that I have and limit my pursuit of things I don't have. Help me to be a good manager of what I have and use it for Your glory and honor. Amen.

JUNE 23

MEMORIALS

Mount Vernon, the stately Colonial mansion overlooking the Potomac River and home of George Washington, should be on the "must visit" list of all who love American history. It is in this beautiful setting that Washington took his bride on their honeymoon. It is from this place that he went off to war to secure independence for the American Colonies. It is here that he died.

Down a little path and just a short distance from his beloved home, George and Martha Washington are buried. No visit to Mount Vernon is complete without standing in reverence at his tomb. Few men in history hold the esteem of George Washington, plantation owner, war hero, father of our country, the first general of the American army, and first president of the United States of America.

With all the love, respect, and honor that we bestow upon this great man, it is notable that nothing at his gravesite is written in praise of him. On the headstone of his grave are these words from John 11:25–26: "I am the resurrection and the life. The one who believes in me will live, even though they die; and whoever lives by believing in me will never die. Do you believe this?" Powerful testimony from one of America's greatest. In the final analysis, what counts in life is not what we do, but what God has done for us.

God's Word: For it is by grace you have been saved, through faith—and this is not from yourselves, it is the gift of God—not by works, so that no one can boast. For we are God's handiwork created in Christ Jesus to do good works, which God prepared in advance for us to do (Ephesians 2:8–10).

Prayer: Father, thank You that it is not by anything that I can do but by Your grace that I have eternal life through Jesus Christ. Amen.

JUNE 24

GET ORGANIZED

Let's face it, our lives are greatly affected by paper: letters, newspapers, magazines, junk mail, etc. We are bogged down and even assaulted by the mass of paper that we handle daily. It is a never-ending battle to avoid being overcome by the clutter of paper on our desks, tables, dressers, and kitchen counters.

Stephanie Winston, founder and director of the Organizing Principle, a New York-based consulting firm, says "there are only four things you can do with a piece of paper: toss it, refer it to someone else, act on it, or file it." She calls it her "TRAF" system. The idea is to never handle the same paper twice.

Handling paper is a matter of priority. The same is true with spiritual matters. Putting God first is a priority decision. It is the most effective way to organize our lives.

God's Word: But seek first his kingdom and his righteousness, and all these things will be given to you as well (Matthew 6:33).

Prayer: Father, help me to get organized in my daily life so that I keep my priorities straight and take care of the most important things first. Amen.

JUNE 25

HUMILITY

There is an old saying that "he who toots not his own horn, the same shall not be tooted." It speaks of self-aggrandizement. The fact is that those who go around bragging about themselves are seldom bragged about by others. Truly humble people do not recognize their humility and are often embarrassed when their humility is acknowledged by others. A truly humble person would never write a book entitled *Humility and How I Achieved It*.

Lewis Dunnington writes in his book *Power to Become*:

> All of the truly great have been humble in spirit. As the years pass, they learn to sense how vast, mysterious, and inexplicable much of our universe really is, and how puny is man's understanding. They have long since passed the place in life where they spend time trying to impress others. Having forgotten themselves, the very integrity of their souls leads them to adopt the inquiring attitude of a little child.[5]

The secret of humility is to forget yourself in the service of others. Perhaps that is why so few are genuinely great.

God's Word: Whoever wants to be great among you must be your servant … just as the Son of Man did not come to be served, but to serve, and to give his life as a ransom for many (Matthew 20:26, 28).

Prayer: Father, help me never to call attention to myself but to keep my focus on helping others. Amen.

---

[5] Lewis Dunnington, *Power to Become* (New York: Macmillan, 1956), 64.

CRITICISM

Psychologists tell us that a common fault with human beings is that we demand of others what we fail to demand of ourselves. The next time you find yourself in a critical spirit, stop and look at your own life. All too often, the faults and failures we see in other people are but a reflection of our faults and failures. We don't like what we see in them because we don't like who we are.

Unrealistic demands of others often result in gossip and harsh judgment. Living with a critical spirit only makes our lives miserable. George Whitfield saw a criminal on his way to the gallows and he said, "There, but for the grace of God, go I!" William Barclay said, "No man can pass judgment on another unless he at least tries to understand what the other man has come through."

You can make a significant difference in your life with more understanding and less criticism. Increase your happiness by finding good in others. In doing so, you will discover the good in yourself. Focusing on the bad in others only reveals the evil in our hearts.

God's Word: Do not judge, or you too will be judged. For in the same way you judge others, you will be judged, and with the measure you use, it will be measured to you (Matthew 7:1–2).

Prayer: Father, forgive my critical spirit. When I see the faults and failures in others, let that be a call for me to correct those same behaviors in my own life. Amen.

JUNE 27

SEARCHING

Late one night, a professor working at his desk shuffled through a collection of papers and junk mail dumped there by the housekeeper. As magazines and letters found their way to the trash can, his attention fell on an article that said, "We have no one to work in the Northern Province of Gabon in the Central Congo. It is my prayer as I write this article that God will lay his hand on one—one on whom already the Master's eyes have been cast—that he or she shall be called to this place to help us."

The professor closed the magazine, laid it aside, and wrote in his diary, "My search is over." Albert Schweitzer surrendered his talents as theologian, organist, writer, humanitarian, philosopher, and physician, then and there, to the Lord's work in Africa.

Have you discovered what God wants you to do with your life? If the search is on, don't give up until you have the answer. If you know what God wants you to do, do it now, and do it with all your heart. There is no greater joy in life than to respond to God's call and discover that the search is over.

God's Word: Then I heard the voice of the Lord saying, "Whom shall I send? And who will go for us? And I said, "Here am I. Send me" (Isaiah 6:8).

Prayer: Father, open my ears to hear Your call. Open my eyes that I may see where You want me to serve. Having heard Your call and having seen Your plan for my life, help me to respond as did Isaiah, "Here am I. Send me!" Amen.

JUNE 28

REJOICE

The biblical word "rejoice" is one of the most vibrant words in scripture. The hymnbook of ancient Israel invited people "to sing for joy to the Lord," and "shout aloud to the Rock of our salvation" (Psalm 95:1). When told of her place in the plan of God, Mary cried, "My soul magnifies the Lord and my spirit rejoices in God my savior" (Luke 1:46–47).

The modern word for rejoicing is "celebrate" or "celebration." To celebrate our faith is to fill our hearts with the joy of Christ. If you are thinking bad thoughts right now, if you feel down and out, start celebrating that you can take all your problems to the Lord. Celebrate that with God you are never alone. Celebrate that God can put faith in your soul, a song on your lips, and hope in your heart. From this moment on you can celebrate life rather than dread it. Turn your thoughts godward. As the hymn writer put it, "Because He lives, I can face tomorrow." That goes for today also.

God's Word: Rejoice in the Lord always. I will say it again: Rejoice! Let your gentleness be evident to all. The Lord is near. Do not be anxious about anything, but in every situation, by prayer and petition with thanksgiving, present your requests to God. And the peace of God, which transcends all understanding, will guard your hearts and your minds in Christ Jesus (Philippians 4:4–7).

Prayer: Father, fill my mind and heart with Your joy. Take away my anxieties and fears and help me to celebrate daily Your presence in my life. Amen.

JUNE 29

LIKE A ROPE

One of the greatest lessons I learned in pastoral leadership came from a layman who loved the Lord and loved the church. It came at a time when our denomination was caught up in a controversy that was tearing us apart. It was a battle between conservatives and moderates, and I was strongly pushing the moderate position.

The layman, Roper Vanhorn, came to the church office and asked if he could speak to me. I invited him in, and after a few words of greeting, he told me how much he appreciated me and how he was concerned for the peace and welfare of the congregation. He was concerned that I was dividing the church by the strong stand that I was taking. He then said, "Pastor, we are like a rope. You can pull us anywhere you want us to go but you can't push us." We talked, prayed together, and then he left.

Alone, I sat at my desk humbled, convicted, and convinced. I wept and prayed, thanking God for that visit. A layman had loved me enough to tell me the truth about myself and about the congregation I served. I too loved the Lord and the church. I knew that my convictions were strong, but Roper convinced me that my ministry would be better served if I pulled the congregation with love rather than pushed them to take sides. His wise words changed my entire approach to ministry.

Many church divisions could be avoided by spiritual leaders understanding that people are like a rope. You can pull them, but you can't push them. You can lead them, but you can't drive them.

God's Word: Love is patient, love is kind. It does not envy, it does not boast, it is not proud. It does not dishonor others, it is not self-seeking, it is not easily angered, it keeps no record of wrongs. Love does not delight in evil but rejoices with the truth.

It always protects, always trusts, always hopes, always perseveres (1 Corinthians 13:4–7).

Prayer: Father, thank you for laymen who will speak truth to their pastor and who promote love. Amen.

JUNE 30

ANGELS UNAWARES

While living in the interior of northeastern Brazil, I was on my way to visit a farmer who owned a building that we were interested in renting for a church start. It was the dry season, and I was told to follow the riverbed for the quickest route to his home.

I soon discovered that my four-wheel-drive jeep was no match for a muddy spot in the riverbed. My car immediately sank up to the running board. I was alone and miles from the nearest town. Rain clouds were visible in the distance. As I sat on the bank of the riverbed, distraught and helpless, suddenly, a group of eight of the largest Brazilian men I had ever seen suddenly appeared out of nowhere with their large Brazilian hoes. After joking with me about my predicament, they got me back in the car, pulled mud away from my tires, and then physically lifted my vehicle out of the mire. Then, they laughed and walked away. All my inquiries about them failed. Little wonder that I believe to this day that they were angels unawares sent by God to get me out of a helpless situation.

Continuing my journey, my visit was successful. The house we rented became a church that is flourishing to this day.

God's Word: Call on me in the day of trouble; I will deliver you, and you will honor me (Psalm 50:15).

Prayer: Father, I have experienced your deliverance both physically and spiritually. Thank you for your power to rescue me when I am helpless. Amen.

JULY 1

EXPLAIN YOURSELF

Sometimes we have trouble expressing ourselves. We try to say something, but it just doesn't come out as we intended. We know what we want to say, but we just don't make it clear to those on the receiving end. Here are a few examples. A woman trying to explain to her insurance adjuster said, "To avoid hitting the bumper of the car in front, I struck a pedestrian." A man told his insurance company, "The pedestrian had no idea which direction to run, so I ran over him." Another man trying to explain his accident said, "When I saw I could not avoid a collision, I stepped on the gas and crashed into the other car."

Trying to explain ourselves to others can get complicated. But we can be confident that God understands the intent of our explanations. When our words don't come out right, we have the assurance that the Holy Spirit interprets for us. When you have trouble explaining yourself to God, just turn to him, knowing that He reads your heart and not your lips.

God's Word: In the same way, the Spirit helps us in our weakness. We do not know what we ought to pray for, but the Spirit himself intercedes for us through wordless groans. And he who searches our hearts knows the mind of the Spirit, because the Spirit intercedes for God's people in accordance with the will of God (Romans 8:26–27).

Prayer: Father, thank You for listening to my heart even when what I say does not always make sense. Amen.

JULY 2

CLEANUP

Anyone who works with computers knows the importance of deleting unused or unnecessary files or programs from their hard drive. Failure to clean up your hard drive slows its performance and can even cause it to crash.

Cleanup is also necessary for our lives. You might recall those resolutions made back in January about the changes you were determined to make this year. How well have you managed your cleanup? July 2 is the halfway point of the year. Perhaps at this halfway point, it is time to reevaluate your cleanup progress.

Clean up means deciding what you need to keep and what you need to discard or delete in your life. Clutter slows you down, hinders your productivity, and can even increase your stress to the breaking point. Ask God to give you the resolve to focus on what is essential and to rid yourself of those things that are tearing you down.

God's Word: Create in me a pure heart, O God, and renew a steadfast spirit within me (Psalm 51:10).

Prayer: Father, help me clean up the clutter in my life, be refreshed by Your Holy Spirit and restored to the joy of my salvation. Amen.

JULY 3

GOD'S CALL

It takes many different professions for the world to function. Not all people are gifted in the same way, and that, by God's design, is a blessing and benefit to society. The truth is that we can use the physical and mental skills God has given us to bless others, and at the same time, through faith, serve and honor God.

Every Christian is God's representative on earth, commissioned to share Christ's love wherever they are. Whether we proclaim Christ at home or abroad is not the question. The question is our relationship with God and our availability to use our gifts and talents to spread the gospel.

It all begins with answering God's call like Samuel, who said, "Speak for your servant is listening" (1 Samuel 3:10), or like Isaiah, who said, "Here am I. Send me!" (Isaiah 6:8). Or Paul, as it is recorded in the King James Version, asking, "Lord, what do you want me to do?" (Acts 9:6). When God calls, your availability to Him is more important than your profession. When you serve Him through your career, then God's call is answered and honored.

God's Word: He has saved us and called us to a holy life—not because of anything we have done but because of his own purpose and grace (2 Timothy 1:9).

Prayer: Father, take my talents and gifts and use them to bring others to Christ. Amen.

JULY 4

DISCIPLINE

Watching the Olympic Games on TV is a thrill and is the next best thing to being there. Each athlete is a winner whether he or she comes away with a gold, bronze, or silver medal or not. That they made it to the Olympics and are part of the competition is an honor in and of itself.

The secret of great athletes is discipline. The discipline to practice, to endure pain, and to keep their minds focused. With their bodies and minds fine-tuned, athletes provide a challenge and inspiration to us all.

The disciplined life is a fulfilled life. Those who focus on a goal and then give their all to achieve it know the joy of successful living.

God's Word: No discipline seems pleasant at the time but painful. Later on, however, it produces a harvest of righteousness and peace for those who have been trained by it (Hebrews 12:11).

Prayer: Father, help me to be disciplined in what I do, realizing that by having a focused life, I can accomplish significant things in my life and bring honor to You. Amen.

JULY 5

NAVIGATION

F. B. Meyer, renowned pastor, evangelist, and inner-city ministry worker in England and the United States, received an important lesson in navigation on one of his many ocean voyages. Coming into port one night during a terrible storm, he noticed that the entrance to the harbor seemed extremely narrow. Standing on the bridge next to the captain, he asked the captain how he would make the turn into the harbor. The captain pointed toward three lights on the shore and explained that they are called "range lights." He said, "When they are all in a straight line, I go right in."

Life is sometimes compared to a storm as heaven is compared to a safe harbor. As a ship captain depends upon "range lights" to get him through the storm and safely into harbor, God has provided "range lights" for us as we navigate through life. If we can align our "range lights"—the Bible, the Holy Spirit as our inner witness, and the circumstances in which we find ourselves—we will arrive safely into the harbor called heaven.

God's Word: I keep my eyes always on the Lord. With him at my right hand, I will not be shaken (Psalm 16:8).

Prayer: Father, as I navigate through life, help me to fix my eyes on You by applying Your Word to my heart and following the guidance of the Holy Spirit in all my circumstances. Amen.

JULY 6

MONEY

If you believe the myth that money is the answer to all your problems, stop for just a moment and consider the lives of Howard Hughes and Aristotle Onassis. Both men had wealth beyond the imagination of most of us. Yet, both died miserable men. If financial wealth is your goal in life, remember that you are devoting yourself to something that can be taken away from you and something that you cannot take with you when you leave this world. Money has never bought anyone peace of mind, nor can it give you health or happiness.

Wealth is more than money. A wife, children, family, and friends, and a right relationship with God are more precious than all the gold in Fort Knox.

There is an investment that pays more significant dividends than any bank, savings & loan, or stocks and bonds can offer—a personal relationship with Jesus Christ. The message of 1 Peter 1:3–4 says: "Praise be to the God and Father of our Lord Jesus Christ! In his great mercy he has given us new birth into a living hope through the resurrection of Jesus Christ from the dead, and into an inheritance that can never perish, spoil or fade. This inheritance is kept in heaven for you, who through faith are shielded by God's power until the coming of the salvation that is ready to be revealed in the last time." Note that this inheritance is nondestructive, not stained, and does not lose value. Best of all, it is eternal.

The choice of the investments you make in life is yours. Choose money, and you will be miserable. Choose Christ, and you will know the meaning of true riches.

God's Word: Keep your lives free from the love of money and be content with what you have, because God has said: "Never will I leave you; never will I forsake you" (Hebrews 13:5).

Prayer: Father, help my choice and my priority in life to be You, knowing that You will provide for my needs. Amen.

JULY 7

JUST THINKING

When was the last time you sat down and did some serious thinking? The world is producing fewer thinkers because our minds are always occupied with noise and activity. Thinking requires a considerable amount of quietness, concentration, and the most important of all elements—time.

Can you imagine the time you would save tomorrow by devoting a few minutes tonight to think through your responsibilities and prioritize them? What a difference it would make if you thought through the discussion you will have with your spouse, children, friend, or boss over differences of opinion. You might save yourself a lot of misery by thinking through the consequences of a marriage, job change, or move.

While you are thinking, how about giving thought to where you are going in life and how you plan to get there—including eternity. Yes, thinking requires time, work, discipline, and patience. It can make the difference between a fulfilled life and one that is wasted.

God's Word: We demolish arguments and every pretension that sets itself up against the knowledge of God, and we take captive every thought to make it obedient to Christ (2 Corinthians 10:5).

Prayer: Father, guide my thoughts so that my decisions and actions will be in obedience to Your will. Amen.

JULY 8

DODGING THE LAW

In 1989, *Time* magazine reported on a small Denver company called "Innovisions Research." The company introduced a line of stealth attachments using microwave-absorbing materials like those in the stealth bomber, which, when fastened to the front of an automobile, reduce the car's visibility to police radar.

The writer of the report said, "It says a lot about our culture's response to authority when we employ the latest high-tech wartime defensive countermeasures to avoid speeding tickets."[6]

There are always those who want to get around the law or be an exception to it. People with evil intent often beat the law with the false conception that they have gotten away with something. What is forgotten is that ultimately we will answer to God. Nothing, absolutely nothing, is hidden from His sight.

God's Word: For we must all appear before the judgment seat of Christ, so that each of us may receive what is due us for the things done while in the body whether good or bad (2 Corinthians 5:10).

Prayer: Father, help me to live with the knowledge that ultimately I am accountable to You for the decisions I make. Do not let me be deceived by thinking that just because someone does not see my misdeeds, I am free to do as I please. Amen.

---

[6] *Time*, 3/13/89, 55.

JULY 9

PROMISES

In times of disappointment or defeat, amid trauma or death, we may easily feel that God has forsaken us. When things do not go our way, when our prayers are not answered, when God appears to be silent, it is hard to see our blessings. Yet, God has promised never to leave us or forsake us (Hebrews 13:5). Jesus, before departing from His disciples, said to them: "I am with you always, to the very end of the age" (Matthew 28:20).

God's promises are not based on our feelings but rather on His will, purpose, and plan. When things do not work out according to our plan, that is not the time to lose our faith or get angry with God. We must remember that God is always faithful to fulfill His promises, but He delivers them on His schedule, not ours. We can be assured that God knows our needs better than we know them. That fact, in and of itself, is a blessing. Take comfort in God's Word for today.

God's Word: So do not fear, for I am with you; do not be dismayed, for I am your God. I will strengthen you and help you; I will uphold you with my righteous right hand (Isaiah 41:10).

Prayer: Father, even when things do not work out like I think they should, and when my prayers are not answered in just the way I want them, open my eyes to see the blessings that You have already given me and the blessing that I don't see that might come in unanswered prayer. Amen.

JULY 10

UNSELFISHNESS

In 1991, the Chicago Bulls won the NBA Championship utilizing outstanding talent and amazing demonstrations of unselfishness. The victory was a team effort. When Disney World offered to fly Michael Jordan and his family to the Florida resort, he agreed to do so only on the condition that the whole team and their families be invited.

On the court and off the court, Michael Jordan became a role model for unselfishness. He is admired for his extraordinary basketball skills, but his unselfish spirit continues to win him friends and admirers.

Practice unselfishness in all you do. The blessings that you will receive for your consideration of others will make your effort worthwhile.

God's Word: Give and it will be given to you. A good measure, pressed down, shaken together and running over, will be poured into your lap. For the measure you use, it will be measured to you (Luke 6:38).

Prayer: Father, help me to live unselfishly, thinking of others and not of myself. Amen.

JULY 11

SPIRITUAL MARKERS

When the Children of Israel crossed the Jordan River and entered the promised land, they were instructed to pick up twelve stones from the river's dry bed and place them on the other side. These stones would serve as a memorial and reminder to future generations that God had shut off the waters of the Jordan so that the people could cross with the ark of the covenant (Joshua 4).

Stones, being abundantly available, were often used as spiritual markers and a reminder of experiences not to be forgotten. Search the scriptures to find when men like Abraham, Jacob, Moses, and others built a spiritual marker to remind them of what God had done in their lives.

Reflect upon the spiritual markers in your life when you have experienced God in a particular way. It might have happened during a revival, a spiritual retreat or camp, a time of sickness, healing, or transformation in your life. It could have happened when your life was spared in a car wreck, flood, or hurricane. A notable spiritual marker is the day you received Christ into your life and found forgiveness for your sins. These spiritual markers remind us of God's love, grace, and transforming power.

God's Word: Praise the Lord, my soul, and forget not all his benefits (Psalm 103:2).
Prayer: Father, thank you for the special moments in my life when I have experienced you at work. Amen.

JULY 12

ATTITUDE

A little girl talking to her mother said, "Mom, I've had such a happy time today." Her mother asked, "What made the difference?" The daughter replied, "Well, yesterday, my thoughts pushed me around. Today I pushed them around."

Being in control of our thoughts rather than allowing our thoughts to control us makes the difference between a good day and a bad one. If negative thoughts are hounding you, push them away. Stop what you are thinking by changing the subject or making that long-promised visit or doing a good deed for someone. Go to God's Word, pray, turn your focus toward God. Ask Him to help you push negative thoughts away.

When the soldiers of Israel looked at Goliath, the Philistine giant, they thought, "He's so big we can never kill him." When young David looked at Goliath with only a slingshot in his hand, he thought, "He's so big, I can't miss." Attitude makes all the difference in the world.

God's Word: And whatever you do, whether in word or deed, do it all in the name of the Lord Jesus, giving thanks to God the Father through him (Colossians 3:17).

Prayer: Father, help my attitude reflect my relationship with You in word and deed. Amen.

JULY 13

COMMITMENT

Nothing significant in life is accomplished without commitment. No athletic team can win without commitment. Just dreaming about being a surgeon, teacher, scientist, or any profession isn't enough to achieve the goal. There must be commitment. Marriages without commitment fail, and for lack of commitment, some marriages never occur. Attending church will never bring the fulfillment that comes with being committed to the Lord.

Meaning and purpose will never come to you without commitment. Say to yourself, "I will do more."

> I will do more than belong—I will participate.
> I will do more than care—I will help.
> I will do more than believe—I will practice.
> I will do more than be fair—I will be kind.
> I will do more than forgive—I will love.
> I will do more than earn—I will enrich.
> I will do more than teach—I will serve.
> I will do more than be friendly—I will be a friend.
> I will do more than live—I will grow.[7]

Don't just think about these things—commit to them.

God's Word: Commit to the Lord whatever you do, and he will establish your plans (Proverbs 16:3).

Prayer: Father, may my commitment to You be a complete surrender of my life. Amen.

---

[7] St. Paul's Evangelical Lutheran Church, Sassamansville, PA, Dr. John Bardsley.

JULY 14

ACCOUNTABILITY

The average church member has little or no idea what is involved in ministering to a large congregation. The Personnel Committee of First Baptist Church, Morehead City, wanted their members to understand and appreciate the work of the staff. In 1993, they requested each staff member to keep a time log on their activities for one month. There was no reluctance on the part of the church staff to comply. They were more than willing to give an account of themselves to the congregation.

From that study, there grew a deeper understanding of what was involved in ministry and a deeper appreciation for the complex work of the church staff. The exercise of accountability resulted in increased prayer support and gratitude for the spiritual responsibilities of the staff.

Accountability, in any position of responsibility, is beneficial and healthy. Ultimately, we are all accountable to a higher authority.

God's Word: So then, each of us will give an account of ourselves to God (Romans 14:12).

Prayer: Father, help me be wise and resourceful in my use of time, knowing that ultimately I am responsible to You and will give an account of how I lived my life. Amen.

JULY 15

THE WRONG MESSAGE

Have you been listening to the subtle messages that are thrown at us every day? "If you drink, don't drive," suggesting that it is all right to drink. Or "Practice safe sex," meaning that it's okay to engage in sexual activity outside of marriage or that there is such a thing as "safe sex." How about sports programs that promote beer or cigarettes as if one could be at his peak athletically by drinking and smoking. Getting the wrong message is bad enough; putting it into practice is foolish. Following the wrong message can tarnish your reputation, destroy your health, or even kill you.

Everything you hear is not trustworthy. Be discerning, be wise, be careful what you believe, and put it into practice. Misinformation presented in attractive ways is always based on half-truths or lies. The attractive message enticing us to do everything our hearts desire never mentions the high risks and serious consequences that follow.

Truth can always be measured by what the Bible teaches. Every message we hear should be weighed by the Word of God. If what we are enticed or challenged to do does not measure up to God's standard, leave it alone. Flee from it. If you want to honor Christ and avoid deception and fatal damage, you must give full attention to the truth.

God's Word: Jesus said, 'If you hold to my teaching, you are really my disciples. Then you will know the truth, and the truth will set you free" (John 8:31).

Prayer: Father, teach me to weigh what I hear and what I do by the truth as it is in Jesus Christ, my Lord. Amen.

JULY 16

INHERITANCE

Today is the anniversary of my father's death. In 1999, he died peacefully at the age of eighty-seven. When I think of my father, Joseph Walter Allard, known to everyone as Joe, I think of all he taught me. He taught me how to throw a ball, how to ride a bicycle, how to shoot a gun, how to fish, crab, and row a boat, how to use power tools, and enjoy woodworking. He taught me how to drive a car and how to respect my elders, saying "Yes, sir" and "No, sir." He taught me to love nature and to take time to ponder the handiwork of God.

But there is so much more. My father taught me to love God and obey Him. Before I entered the first grade, he had taught me most of the stories of the Bible. He taught me by example that spiritual things are far more important than material things. He taught me that it's only the eternal that lasts. My father didn't give me a lot of this world's goods, but He gave me something far more important. He gave me the best—he introduced me to God.

God's Word: Start children off on the way they should go, and even when they are old, they will not turn from it (Proverbs 22:6).

Prayer: Father, thank You for my father, who introduced me to You and set me on the path to eternal life and joyful service. Amen.

JULY 17

STANDING TALL

The most subtle form of suffering inflicted upon prisoners in the days of the Spanish Inquisition was to put a man in a dungeon where the ceiling was not high enough for him to stand to his full height. Confined in such quarters, the prisoner was powerless to stand straight or breathe deeply with his head held high. The Spanish had learned that the quickest way to break a man's spirit was to keep him from standing tall.

Sin limits our ability to stand tall, hold our heads up, and walk with confidence. Notice how any criminal apprehended by police cowers before cameras. They cover their head or hide their face and often bend over low to avoid recognition.

Forgiveness from God, on the other hand, enables us to walk straight and tall. The Christian faith enables us to grieve over our sins, but forgiveness gives us liberty and joy.

God's Word: Therefore, there is now no condemnation for those who are in Christ Jesus, because through Christ Jesus the law of the Spirit who gives life has set you free from the law of sin and death (Romans 8:1).

Prayer: Father, thank You for setting me free from the bondage of sin. I can stand tall because I have repented of my sins and found forgiveness through Jesus Christ. Amen.

JULY 18

COMPASSION

In revisiting the story of the prodigal son in the Gospel of Luke, I was led to think in a way I had not considered before. Previously, most of my thoughts were about the son and how he squandered his life. On this visit, I realized that the principal character was the father and not the son or his brother.

The father represents the loving, forgiving, receiving heavenly Father. Like God, he focused, not on the wrong that his son had done, but on that the son came home. The father loved his wayward son so much that he never stopped looking for him to return. He didn't chase after his son, scold him, condemn him, or reject him. He just waited and kept the door open. When the son returned, the father was filled with joy. He embraced his son, threw a big welcome party, and welcomed him home. With a Father like God, why would anyone not want to come home?

God's Word: But you, Lord, are a compassionate and gracious God, slow to anger, abounding in love and faithfulness (Psalm 86:15).

Prayer: Father, there are no words to express my gratitude for the love, compassion, forgiveness, and grace you have shown to me, a sinner. Thank you for receiving me into your kingdom and filling my life with joy and purpose. Amen.

JULY 19

PERSPECTIVE

He was long past his prime. He shouldn't have been in the ring at all. In the third round, he took a tremendous blow to the jaw that sent him to the mat, flat on his back. As he attempted to stagger up, his manager yelled, "No, no, no! Stay down until nine!" The dazed boxer asked, "What time is it now?"[8]

Sometimes we are so dazed by the knockout blows of life's problems that we have no idea where we are, what we are doing, or what time it is. When you are down and close to being knocked out, you need a personal relationship with Jesus Christ. A relationship with Jesus can give you a proper perspective on life. With Jesus in your life, you can get your head cleared and your heart cleansed by confessing your sins and receiving the forgiveness He alone can offer. If sin has you on the mat, only Jesus can raise you up. Don't you think it's time to surrender to Him?

God's Word: "Come now, and let us settle the matter," says the Lord, "Though your sins are like scarlet, they shall be as white as snow; though they are red like crimson, they will be like wool" (Isaiah 1:18).

Prayer: Father, I confess that the problems of life and my sins have knocked me down and left me in a daze. Help me, by faith, to surrender my life to You and get the proper perspective for a meaningful life. Amen.

---

[8] Pastor's Professional Research Service, Seven Worlds Corp., Knoxville, TN, July/August/ September 1992.

JULY 20

THE BIBLE

The Bible is not a book of magic. If you start reading it, all your problems won't mysteriously disappear. If you carry it in your car, it won't protect you from having a wreck. If you carry it close to your heart, it won't necessarily stop a bullet. The Bible is not a magician's wand or a fortune teller's tarot card. The Bible is not a good luck charm to be pulled out in times of emergency or danger.

The most critical part of your being is your soul. What profit is it if you feed your body and starve your soul? If you are willing to spend time daily feeding and exercising your body, why would you not feed and exercise your soul? A healthy body and a healthy soul will put balance in your life and enable you to be a valuable servant of the Lord. A wise man wrote about the Bible: "This book will keep you from your sins, or your sins will keep you from this book."

God's Word: Therefore everyone who hears these words of mine and puts them into practice is like a wise man who built his house on the rock (Matthew 7:24).

Prayer: Father, Your Word is a road map for daily living and a guide to eternal life. Help me to hunger and thirst for the truth that it provides. Amen.

JULY 2L

TRUST

It is amazing how God customizes His methods to individual needs. In his book *Experiencing God*, Henry Blackaby calls attention to how God works in diverse ways in different situations. For example, when God led Israel to the Red Sea, He parted the waters so they could cross on dry land. But when the Children of Israel reached the Jordan River, He required the priest to put his foot into the water before He stopped the downward flow. On one occasion, God told Moses to strike the rock to receive water, and on another occasion, He instructed Moses to speak to the rock.

An inquiring mind cannot help but wonder why God required different methods to accomplish His purpose. The answer lies in that God wants us to trust Him rather than His methods. We can easily fall into the rut of trusting methods, traditions, and ideas, but there is no substitute for simply trusting God.

God's Word: The Lord is my strength and my shield; my heart trusts in him, and he helps me. My heart leaps for joy, and with my song I praise him (Psalm 28:7).

Prayer: Father, thank You for the strength and protection that You give me every day. Accept my praise and thanksgiving for Your presence in my life, and help me to trust You without reservation. Amen.

JULY 22

COMFORT

We all seek comfort in times of trials, tribulations, sickness, death, war, or even threats. The word "comfort" comes from the Latin *comfortare*. If you break the word down, "com" means "with," and "fort" means strength. To comfort someone or to be comforted means strengthen greatly, support, cheer up, bring solace, or shore up the mood.

Comfort in times of difficulty does not come from drugs, alcohol, immorality, overeating, or going on a spending spree. The biblical solution for comfort is to turn to God, asking for strength and boldness to see the problem through. Early Christians never asked God to relieve their pain but rather to give them the strength to endure. They did not ask, "Why me?" They did not complain in adverse circumstances but instead sang hymns, praised God, and prayed to be faithful witnesses.

God's Word: Praise be to the God and Father of our Lord Jesus Christ, the Father of compassion and the God of all comfort, who comforts us in all our troubles, so that we can comfort those in any trouble with the comfort we ourselves receive from God (2 Corinthians 1:3–4).

Prayer: Father, I thank You for the comfort that you give me. Your love and presence lift me in my times of distress. As You comfort me, help me be ready and willing to comfort others in their time of need. Amen.

JULY 23

THE LIGHT IS ON

A well-known motel advertisement says, "We'll leave the light on." I'm reminded of a young girl who ran away from home and brought tremendous grief and anxiety to her widowed mother. After years of throwing herself away, she, like the prodigal son—broken and spent—made her way back to the homeplace. Arriving late at night, she was surprised to see the light on and the front door unlocked. Her aged mother awoke and embraced her wayward daughter, and the two talked through the night. When the daughter asked about the light being on and the door unlocked, the mother said, "The light has never been out since you left, nor has the door been locked."

In the night of our spiritual rebellion, in the despair of our sinful ways, God has the light on and the door open for our repentance and return. All we must do is come home.

God's Word: If we confess our sins, he is faithful and just and will forgive us our sins and purify us from all unrighteousness (1 John 1:9).

Prayer: Father, thank You for keeping the light on and the door open for me to recognize my sins, repent, and come home to You. Amen.

JULY 24

THE MAIN THEME

I love the story of the little fellow who returned to his mother after his first day in Sunday school. "Who was your teacher?" she asked. "I don't remember her name," he replied, "but she must have been Jesus's grandmother because she didn't talk about anyone else."

In many churches, the Sunday school hour has turned into a social hour, a party planning session, or conversation about things that people can talk about at any other time. If you belong to such a class, perhaps it would be appropriate to discuss using the hour to talk about Jesus with your class members.

Whether it is Sunday school or worship, our minds ought to be focused on Jesus. Knowing and serving Him should be the central theme and purpose for Sunday school. It's a sad commentary on the church when sacred time is spent on everyone and everything except Jesus.

God's Word: The Lord looks down from heaven on all mankind to see if there are any who understand, any who seek God (Psalm 14:2).

Prayer: Father, as the writer of Ecclesiastes so beautifully expressed it, "There is a time for everything." As Christians, discipline us to use our time in Sunday school and worship to focus Jesus. Amen.

JULY 25

MOVE THE FENCE

A man bought a home in a rather plush neighborhood only to discover that his neighbor's fence extended one foot into his property. He threatened to sue his neighbor. "That won't be necessary," the neighbor said. 'My boys and I will move the fence."

Some folk are eager to fight and inflict pain, while others are peacemakers. Which one are you? In the Sermon on the Mount, Jesus said, "Blessed are the meek, for they will inherit the earth. Blessed are the peacemakers for they will be called children of God" (Matthew 5:5, 9).

Peacemakers are those who have peace in their hearts. Those looking for a fight have a heart filled with anger and unresolved tension. True peace can only be found in the "Prince of Peace"—Jesus Christ. When the peace that Christ gives dominates your heart, you will seek peace and be at peace with others. It is a choice you make. Live in peace and enjoy life or live without it, be miserable, and make others miserable.

God's Word: The meek will inherit the land and enjoy peace and prosperity (Psalm 37:11).

Prayer: Father, help me be at peace with You so that I can be a peacemaker. Amen.

JULY 26

WHIRLWIND

Solomon, reportedly being the wisest man who has ever lived, said,

> I have seen all the things that are done under the sun; all of them
> are meaningless, a chasing after the wind. (Ecclesiastes 1:14)

It doesn't take more than a casual look at what goes on in our world to realize that many people are chasing after the wind. Such a pursuit turns into a whirlwind of meaninglessness.

Have you pursued one avenue of happiness after another to the extent that you have lost your direction? You find yourself as confused as if you were in a corn maze at Halloween. The truth is that life without God is a whirlwind—a meaningless whirl of activity that leaves you empty and devastated. The whirlwind will never end until you allow God to take control of your life. Don't ignore a truth that a wise man discovered the hard way. Open your life to God and stop chasing the wind.

God's Word: Be still, and know that I am God; I will be exalted among the nations, I will be exalted in the earth (Psalm 46:10).

Prayer: Father, in the whirlwind of life, give me calm, peace, and guidance and help me focus on eternity and the things that really matter. Amen.

JULY 27

REMEMBER YOUR CALL

We were appointed missionaries to Brazil on March 10, 1966, by the Foreign Mission Board of the Southern Baptist Convention. We will never forget that special night when Executive Director Dr. Baker James Cauthen delivered a challenging message to the missionary candidates. He acknowledged the call that we had received to carry the gospel to distant lands, the challenge and adventure we would face, the excitement of going, and the work God would do through us.

Dr. Cauthen also spoke of hardships that we would encounter. He said that there would be times of trials and tribulations, times of discouragement and depression, times when a missionary colleague would let us down or disappoint us, and times of homesickness. He mentioned physical diseases that we could encounter, political upheaval, and even threats to our lives. Then, he said, "In those times, remember your call."

With all the challenge and excitment we encountered in Brazil, we found Dr. Cauthen's words prophetic. More than once in situations we faced, the words "remember your call" anchored our souls, kept us from giving up, and steadied our course. The words of Christ, "I am with you always, to the very end of the age" (Matthew 28:20) gave us assurance that we were not alone and kept us focused on our mission.

In whatever work you find yourself in, you may face the same challenges and discouragements. As a Christian, you are also a missionary and ambassador of Jesus Christ. So, "remember your call."

God's Word: Therefore, since we are surrounded by such a great cloud of witnesses, let us throw off everything that hinders and the sin that so easily entangles. And let us run with perseverance the race marked out for us, fixing our eyes on Jesus, the pioneer and perfecter of faith (Hebrews 12:1–2).

Prayer: Father, in my trials and disappointments, help me to keep my eyes on Jesus and remember my call. Amen.

JULY 28

STUBBORNNESS

Has anyone ever called you stubborn? There is perhaps a stubborn streak in all of us. Sometimes we pride ourselves on being stubborn, and at other times we may be unaware of just how stubborn we are and how it affects those around us.

Examples of stubbornness are legion. Think of those who will not leave their property when told that they are in the path of a hurricane, flood, or tornado. Think of those who refuse to get a vaccine when a serious disease threatens the community. Think of those who hear the gospel but refuse to repent of their sins because they don't want to give up their lifestyle.

Stubborn people often rob themselves of life's greatest blessings. Stubbornness is not a trait to be proud of, nor does it often win awards. Rather, it is a sin from which we need release. God's power of forgiveness can turn stubbornness into submissiveness and bring joy and peace you can never know in any other way.

God's Word: Do not be like the horse or the mule, which have no understanding but must be controlled by bit and bridle or they will not come to you (Psalm 32:9).

Prayer: Father, forgive me for my stubborn, rebellious spirit. Help me to know the peace and joy of surrendering to the guidance of Your Holy Spirit. Amen.

JULY 29

PERSISTENCE

In 1998, Steve Fossett made his fourth attempt to circle the globe in a hot air balloon. On his sixth attempt in 2002, he succeeded. The duration and distance of this solo balloon flight were fourteen days, nineteen hours, fifty minutes to landing after 20,626.48 statute miles.

Fossett, an American businessman and a record-setting aviator, sailor, and adventurer, was the first person to fly solo nonstop around the world in a balloon and a fixed-wing aircraft. His amazing success can be summed up in one word—persistence.

Persistence wins. Every great achiever experienced many failures before success came. Persistence made the difference. Whatever you are working on that is worthy of your time, don't give up. Keep on keeping on. Hang in there; don't get discouraged, and be persistent. Perseverance is the path to overcoming our difficulties. By persevering, we grow and increase our self-esteem.

God's Word: Let your eyes look straight ahead; fix your gaze directly before you. Give careful thought to the paths for your feet and be steadfast in all your ways (Proverbs 4:25–26).

Prayer: Father, help me to be persistent and determined in living my life for You. Amen.

JULY 30

DOUBT YOUR DOUBTS

Doubt is not a sin, but it can lead to sin. There is nothing wrong with an enquiring, open mind, questioning, examining, and processing what is presented to you. But we must guard against the danger of allowing doubt to overtake us.

Doubt is Satan's bait. Satan was able to persuade Eve to partake of the forbidden fruit because he put doubt in her mind about what God had said. Thomas, the disciple, doubted the resurrection of Jesus until he saw Jesus with his own eyes. John Mark doubted his call to missions, turned around at the halfway point, and went home.

The antidote to doubt is faith. We must learn to doubt our doubts by disregarding feelings that can be deceptive and by embracing faith and trust in the Word of God. When you face doubt, stop and question why you are doubting. Look to Jesus and not to yourself. Listen to Him who has never told you a lie or failed to fulfill a promise. Cast your burden on the Lord, and He will sustain you. Doubt your doubts!

God's Word: Each person is tempted when they are dragged away by their own evil desire and enticed. Then, after desire has conceived, it gives birth to sin; and sin when it is full-grown, gives birth to death (James 1:13–15).

Prayer: Father, teach me to doubt my doubts and to trust Your Word rather than my feelings. For every doubt that enters my mind, reinforce my faith and trust in You and Your faithfulness. Amen.

JULY 31

PRAYER

Do you have trouble praying? Jesus tells us how to pray in the Sermon on the Mount. Listen to Him!

"Ask and it will be given to you; seek and you shall find; knock and the door will be opened to you. For everyone who asks receives; the one who seeks finds; and to the one who knocks, the door will be opened ... If you, then, though you are evil, know how to give good gifts to your children, how much more will your Father in Heaven give good gifts to those who ask him!" (Matthew 7:7–8, 11).

Don't make prayer difficult. Prayer is talking to God as you would a friend. And when you lack words, the Holy Spirit interprets for you. Don't bow to the old argument that God knows everything, and it is useless to tell him what He already knows. While that is true, it is also true that God wants to know that you know your need. He wants to hear it from your lips. So, ask, seek, knock, and then look for God's response.

God's Word: But, when you pray, go into your room, close the door and pray to your Father, who is unseen. Then your Father, who sees what is done in secret, will reward you (Matthew 6:6).

Prayer: Father, thank You for wanting to hear me express my thoughts to You. Thank You for listening and for responding to my needs according to Your will. Amen.

AUGUST 1

THINGS VS. RELATIONSHIPS

Are you a "people person" or a "things person"? Dr. Raymond Flannery Jr. of the Harvard Medical School says, "We've stopped focusing on the truly important things in life–good relationships with the people we love … and stress ourselves trying to acquire and make use of everything that's in sight."[9]

Most people have more gadgets and machines to attract their attention than time permits to use them. Just observe a group of young people gathered in a room with full focus on their smartphones, iPad, or game gadgets rather than engaging in conversation with each other.

Our electronic devices and things have taken priority over our quest to expand and build human relationships. There is a great void in our lives when we had rather interact with a gadget than with a family member or friend. No gadget can share the pain or loneliness you feel in your heart. No gadget can comfort you or counsel you in times of grief, sickness, or tragedy. No gadget can laugh or cry with you or respond to your need like another human being. Enhance the quality of your life by focusing on people and relationships rather than things.

God's Word: Be devoted to one another in love. Honor one another above yourselves (Romans 12:10).

Prayer: Father, help me to value human relationships over gadgets and things. Help me to make friends by being a friend. Amen.

---

[9] Dr. Raymond B. Flannery Jr., "Stress—The Secrets of Stress-Resistant People," Bottom Line\Personal, vol. 12, no. 13, July 15, 1991, 1.

AUGUST 2

HATRED

Hatred is cancer of the soul, just like cancer is a disease of the body. Like cancer, hatred will eat you alive, destroy and kill you. Hatred is a sin not just against someone else but against God. 1 John 2:11, 15, says: "Anyone who hates a brother or sister is in the darkness. They do not know where they are going because the darkness has blinded them ... Anyone who hates a brother or sister is a murderer, and you know that no murderer has eternal life residing in him."

The opposite of hate is love. In 1 John 4:8, we read: "Whoever does not love does not know God." If you call yourself a Christian and hold hatred in your heart, it is imperative that you *acknowledge* your sin, repent, and ask God to forgive you. If you can't do that, then you must recognize the stark truth of God's Word. Without love in your heart, you really don't know God. Without love in your heart, you cannot be a Christian. Just saying that you are a Christian does not make you one. Jesus said of Christians, "Thus, by their fruit you will recognize them" (Matthew 7:20).

God's Word: Likewise, every good tree bears good fruit, but a bad tree bears bad fruit ... Every tree that does not bear good fruit is cut down and thrown into the fire (Matthew 7:17,19).

Prayer: Father, guard me against the sin of hating. Let Your love dominate my heart, my thoughts, and my actions so that others can see Jesus in me. Amen.

AUGUST 3

SALVATION

A manager of a ten-story office building was informed that a man was trapped in an elevator between the second and third floors. He rushed to the grillwork under the stalled elevator and called to the passenger, "Keep cool sir; we'll have you out soon. I've phoned for the elevator mechanic." There was a brief pause, and a tense voice replied, "I am the elevator mechanic."

There are situations in which we cannot deliver ourselves. If a cruise ship stops in the middle of the ocean, passengers cannot simply get out and push. If a man is drowning, he cannot save himself by grabbing his hair and lifting it up. Salvation in such circumstances must come from an outside source.

The fact is that we cannot save our souls, forgive our sins, put peace in our hearts, or give ourselves eternal security. Our help must come from an outside source. That source, of course, is Jesus, who died on the cross to save us from our sins. Without Jesus to save us, we are as helpless as the mechanic caught in his elevator or passengers aboard a stranded cruise ship.

God's Word: "Sirs, what must I do to be saved?" They replied, "Believe in the Lord Jesus, and you will be saved—you and your household" (Acts 16:30–31).

Prayer: Father, thank you for sending your Son, Jesus Christ, to die on the cross to save me from my sins. I confess that I am a sinner. I repent of my sins, and I ask Jesus to come into my life. Amen.

AUGUST 4

FRIENDS

Do you have more acquaintances than close friends? Most people do. Friends vary. Fair-weather friends hang around as long as you can do something for them or because it is to their advantage. True friends stick with you through thick and thin but are hard to find. While having lunch with a man, Henry Ford surprisingly asked him, "Who is your best friend?" With no immediate response, Henry gave him the answer in one short sentence. "Your best friend is he who brings out the best that is within you."

We sometimes sing "My Best Friend Is Jesus," and another song says, "No one ever cared for me like Jesus." Both songs are true. In the Bible, Jesus calls us friends and gives us the definition of a true friend: "Greater love has no one than this: to lay down one's life for one's friends" (John 15:13). Jesus proved true friendship by laying down his life to save us from our sins. And no one can bring out the best in you like Jesus.

God's Word: One who has unreliable friends soon comes to ruin, but there is a friend who sticks closer than a brother (Proverbs 18:24).

Prayer: Father, thank You for true friends. I am blessed to have them in my life. Thank You also for Jesus, who is my friend, Savior, and Lord. Amen.

AUGUST 5

WORSHIP

In the "Arabian Nights," Sinbad the sailor warned his shipmates about a great magnetic rock in the Indian Ocean that would draw all the nails and bolts out of passing ships. The ships would then collapse and sink. The distracting influences of this world are like Sinbad's magnetic rock that loosens the nails and bolts holding families and individual lives together.

Worship allows us to tighten up the spiritual nails and bolts of our lives against destructive forces. Worship keeps us intact in a world that wants to pull us apart. Worship has the power to restore, heal, strengthen, and guide our decisions and to repel the forces of evil. Worship puts you in the right relationship with God and our fellowman.

Worship with your family in the quiet of your home. Worship with God's family in the church of your choice. Worship alone walking on the beach or a mountain or forest trail. The place of worship is not as important as the experience of worship, but whatever you do—worship.

God's Word: Worship the Lord in the splendor of his holiness (Psalm 29:2).

Prayer: Father, let my worship of You be a priority in my life. Help me to understand that no amount of goodwill, good Intentions, or service rendered can substitute for my adoration, praise, and thanksgiving for who You are. Amen.

AUGUST 6

CRITICISM

Do you feel the need to criticize someone? Criticism can be helpful and even redemptive if offered with the proper motive and a spirit of helpfulness. On the other hand, criticism can be offensive and counterproductive if not presented in the proper way.

A careful reading of Revelation 2:2–4 gives insight into a constructive way to offer criticism. The model for criticism here is three compliments to one criticism. There is added value if the compliments are in the same area as the criticism. Compliments give reassurance that the person receiving the criticism has value, is not a failure, and is encouraged to continue growing and improving. Encouragement outweighs criticism when the motive behind it is to be helpful and not destructive.

God's Word: Speaking the truth in love, we will grow to become in every respect the mature body of him who is the head, that is, Christ. From him the whole body, joined and held together by every supporting ligament, grows and builds itself up in love, as each part does its work (Ephesians 4:15–16).

Prayer: Father, help my criticism of others to be made in love with a desire to help, not hinder, to be constructive, not destructive, to restore, not destroy, to build up, not tear down. Amen.

AUGUST 7

TRUE GREATNESS

Columnist Jack Anderson reminds us that when Thomas Jefferson was elected president of the United States, he checked into a Washington rooming house like any ordinary citizen, walked to his inauguration, and was sworn in. Friends swarmed about him to congratulate him, and then he left to walk alone to his rooming house. When he got there, dinner was already being served. There wasn't a plate left at the table. History records that no one offered him a plate. The president returned to his room that night without dinner or complaint. Jefferson considered himself a servant of the people, not a master.

Great men and women are humble. They are not greedy, selfish, or arrogant. They do not complain when inconvenienced, nor do they make demands for themselves. They always look out for the best interest of others.

God's Word: Whoever wants to become great among you must be your servant, and whoever wants to be first must be your slave—just as the Son of Man did not come to be served, but to serve, and to give his life as a ransom for many (Matthew 20:26–28).

Prayer: Father, as Jesus set the example for true servanthood and as Thomas Jefferson modeled it in his life, help me to aspire to be a servant whose life is pleasing and useful to You. Amen.

AUGUST 8

LESSONS FROM HOMING PIGEONS

Growing up, I was always fascinated by the homing pigeons that our neighbor, Mr. Pittman, raised. Mr. Pittman was a traveling salesman and was often away from home for days and weeks at a time. With his homing pigeons, he could send messages and even money back home to his family.

The instinct of a homing pigeon, also called a carrier pigeon, is so strong that these birds can fly more than a thousand miles over unfamiliar territory and never fail to find their way home.

If a bird can find its way home from such a great distance and if, like Isaiah, the prophet says, "The ox knows his master, and the donkey his owner's manger" (Isaiah 1:3), why is it that human beings have so much trouble discovering that peace and fulfillment in life only come from a personal relationship with Jesus Christ?

We who pride ourselves on intelligence and who live in the most advanced information age the world has ever known would do well to take a few lessons from birds, oxen, and donkeys.

God's Word: But ask the animals, and they will teach you, or the birds in the sky, and they will tell you; or speak to the earth, and it will teach you, or let the fish in the sea inform you. Which of all these does not know that the hand of the Lord has done this? In his hand is the life of every creature and the breath of all mankind (Job 12:7–10).

Prayer: Father, the birds of the air, the beast of the fields, and all of nature have so much to teach us. Help me to learn from the creatures of Your creation how to be faithful and useful to You. Amen.

AUGUST 9

CONSUMED BY SUCCESS

Consumed by Success is the title of Athena Dean's book that deals with climbing the ladder of success. The subtitle of the book is especially insightful. It reads: *Reaching the Top and Finding God Wasn't There.*

The book has to do with those who are so success-driven that they neglect God, their spouses, and their children. For the love of money, they gain the world and lose their family and soul.

If your primary goal in life is money and success, you have completely missed the point of what life is all about. It's a terrible thing to come to the end of life and know that you have thrown it away on something that can't last and something you can't take with you.

God's Word: What good is it for someone to gain the whole world, yet forfeit their soul? Or what can anyone give in exchange for their soul (Mark 8:36–37)?

Prayer: Father, help me to be focused on You so that any success that comes to me brings You Glory and Honor. Amen.

AUGUST 10

REGRETS

Regrets! We all have them. We regret that we did not do what we should have done. For months, I told myself that I needed to go and visit a cousin of mine who was sick. For one reason or another, I kept putting the visit off until a more convenient time. Then word came that my cousin had died. I was not only shocked; I was also ashamed. Now, I live with the thought that because of my procrastination, I missed a golden opportunity that will never return.

Is there someone you need to visit? Is there a call you need to make? Is there a letter you need to write? Is there something you have been telling yourself you need to do, but you have put it off? Is there something you need to say to someone before it is too late? Stop putting it off! Stop making excuses! You don't have to live with regrets. Do what you need to do now!

God's Word: If anyone, then, knows the good they ought to do and doesn't do it, it is sin for them (James 4:17).

Prayer: Father, I know in my heart that procrastination leads to deep regrets. I know that putting off until tomorrow what I need to do today adds to my anxiety and stress. Help me to stop making excuses and do what I need to do today. Amen.

AUGUST 11

BEING SPIRITUAL IN A MATERIAL WORLD

God's call to each of us is to be spiritual in a material world. We are admonished to be in the world but not of the world. As someone wisely said, "It is all right for the boat to be in the ocean; it is not all right for the ocean to be in the boat."

We are called upon to be witnesses of our faith in Jesus Christ. We are called to be ambassadors of the King of Kings. Being spiritual in a material world is a matter of focusing on things that are eternal rather than temporary.

Concentrating on spiritual things results in acknowledging that God is the owner of everything, and we are his servants and stewards. Then, we allow God to work through us, so that money and possessions are under His control and do not control us. The spiritual-minded person is generous in meeting the needs of others, faithful in serving God, and content with what they have rather than focusing on what they don't have. The spiritual-minded live for Christ and not for self.

God's Word: Fight the good fight of the faith. Take hold of the eternal life to which you were called when you made your good confession in the presence of many witnesses (1 Timothy 6:12).

Prayer: Father, the lure of the world pulls strong. Help me to keep my eyes on Jesus and hide Your Word in my heart that I might not sin against You. Amen.

AUGUST 12

BEAUTY

Read the psalms, and you will immediately discover the psalmist's love for the beauty and majesty of nature. The psalms speak of the sea, the mountains, the valleys, the hills, green pastures, trees, still waters, the heavens, stars, the moon, and much more.

Get in touch with the beauty around you today. Stop and take it in. Marvel at the beautiful world God has given you to enjoy. Smell the roses, watch the birds, squirrels, the rabbits and deer, the bees and ants. Let nature calm your soul.

The more you get in touch with nature, the more peaceful you will become. The more you understand nature, the more you will stand in awe of the God who created it.

God's Word: The earth is the Lord's and everything in it, the world, and all who live in it (Psalm 24:1).

Prayer: Father, help me each day to pause and observe this beautiful world that You have made. In the majesty of nature, let me worship You and experience Your peace. Amen.

AUGUST 13

GOD'S PROMISES

Everette R. Storms, a Canadian school teacher, is credited with reading the Bible twenty-seven times in eighteen months with the sole purpose of counting all the promises of God to man. He concluded that 7,487 promises fit the category.[10] Whether that number is accurate or not is debatable. The number of promises is not important. What is important is God's faithfulness in fulfilling His promises.

It is a good spiritual exercise to meditate upon the promises of God. For example, the promises of his presence, comfort, strength, power, forgiveness, grace, mercy, eternal life, etc. What we know and experience is that human promises are made and broken at an alarming rate. On the other hand, God is faithful to His Word.

God's Word: God is not human, that he should lie, not a human being, that he should change his mind. Does he speak and then not act? Does he promise and not fulfill (Numbers 23:19)?

Prayer: Father, Your Word is truth. Thank You that I can always count on Your Word and Your promises. Help me to be faithful in receiving Your Word and applying it to my life. Amen.

---

[10] Herbert Lockyer, *All the Promises of the Bible*, Zondervan, Grand Rapids, MI, 1973, 10.

AUGUST 14

BLAME

Gary Chapman, popular marriage counselor and best-selling author of *The 5 Love Languages*, has solid counsel for marriage partners who are constantly blaming their spouse for all the problems in a marriage relationship. Chapman explains that it is wasted energy trying to change your spouse. It is far better to work on our problems. Each one of us has peculiarities, quirks, and habits. With God's help, we can change our ways and, in the process, improve our marriage relationship.

There are no perfect marriages. Adjustments must be made; differences and difficulties must be recognized and overcome if a marriage is to succeed. Playing the blame game is detrimental to a healthy marriage. Allowing God to be the head of the household combined with a love for each other, a good dose of patience and understanding, and a willingness to compromise can go a long way in building a healthy relationship.

God's Word: You hypocrite, first take the plank out of your own eye, and then you will see clearly to remove the speck from your brother's eye (Matthew 7:5).

Prayer: Father, before I criticize and judge my spouse, give me the wisdom to recognize and correct my faults. In my marriage, give me patience, understanding, and love, along with a strong commitment to making my marriage work, with Your help. Amen.

AUGUST 15

LOST BLESSINGS

We are accustomed to hearing the names of the early biblical patriarchs in this order: Abraham, Isaac, Jacob, and Joseph. The correct order should have been Abraham, Isaac, Esau, and Joseph. The reason that Jacob's name appears instead of Esau's is that Esau failed to control his appetite and forfeited the family blessing by selling his birthright to Jacob for a bowl of soup.

Many people lose the blessings that God has intended for them because they cannot control their appetites, greed, or jealousy. Spur of the moment decisions are foolishly made because human desire exceeds wisdom. Thoughtlessly yielding to human appetite overcomes self-control, which results in catastrophe and loss of blessing.

Make certain that your desires are within the will of God. We have the choice to live within God's will or lose His blessings.

God's Word: If my people, who are called by my name, will humble themselves and pray and seek my face and turn from their wicked ways, then I will hear from heaven, and I will forgive their sin and will heal their land (2 Chronicles 7:14).

Prayer: Father, knowing the loss of blessings that awaits me when I disregard Your will and yield to my sinful desires and appetites, help me to think before I act. Amen.

AUGUST 16

I KNOW THEM!

About believers, Jesus said, "I know them" (John 10:27). Stop and ponder what He said. There is no blessing greater than being known by Jesus. Do you have the assurance that Jesus knows you?

You may say you are a Christian. You may even be a member of the church. Perhaps you have a leadership role in the church as a deacon, Sunday school teacher, or serve on a committee, but none of those positions or responsibilities guarantees that Jesus knows you. You may impress your church or society with your charitable giving or your deeds of kindness. You may go out of your way to be kind to widows or strangers, but those characteristics do not guarantee that Jesus knows you. You may be known by community leaders and people in high places, but those acquaintances do not guarantee that Jesus knows you.

To be known by Jesus, you must acknowledge that He is the Son of God and that He died on the cross to save you from your sins. You must acknowledge your sins, repent, and ask God to forgive you and to come into your heart and life. You must commit to serving Him, obeying Him, and honoring His name in all that you do.

God's Word: Not everyone who says to me, "Lord, Lord," will enter the kingdom of heaven, but only the one who does the will of my Father who is in heaven (Matthew 7:21)

Prayer: Father, help me to understand that You know me not by my good character or good deeds or even by my standing in the community but by my commitment to do Your will. Amen.

AUGUST 17

REPEATED MISTAKES

Two men were watching a western on television. As the hero rode on horseback toward the edge of a cliff, one man said, "I bet you $50 he goes over the cliff. "You're on," said the other man. The hero rode on, straight over the cliff. Being a sportsman, the other man handed over the money. The first man looked at it and said, "You know, I feel a bit guilty about taking this money. I've seen this film before." "So have I," said the second man, "but I didn't think he'd be stupid enough to make the same mistake again."[11]

How often do you keep making the same mistake? Life is not fixed like a movie. Sins do not have to be repeated. Jesus told the woman who had been caught in the act of adultery, "Go now and leave your life of sin" (John 8:11). In other words, change your life. Don't repeat your sins.

God's Word: If we deliberately keep on sinning after we have received the knowledge of the truth, no sacrifice for sins is left, but only a fearful expectation of judgment and of raging fire that will consume the enemies of God (Hebrews 10:26–27).

Prayer: Father, Your grace and forgiveness offered to me through Your Son, Jesus Christ, has come to me at a great price. Help me to avoid the foolishness and danger of repeated sins. Amen.

---

[11] *Illustration Digest*, Sept.-Oct. 1991, 14.

AUGUST 18

BEING USEFUL

Harvey Knowles, a good friend of mine, wakes up every morning with a plan to do something good for someone during the day. He brings cheer to those who are having birthdays by calling or personally visiting them so that he can play "Happy Birthday" on his harmonica. He tries to bring a word of encouragement or praise to everyone he meets. He's not good with tools or machinery, but he is great at connecting those who have a need with someone who can take care of their problem. His positive attitude lifts people's spirits. Mention any subject, and Harvey has a good story to match the situation.

There is an abundance of good to be done while we live on this earth. Needs are everywhere. We have the choice to be detached or involved, to be useful or useless. Perhaps the greatest test of your character is your willingness to make a difference in someone's life. A quote in a church bulletin caught my attention: "Find a need and meet it! See a wound and heal it!" In other words, don't just stand there—do something! Be useful.

God's Word: Therefore, as we have opportunity, let us do good to all people, especially to those who belong to the family of believers (Galatians 6:10).

Prayer: Father, help me to serve others in love. Amen.

AUGUST 19

THE HOUSE YOU BUILD

An elderly carpenter decided to retire and spend more time with his family. His boss hated to see him go but asked him as a favor to build one more house. The carpenter agreed. However, it soon became apparent that his heart was not in his work. He took shortcuts, used inferior materials, and covered up his poor workmanship with wallpaper and sheetrock.

When the house was completed, the contractor handed the keys to the carpenter and said, "this is your house—it is my gift to you for your years of service. The shocked carpenter was now terribly embarrassed, ashamed, and disappointed. He built an inferior house that he now owned but didn't want.

Take care of how you build your life. You own it; will have to live in it and give an account for it.

God's Word: And whatever you do, whether in word or deed, do it all in the name of the Lord Jesus, giving thanks to God the Father through him (Colossians 3:17).

Prayer: Father, help me to do the absolute best that I can in building my life, knowing that in the end, I own it. I am accountable for my life, and I will have to live with what I have done. Amen.

AUGUST 20

LEAVING IT ALL

When we were missionaries in Brazil, one of the richest men in the country was our neighbor. Tragically, he died in a plane crash. Someone asked, "What did he leave his family?" The response was, "everything."

No matter how prosperous you are, you won't take it with you when you die. For this reason, you need to be laying up treasures in heaven and not on earth. The treasures you store in heaven will be with you for eternity. The treasures you amass on earth will remain here. Which treasures are the most important to you?

God's Word: Do not store up for yourselves treasures on earth, where moths and vermin destroy, and where thieves break in and steal. But store up for yourselves treasures in heaven, where moths and vermin do not destroy, and where thieves do not break in and steal (Matthew 6:19–20).

Prayer: Father, give me wisdom and discernment to live and work for that which will not perish and which will not be taken away from me. Amen.

AUGUST 21

CHILDREN

Do you love and appreciate your children? Sadly, some parents do not. The most disturbing words I ever heard from a mother's lips were, "I wish my daughter had never been born. Psalm 127:3 says, "Children are a heritage from the Lord, offspring a reward from him."

Children are not burdens to bear. They are not excuses to keep parents from serving the Lord. They are not liabilities or write-offs for income tax. They are not punching bags for frustrated adults or just mouths to feed. Children are gifts from God to be loved, appreciated, protected, and guided.

Parenting is a serious responsibility accountable to God. Children are to be brought up in the nurture and admonition of the Lord. They learn more from the life you live and the example you set before them than from anything you will ever say.

God's Word: Like arrows in the hands of a warrior are children born in one's youth. Blessed is the man whose quiver is full of them. They will not be put to shame when they contend with their opponents in court (Psalm 127:4–5).

Prayer: Father, thank You for the precious children that You have given me. I am so blessed to have them. Help me to be a role model guiding their lives to love and serve You all the days of their lives. Amen.

AUGUST 22

PROBLEMS

Have you ever thought about thanking God for your problems? Have you ever been told that having problems is a good thing? Problems are challenges, not obstacles. Problems are good for you, not bad. Problems can bring out the best in you, challenge your creativity, enhance your solving skills. Problems can mold your character, give you patience, help you recognize your limitations, and even increase your faith and dependency upon God.

The next time you face a difficulty, an obstacle, an interruption, a frustration, thank God and look for the lesson He is trying to teach you. There is strength in struggle. Accepting your problem as an opportunity to grow and mature will do far more for you than throwing up your hands in defeat or cursing your situation. By relying upon God rather than himself, apostle Paul knew that he could face anything with Christ's strength. If Paul could do that, so can you.

God's Word: My God will meet all your needs according to the riches of his glory in Christ Jesus (Philippians 4:19).

Prayer: Father, thank You for being with me in the good times and the bad, when things are easy and when they are difficult. Thank You that I do not have to face my problems alone because You are my help and strength. Amen.

AUGUST 23

THANKSGIVING
AND CHRISTMAS

You've heard of "Christmas in August," but have you ever thought about "Thanksgiving in August"? Yes, I know that Christmas comes in December and is preceded by Thanksgiving in November. But are we not challenged to live the Christmas spirit and have Thanksgiving in our hearts throughout the year?

From my earliest childhood, I was taught a little chorus that often comes to mind.

> "Thank you, Lord, for saving my soul.
> Thank you, Lord, for making me whole.
> Thank you, Lord, for giving to me
> Thy great salvation so rich and free."

God's greatest gift to us is His Son, Jesus. He came into this world to save us from our sins. He lived, taught, healed, died, and rose again so that we could have life eternal with Him. God's greatest, unspeakable, amazing gift is worthy of our daily thanksgiving.

God's Word: I will give thanks to you, Lord, with all my heart; I will tell of all your wonderful deeds. I will be glad and rejoice in you; I will sing the praises of your name, O Most High (Psalm 9:1–2).

Prayer: Father, I thank You for sending Your Son, Jesus Christ, to save me from my sins and to give me eternal life. Amen.

AUGUST 24

STRICTNESS

Psychologist and popular TV personality Dr. Joyce Brothers reminds us that strictness, considered by some as an old-fashioned method of parenting, may be coming back into style. A study of almost two thousand fifth- and sixth-graders, some of whom have been reared by strict parents, others by permissive ones, produced some surprising results.

The children who had been strictly disciplined possessed high self-esteem and were high achievers, socially and academically. What these children said revealed that they were happier than the undisciplined children. They loved the adults who made and enforced the rules they lived by.[12]

Modern research has only verified biblical truth. The genuinely happy child, the productive child, is the one who knows discipline.

God's Word: No discipline seems pleasant at the time, but painful. Later on, however, it produces a harvest of righteousness and peace for those who have been trained by it (Hebrews 12:11).

Prayer: Father, I thank You for parents who love their children enough to discipline them so that they will grow up to be responsible, respected, and productive. Amen.

---

[12] Dr. Joyce Brothers, "The Power of Love," *Good Housekeeping*, Sept. 1985, 103.

AUGUST 25

KEEPING RECORDS

As I sat in the waiting room of my doctor's office, my eyes caught the multicolored tabs on rows of files that were on the shelves behind the receptionist. Each folder represented a patient and vital medical history that had been recorded for future reference. Record keeping is a time-consuming task, yet it is extremely important to the doctor as well as the patient.

Record keeping is essential in almost every area of life. The human mind is marvelous, but no one can remember all the details that are important to our well-being. Record keeping is essential to be responsible and accountable.

Scripture tells us that God also keeps records. The hairs of our head are numbered. God knows where we are always, what we are thinking, and what we are doing. He knows those who love Him and those who don't. There is nothing hidden from Him. The Bible speaks of the book of life and the names of those written in it who have been forgiven for their sins. Is your name in God's book of life?

God's Word: The one who is victorious will, like them, be dressed in white. I will never blot out the name of that person from the book of life, but will acknowledge that name before my Father and his angels (Revelation 3:5).

Prayer: Father, thank You for the security and peace that I have knowing Jesus as my Savior. I am at peace knowing that my name is recorded in the book of life. Amen.

AUGUST 26

KEEP THE MESSAGE CLEAR

It's a fact that the message of the church is not always clear. A congregation advertised the topic of the pastor's Sunday sermons on their highly visible outdoor church sign. The 11:00 a.m. message was entitled, "Jesus, Walking on Water." The 7:00 p.m. Topic was "Searching for Jesus."

From the gospel narrative, it is evident that Jesus successfully walked on water. It was the disciple, Simon Peter, who sank for failure to keep his eyes on Jesus. The truth is that people with sinful frailties like those of Simon Peter are searching for Jesus even though they may not always understand that they truly need Him. The clear message of God's Word is that Jesus, who could walk on water, has the power to save those who are searching for the answers to life's meaning.

God's Word: Write down the revelation and make it plain on tablets so that a herald may run with it (Habakkuk 2:2).

Prayer: Father, help me in word and deed to make the message of Jesus Christ clear and understandable. Amen.

AUGUST 27

DO IT YOURSELF

I have many "do it yourself" books. I have one for building shelves and storage space, another that covers every subject from emergency repairs to furniture making. Friends have loaned me books on such subjects as car repair, fishing, and camping.

As much as I like these "do it yourself" books, and as often as I refer to them, I have a problem. Things don't work out for me as easily as the author indicates. I know that the author is not at fault. It's me! I have discovered that in the long run, it is cheaper to hire an expert and get the job right the first time.

Some people have the same difficulty with the Bible. But there is a notable difference between a "do It yourself" book and the Bible. The authors of my "do It yourself" books don't come to my aid when I get in trouble. But God is always present and waiting for my call. I not only have God's book, but I also have Him, and He has me.

God's Word: Hear my prayer, Lord; let my cry for help come to you. Do not hide your face from me when I am in distress. Turn your ear to me; when I call, answer me quickly (Psalm 102:1–2).

Prayer: Father, so many times I mess up when I try to do it myself. Help me to know that You are always with me and that You have given me the Holy Spirit to help me in every situation. Amen.

AUGUST 28

STRENGTHS AND WEAKNESSES

A student filled out his college admission application and listed his strengths in the following manner: "Sometimes I am trustworthy, loyal, helpful, friendly, courteous, kind, obedient, cheerful, thrifty, brave, clean, and reverent." Where the form said, "List your weaknesses," he wrote, Sometimes I am trustworthy, loyal, helpful, friendly, courteous, kind, obedient, cheerful, thrifty, brave, clean, and reverent."

Isn't it true that in our strengths, we also find our weaknesses? No one is perfect, but if we turn our lives over to Jesus Christ, most of us can be better than we could be without Him. God is not looking for perfect people, just those who will accept His forgiveness and be faithful to Him.

God's Word: He has shown you, O mortal, what is good. And what does the Lord require of you? To act justly and to love mercy and to walk humbly with your God (Micah 6:8).

Prayer: Father, You know my strengths and weaknesses, and You still love me. Thank You for accepting me just as I am and for molding me into the person You want me to be. Amen.

AUGUST 29

IDENTIFICATION

The noted nineteenth-century political cartoonist Thomas Nast once attended a party with a group of friends. Someone asked him to draw a caricature of everyone present. With a few skilled strokes of his pencil, the task was done. The sketches were passed around for the guests to identify. Everyone recognized the other persons in the room, but hardly anyone recognized their own caricature.

It is not unusual for us to fail to recognize some of our characteristics and habits. What we so often criticize in others is indeed but a reflection of the flaws in our own lives. If we were more adept at self-identification, we might be more prone to make some needed changes. Think about that the next time you judge another person.

God's Word: For in the same way you judge others, you will be judged (Matthew 7:1).

Prayer: Father, when I am tempted to judge others, help me to look within myself to see the same faults. Forgive me for recognizing the faults of my neighbor and being blind to the very same faults in my own life. Amen.

AUGUST 30

UPDATING

Iberia Airlines flight 610 was a scheduled domestic passenger flight from Madrid to Bilbao, Spain. On February 19,1985, the Boeing 727-200 flight crashed into a television antenna on the summit of Mount Oz Bisque near Bilbao. All 141 passengers and seven crew members on board died. The crash was the deadliest aviation disaster in Basque County and Iberian history. An investigation into the cause of the crash revealed that the pilot disregarded the autopilot system warning and failed to update a map showing the location of the television tower.

Hardship, burdens, pain, tragedy, and grief come our way because we ignore warning signals and fail to make necessary upgrades in our lives. Negligence is costly, and death often gives no warning.

If you are not up-to-date in your relationship with God, you are in as much danger as the pilot who ignored his instruments and failed to upgrade his map. Your death could be an eternal disaster, not to mention the unresolved grief it will bring to your loved ones, who cannot be assured that your soul is in heaven. Today is the time to get up-to-date with God!

God's Word: "I tell you, now is the time of God's favor, now is the day of salvation (2 Corinthians 6:2).

Prayer: Father, failing to upgrade my relationship with You can be spiritually deadly. Help me to pay attention to Your Word, heed it, confess my sins and submit to Your plan for my life. Amen

AUGUST 31

GOING TO THE SOURCE

In his book *Satisfying People*, Calvin Ratz tells of a study by the White House Office of Consumer Affairs, which revealed the frustration and dissatisfaction of the retail business management. They complained that rather than reporting to them, customers are more likely to tell their friends when they are unhappy with a product or service. On average, unhappy customers are likely to tell at least ten friends about their dissatisfaction.

What happens in the business world also happens in the church. The average church member will talk to some church members about a problem or dissatisfaction rather than going to those who may be able to correct the problem or at least address it. As a result, the malady spreads through the congregation, damaging relationships and the witness of the church.

If you have a complaint or dissatisfaction, sharing the discontent with those in authority is more likely to get positive results. In like manner, taking your concern directly to the Lord can be more effective than complaining to friends.

God's Word: Cast your cares on the Lord and he will sustain you; he will never let the righteous be shaken (Psalm 55:22).

Prayer: Father, I am comforted knowing that I can come directly to You with my concern knowing that You can help me when others can't. Help me also to be beneficial to those in authority by telling them my concerns rather than spreading my discontent to those who can do nothing about it. Amen.

SEPTEMBER 1

AN EMERGENCY GOD

Most people never think about the spare tire tucked away in the trunk of their car until they have a flat tire. Interesting that people treat God the same way. They never think about Him or consult Him until an emergency arises.

When things are going well—we have a good job, good health, and money in the bank—there is a tendency to forget God. But let a death, trauma, loss of a job, or a terminal disease invade our lives—then we remember to call out to Him for help.

God doesn't mind us calling on Him when we are in trouble, but put ourselves in His place. If we only had friends call on us when they needed help, what kind of relationship do you think we would have with them?

How fortunate we are that God is a God of love, mercy, and grace. A God like that deserves more from us than an emergency call. Having an up-to-date relationship with God will avoid the embarrassment and shame of calling upon Him only when we have a problem.

God's Word: I sought the Lord, and he answered me; he delivered me from all my fears (Psalm 34:4).

Prayer: Father, I want my relationship with You to be up-to-date. Help me to be so close to You that I don't have to be embarrassed to call on You in an emergency. Amen.

SEPTEMBER 2

BUILDING

If you have ever gone through the process of building a home, you know about the months, days, and hours that you put into the planning. Then, in the construction phase, there are daily visits to the building site, constant consultation with the contractor, and last-minute alterations. Building a house is a major investment of time and money. You want to be pleased with the results.

Building a life is of far greater importance and requires no less investment in all the details. Being careful in the building of your life means establishing a strong personal relationship with God: feeding your soul on His Word, feeding your mind on those things that build character, integrity, morals, ethics, honesty, trustworthiness, kindness, love, patience, and generosity.

God has made a significant investment in you. He created you in His image. He sent His Son to die for your sins. He offers you His love, grace and forgiveness, and eternal life. His concern for you cannot be measured. Earthly dwellings come and go, but you have been created for eternity. Should you not give greater detail to your eternal life than to this temporary one on earth?

God's Word: For we are co-workers in God's service; you are God's field, God's building (1 Corinthians 3:9).

Prayer: Father, thank You for the investment You have made in my life. Help me to take care of how I build my life by giving attention to eternal things. Amen.

SEPTEMBER 3

THE ROAD TO DESTRUCTION

The road to destruction is laid out for us in the third chapter of Genesis. Satan's method for destroying us begins with doubting God's Word. Once we doubt the Word of God, it is easy to disobey. When we disobey God, we dethrone Him and enthrone ourselves. In other words, instead of allowing God to control our lives, we decide to control our destiny. In so doing, we disgrace ourselves because we are incapable of saving our souls. At that point, we are helpless and lost.

God calls us to give an account for our sins and the careless decisions we make. He is grieved by the separation that sin has caused between us. The road to destruction is the road that Satan wants us to travel, but God offers us a road to eternal life with Him.

The road we follow is our choice. We choose death or life. Which road have you chosen?

God's Word: The Lord is not slow in keeping his promise, as some understand slowness. Instead he is patient with you, not wanting anyone to perish, but everyone to come to repentance (2 Peter 3:9).

Prayer: Father, You are a gracious, merciful, and patient God. Even so, help me not to be slow in confessing my sins and surrendering my life completely to You. Amen.

SEPTEMBER 4

BAILIFF FARMER

In researching my family history, I discovered that my great-grandfather, Laurence Allard, was by profession a "bailiff farmer" in Kent County, England. In the 1800s, large landowners employed managers or supervisors to oversee the business of their farms. They were called "bailiff farmers." It was their responsibility to manage all aspects of the farm business, oversee farm laborers, and buy and sell produce and equipment.

To qualify for the position of bailiff farmer, a person had to be competent with figures and keeping accounts. He must have a range of knowledge and experience in farming and a willingness to learn more and keep up-to-date with new ideas. He must be intelligent, reliable, hard-working, honest, energetic, and innovative. A bailiff farmer was a valued employee and well-compensated. He was accountable to the land owner. The quality of his work could make or break the landowner.

Have you ever considered that God has made each of us bailiff farmers? We are God's managers put in charge of caring for the earth and our fellow man. God is the owner who holds us accountable for how we manage that which has been entrusted to us.

God's Word: The Lord God took the man and put him in the Garden of Eden to work it and take care of it (Genesis 2:15).

Prayer: Father, help me to be wise and resourceful in taking care of all that You have entrusted to me. Help me to live and work with a clear understanding that You are the owner, and I am the manager accountable to You. Amen.

SEPTEMBER 5

COMMITMENT

Polycarp, the Christian bishop of Smyrna, in his middle eighties, was taken into a stadium and told to renounce Christ or die. He responded, "Eighty and six years I have served Him, and He did me no wrong. How can I blaspheme my King that saved me?" With those words, he was tied to a stake, burned alive, and then stabbed because the flames did not take his life.

It is hard to imagine such a horrible death. But focus on the steadfast commitment of a man who would not renounce his Savior, Jesus Christ. The death of Polycarp begs the question for all of us: "If you were put on trial for your faith in Christ, would there be enough evidence to convict you?" If you were told to renounce your faith or die, would you choose death or life? These are sobering questions.

Those who died for their faith inspire and challenge us all. Their deaths stand in history as testimonies to unshakable faith. Their convictions inspire all of us. On the other hand, those who renounced their faith are mostly forgotten. Their cowardness leaves us cold and empty and underlines Jesus's teaching that those who save their lives lose them while those who lose their lives for Christ's sake, gain them.
What is your level of commitment?

God's Word: Do your best to present yourself to God as one approved, a worker who does not need to be ashamed and who correctly handles the word of truth (2 Timothy 2:15).

Prayer: Father, In the light of the steadfast faith of a man like Polycarp, I can only pray, "keep me faithful." Amen.

SEPTEMBER 6

FORGIVENESS

A very sincere person asked me if you must forgive someone who has wronged you to receive the forgiveness of God. Dr. John A. Redhead helps to answer that question in his book *Learning to Have Faith*. He imagines a man with two buckets—one filled with water and the other with oil. Both buckets are filled to the brim. Only an empty bucket can be filled, and, besides, oil and water do not mix.

Now imagine that one of those buckets is you and the other is God. God wants to pour His forgiving love into your life, but your life is filled with sin. Furthermore, God's loving mercy and your unforgiving spirit won't mix. Did not Jesus teach us in the Lord's Prayer, "Forgive us our debts, as we also have forgiven our debtors"? Hopefully, the prayer that Jesus taught answers the question.

God's Word: Get rid of all bitterness, rage and anger, brawling and slander, along with every form of malice. Be kind and compassionate to one another, forgiving each other, just as in Christ God forgave you (Ephesians 4:31–32).

Prayer: Father, cleanse my heart and mind of all evil. Free me from the slavery of anger and slander. Give me compassion and forgiveness toward my fellow humans as You have shown compassion and forgiveness to me. Amen.

IF YOU REALLY BELIEVE!

The soprano soloist had just finished singing "I Know That My Redeemer Liveth," from Handel's *Messiah*. Instead of praise, the conductor asked, "My daughter, you do not really know that your redeemer lives, do you?" The singer squirmed a little, then said, "Why, yes, I believe I do." "Then sing it!" He commanded. "Tell it to me so that I'll know you have experienced the joy and power of it."

The soloist sang it again, this time with all the joy and passion that the song deserves. She brought tears to the eyes of everyone in the room. Even the conductor wiped his eyes and said, "You do know, for this time you have told me."[13]

If you truly believe that your redeemer lives, then proclaim it and live it in such a way as to convince others.

God's Word: Let your light shine before others, that they may see your good deeds and glorify your Father in heaven (Matthew 5:16).

Prayer: Father, I pray that others will see Jesus in me. Amen.

---

[13] Norman G. Wilson, "The Salvation of Jesus the Messiah," *Wesleyan Advocate*, Dec. 1992, 23.

SEPTEMBER 8

ROLE MODEL

According to Webster's Dictionary, a role model is "a person who is unusually effective or inspiring in some social role, job, etc., and so serves as a model for others." There is someone who sees you as a role model. It may be your son or daughter, a neighbor, friend, or acquaintance. Your life is noticed. A person that you don't even know could be imitating you right now.

Following Jesus's death and resurrection, He was absent from His disciples for some time. They were perplexed and discouraged. It was then that Simon Peter decided to quit his ministry and return to his fishing business. His role model status influenced the other fishermen to do the same. Jesus appeared to them and questioned Simon Peter's decision by asking him three times, "Do you love me?" Then, Jesus challenged Simon Peter to return to his call and "feed my sheep."

Because we are role models to someone, it behooves us to be careful how we live. Be certain that you are leading people in the right direction.

God's Word: Watch your life and doctrine closely. Persevere in them, because if you do, you will save both yourself and your hearers (1 Timothy 4:16).

Prayer: Father, keep me aware that I will be held accountable for the influence I have on other people. Help me to lead by example in ways that will result in good and not evil. Amen.

SEPTEMBER 9

AMBITION

A young professional once told me that his greatest desire in life was to become a millionaire. I was reminded of Henry Ford, who asked one of his auto engineers to name his chief ambition in life. Without hesitation, the man replied, "To become very rich. Everything else is secondary." Sometime later, Henry Ford gave the young man a small package that contained a pair of metal-rimmed eyeglasses. Ford had replaced the glasses with a pair of silver dollars. He suggested the man put them on, and then he said, "Tell me what you see!" The engineer replied, "The money blocks out everything." The inventor then suggested, "Maybe you should rethink that ambition of yours."[14]

If your only goal in life is to become rich, make certain that it is a treasure you can take with you into eternity and not one that can be taken away from you on earth.

God's Word: Do not store up for yourselves treasures on earth, where moths and vermin destroy, and where thieves break in and steal. But store up for yourselves treasures in heaven, where moths and vermin do not destroy, and where thieves do not break in and steal (Matthew 6:19).

Prayer: Father, knowing that You will provide what I need in this life helps me to focus on eternal things. Amen.

---

[14] King Duncan, Dynamic Illustrations, The Pastor's Professional Research Service, Seven World's Corp., Knoxville, TN, April/May/June 1993.

SEPTEMBER 10

SUFFERING

An epitaph on a grave maker read, "I told you I was sick." You may not understand why others do not feel the extent of your pain. A wise man once said, "Only the wearer knows how badly the shoe pinches."

Soren Kierkegaard, one of Christianity's great thinkers, said on his deathbed, "My life is a great suffering, unknown by others and incomprehensible." No person can adequately communicate the intensity of his pain, nor is any human being fully capable of measuring the suffering of others. When we tell others, "I know how you feel," unless you have experienced what they are experiencing, you are just fooling yourself and not being truthful.

If you want to genuinely help someone who is suffering, let them tell you how they feel rather than pretending that you understand, when you don't.

God's Word: Finally, all of you, be like-minded, be sympathetic, love one another, be compassionate and humble (1 Peter 3:8).

Prayer: Father, help me to be honest with those who suffer, not pretending that I know their pain when I don't. But help me to communicate my love and concern for them through kindness and prayer. Amen.

SEPTEMBER 11

PAYDAY

Dr. R. G. Lee was one of the most profound, effective, and entertaining preachers in Southern Baptist history. He was pastor of the Bellevue Baptist Church in Memphis, Tennessee, for thirty-three years and was famous for his sermon "Payday Someday," preached over twelve hundred times in pulpits across America.

His sermon was based on the judgment of God and the wickedness of King Ahab and Queen Jezebel, who had their neighbor, Naboth, murdered because he refused to sell them his vineyard. The story is told in 1 Kings 21.

The point of the sermon "Payday Someday" is that you may be living in the fast lane of today, wildly taking advantage of others, enjoying your pleasures, and fulfilling your selfish desires, but as sure as you are breathing, a day of accountability is coming. You will answer to God for your sins. Sinful debt cannot be paid with good deeds. Sins can only be forgiven by the grace of God, who permitted His Son, Jesus Christ, to die on the cross for you—repenting and accepting Jesus Christ as your Savior is the only way that you can find forgiveness and avoid judgment.

God's Word: Do not be deceived: God cannot be mocked. A man reaps what he sows (Galatians 6:7).

Prayer: Father, help me to understand that absolutely nothing is hidden from You, not even my most secret thoughts. Remind me every day that I will answer to You for everything. Amen.

SEPTEMBER 12

CONSISTENCY

We had just moved into our new home in Boone, North Carolina, and my wife said that she needed a clothesline in the backyard. We were given a set of T-bars no longer being used—just right for a clothesline. Fred Castle, one of our deacons, volunteered to help me with the project. Once the steel T-bars had been extracted from the ground, a sizable amount of concrete that encased the bars had to be removed.

Fred handed me a large sledgehammer and said, "See if you can break the concrete." I started hitting the concrete with lots of force and at various angles, only to have the sledgehammer bounce off it. Finally, exhausted from the effort, I stopped to get my breath. Fred was laughing at me and said, "You want to see how it's done?" I said, "show me." Fred took three hard, consistent strikes at the same spot on the concrete, and it fell off in two complete pieces. In a simple way, Fred Castle taught me the benefits of consistency.

Inconsistency is a critical problem for many. For example, some people move from one church to another looking for the perfect one, and others jump from one job to another. Still, others marry and divorce multiple times.

If there is one quality that God desires in our Christian life, it is consistency. The most scathing condemnation was directed at the Church of Laodicea. "I know your deeds, that you are neither cold nor hot. I wish you were either one or the other! So because you are lukewarm—neither hot nor cold—I am about to spit you out of my mouth" (Revelation 3:15–16). The word "consistency" is not in the Bible. But the idea is found in the words "steadfast," "stand fast," "perseverance," and "faithful." How much consistency is in your life?

God's Word: Therefore, my dear brothers and sisters, stand firm. Let nothing move you. Always give yourselves fully to the work of the Lord because you know that your labor in the Lord is not in vain (1 Corinthians 15:58).

Prayer: Father, help my witness for You be consistent so that I will honor you and be a positive witness for others. Amen.

SEPTEMBER 13

A BEAUTIFUL PACKAGE

I read about a New York cab driver who was having a problem disposing of his trash. He decided to package it in beautiful wrapping paper tied up with a pretty ribbon on it. The next morning, he placed the attractive package on the back seat of his cab. Just as expected, by evening, the package was gone. A sly passenger had tucked the beautiful package under his arm as he exited the cab, thinking, of course, that the driver was completely unaware of the theft. Imagine the passenger's surprise when he opened the attractive package only to find rotten potatoes, banana peelings, and dirty paper.

Satan wraps every temptation in a beautiful package and watches with glee as people take the bait, thinking all the while that they are getting something of value. You've heard the expression that "all that glitters is not gold." Temptation is always wrapped in attractive packages; that's the way the Devil deceives us to do evil.

God's Word: Be alert and of sober mind. Your enemy the devil prowls around like a roaring lion looking for someone to devour. Resist him, standing firm in the faith, because you know that the family of believers throughout the world is undergoing the same kind of sufferings (1 Peter 5:8–9).

Prayer: Father, keep my mind focused on You so that I will overcome any temptation to take something that does not belong to me, no matter how attractive it may appear. Amen.

SEPTEMBER 14

INTEGRITY MODELED

In March 1993, I was thrilled by the story of a California couple that found a wallet containing $2,394. At the time, both husband and wife had lost their jobs and were sleeping in their car. They did not know where they would get their next meal or when a job opportunity would open to them. It was in those circumstances that they found the lost wallet. They could have kept the money and spent it on themselves. Instead, they turned it in because it was the right thing to do.

People of less character would have kept the money. But the integrity of this couple led them, without question, to give up what was not rightfully theirs. Their integrity did not go unnoticed. When the story was reported, the public was shocked that the wallet owner offered no more than a "thank-you!" But generous, respectful people offered the couple an apartment rent-free. Others came forward with cash and job offers.

The destitute California couple modeled integrity, and God rewarded them. In a day of bad news, the good news is refreshing. That's why God's Word stands out in contrast to all the adverse news that reaches our ears. Those who live by the Word of God and model integrity are not overlooked by God.

God's Word: Better the poor whose walk is blameless than the rich whose ways are perverse (Proverbs 28:6).

Prayer: Father, thank You for people of integrity who will deny themselves to do what is right. Help me to be that kind of person. Amen.

SEPTEMBER 15

WARNINGS AND HUMAN NATURE

In every hurricane, tornado, fire, or winter storm, there are stories of individuals who ignore the warnings to prepare or evacuate. For whatever reason, some think that they can beat the odds.

Human nature is as the Bible describes. We are told to prepare for death and eternity by repenting of our sins and accepting Jesus Christ as our Savior. But just as people ignore storm warnings, they also ignore spiritual truth, live as they please, and expect to escape judgment.

When the Bible says, "I tell you, now is the time of God's favor, now is the day of salvation" (2 Corinthians 6:2), believe it. To ignore His Word or harden your heart could be an eternal mistake.

God's Word: See to it, brothers and sisters, that none of you has a sinful, unbelieving heart that turns away from the Living God. But encourage one another daily, as long as it is called "Today," so that none of you may be hardened by sin's deceitfulness (Hebrews 3:12).

Prayer: Father, help me never to be so foolish that I disregard warnings of danger or turn a deaf ear to the truth of Your Word. Amen.

SEPTEMBER 16

SIDETRACKED

The story is told of a bloodhound that started a hunt chasing a large buck. A fox crossed the path, so the hound chased the fox. In a short time, a rabbit crossed the path, and the hound chased the rabbit. Then a mouse crossed the path, and the hound chased the mouse into a hole. The hound began his hunt on the trail of a magnificent buck and ended up watching a mouse hole!

It is a tragedy to have your eyes on a worthy goal only to be distracted to the point of insignificance. Yet, human beings are often like the bloodhound. We start on a magnificent journey with noble ambitions and goals only to be sidetracked with less important objectives.

Those who win the race are those who don't take their eyes off the goal. Winners never look back, and they refuse to give attention to lesser things.

God's Word: I press on toward the goal to win the prize for which God has called me heavenward in Christ Jesus (Philippians 3:14).

Prayer: Father, there are so many distractions in life's journey. Help me to keep my eyes fixed on You so that I will be faithful in what You have called me to do. Amen.

SEPTEMBER 17

REFUGE

Everyone dreams of a vacation, but most people think about far-away places and extended time from home. Some dream of ocean cruises, expensive dining, or luxury hotels but back away from such adventures because of the high price tag.

Let me suggest a minivacation at home. You won't have to pack a bag, drive a long distance, pay an expensive hotel bill, or sleep in a strange bed. But you will need a creative imagination. Imagine that you are thousands of miles away from home, free from worries, schedules, and responsibilities. In your mind, you can be at the beach bathing in the sun or hiking a mountain trail or taking a walk through the forest. You can take a day off, sleep in, read that book that you have put off for months. Imagine yourself refreshed, rested, and released from stress. Take a deep breath. It is amazing what our thoughts can do for us.

In the busiest of times when the pressures of the world were closing in on him, Jesus found a way to get away from it all. We come apart, or we fall apart. We are wise to take a break, to get away for a while, to change the scenery, to divert our mind from daily stress. For our mental, physical, and spiritual health, we must find a place of refuge.

God's Word: Then, because so many people were coming and going that they did not even have a chance to eat, he said to them, "Come with me by yourselves to a quiet place and get some rest." So they went away by themselves in a boat to a solitary place (Mark 6:31–32).

Prayer: Father, help me to recognize my need to separate myself from the busy world and pressing responsibilities. Help me to find a quiet place, even if it is in my own home. Amen.

SEPTEMBER 18

FRIENDS

Are you one of those fortunate people who have a close friend who fills your heart with joy each time you are with him or her? I'm talking about a friend with whom you can just be yourself. You can laugh or cry with that person and share the deepest secrets of your heart in confidence that you will not be betrayed. Do you have a friend who brings out the best in you, challenges you to noble living, and dares to tell you the truth about yourself? Do you have a friend who forces you to think deeply about your decisions and your faith? Do you have a friend with whom you feel comfortable because you know deep down in your heart that he or she accepts you as you are and loves you despite your faults? If so, you are rich indeed and truly blessed.

I have a feeling that apostle Paul had friends as I have described because about them, he said, "I thank my God every time I remember you" (Philippians 1:3). Can you thank God every time you think of your friend?

God's Word: One who has unreliable friends soon comes to ruin, but there is a friend who sticks closer than a brother (Proverbs 18:24).

Prayer: Father, thank You for friends who are trustworthy, who tell me the truth, accept me for the person I am, and keep my best interest at heart. Amen.

THE CULT OF SELF

With the name David Koresh and Waco—a place of tragedy on the map of America—our ears perk up when we hear the word "cult." In general, we think of cults as being a group of people following a fanatical leader. But what about the cult of self where individual selfishness, greed, personal rights, personal demands, the "what can I get out of it attitude" abounds?

The trend today is isolation from our neighbors, retreating to the security of our homes, our interests, the TV, iPad, or internet. The cult of self is in the attitude. If it doesn't affect me, then I don't want to know about it, or I want what I want no matter who it hurts or what it costs. The cult of self is "me first."

May God open our eyes to see the needs of others and respond to them with love and compassion. Jesus looked upon Jerusalem and wept. When have you wept over the sins of your city or country? When have you wept over your sins?

God's Word: Do nothing out of selfish ambition or vain conceit. Rather, in humility value others above yourselves, not looking to our own interests but each of you to the interests of the others (Philippians 2:3–4).

Prayer: Father, as You have blessed me, help me to be a blessing to others and especially to those in need. Amen.

SEPTEMBER 20

THE GOOD OLE DAYS

Do you find yourself longing for "the good ole days"? Read this commentary published in the *Atlantic Journal*, June 16, 1833.

The world is too big for us. Too much going on, too many crimes, too much violence, and excitement. Try as you will you get behind in the race … it's an incessant strain to keep pace … and still, you lose ground. Science empties its discoveries on you so fast that you stagger beneath them in hopeless bewilderment. Everything is high pressure. Human nature can't endure much more.

For those prone to call yesterday "the good ole days," this article reminds us that those days weren't much different from our present time. Fortunately for us, the God who held the future in1833, still holds it today.

God's Word: But I trust in you, Lord; I say, "You are my God." My times are in your hands. (Psalm 31:14–15).

Prayer: Father, You are the same yesterday, today, and tomorrow. Help me to serve You faithfully. Free me from fear, apathy, and compliancy and give me courage and determination to make a difference. I pray in Jesus's name. Amen.

SEPTEMBER 21

ON SHOWING COMPASSION

It has been my fortunate experience as a pastor to have had individuals in my congregations who have been extremely blessed financially. They have been devoted servants of God who have compassion for the less fortunate. These individuals have privately told me that if I ever find a need that cannot be met with the benevolent funds of the church, to let them know. They were not interested in publicity. On the contrary, they wanted no attention drawn to themselves. The need was to be met, but the giver of the gift was to remain anonymous. If someone were to ask about the source of the gift, I was told to say, "Give God the glory!"

Because of their compassion, a family who had no insurance had their roof replaced after a hurricane. Groceries were provided for a family whose wife was sick, and the husband had lost his job. A car with mechanical problems was repaired. The list goes on.

Compassion is also shown by volunteer organizations such as Baptist Men, who restore homes damaged by storms and build ramps so that the handicapped can access their homes in wheelchairs. Thousands are provided meals in times of disaster; dental and medical services are provided to those who would otherwise go untreated. We are most like Jesus when we show compassion.

God's Word: Finally, all of you, be like-minded, be sympathetic, love one another, be compassionate and humble (1 Peter 3:8).

Prayer: Father, thank You for compassionate servants who inspire us and whose devoted service to "the least of these" challenges us all to follow their example. Amen.

SEPTEMBER 22

STRIVE FOR EXCELLENCE

I don't recall ever meeting a person who wanted to go to a mediocre doctor. No one I know wants to take their car to a mediocre mechanic or deposit their money in a mediocre bank. The fact is that most people want the best when it comes to medical care, car repair, or financial confidence.

Webster defines "mediocrity" as moderate or low excellence—ordinary. The amazing thing about human nature is that those who adopt mediocrity as a lifestyle cannot tolerate it in others.

Through the years, I have benefited from the writings of Dr. Charles Swindoll, respected author and pastor of Stonebriar Community Church, Frisco, Texas. He has written a book called *Living Above the Level of Mediocrity*, and has adopted a policy of excellence. If we appreciate excellence in others, why not pursue it in our own lives? Someone said, "God don't make junk." That is why He made us "in His image." Being made "in His Image," why should we strive for anything less than excellence?

God's Word: But you are a chosen people, a royal priesthood, a holy nation, God's special possession, that you may declare the praises of him who called you out of darkness into his wonderful light (1 Peter 2:9).

Prayer: Father, as You have given me immense value by making me in Your image, help me to strive for excellence in all that I do. Amen.

SEPTEMBER 23

LOOKING ON THE BRIGHT SIDE

A tsunami is defined as a huge sea wave caused by a great disturbance under the ocean, as a strong earthquake or volcanic eruption. The consequences can be devastating. Life, like nature, can also have tsunamis, which we are more accustomed to calling trauma. How we react when it seems the world is caving in around us or falling apart can make a big difference in the outcome. It is in tsunami life experiences that our faith is tested the most. Hear the words of the prophet Habakkuk, who had every reason to despair:

> Though the fig tree does not bud and there are no grapes on the
> vines, though the olive crop fails and the fields produce no food,
> though there are no sheep in the pen and no cattle in the stalls,
> yet I will rejoice in God my Savior.
> The Sovereign Lord is my strength; he makes my feet
> Like the feet of a deer, he enables me to tread on the heights.
> (Habakkuk 3:17–19)

When everything you thought was nailed down starts coming up, when you are hit with waves of trauma, remember Habakkuk. Cling to God—your Savior and your strength, who is totally capable of seeing you through the storm. Look on the bright side!

God's Word: Lord, I have heard of your fame; I stand in awe of your deeds, Lord. Repeat them in our day, in our time make them known; In wrath remember mercy (Habakkuk 3:2).

Prayer: Father, when life seems to be crashing down upon me, give me the faith of Habakkuk to rejoice in You and to lean upon Your strength to get me through. Amen.

SEPTEMBER 24

PROMOTING LOVE

In the aftermath of the April 19, 1995, Oklahoma bombing, America was brought face-to-face with the devastation caused by hatred. President Bill Clinton took a biblical theme when he addressed the tragedy:

> Let us let our own children know that we will stand against the forces of fear. When there is talk of hatred, let us stand up and talk against it. When there is talk of violence, let us stand up and talk against it. In the face of death, let us honor life. As Saint Paul admonished us, let us not be overcome by evil, but overcome evil with good.[15]

In a world of violence and hatred, as followers of Jesus Christ, we must dedicate ourselves to love, kindness, and peace. Love is the greatest gift of all. Love never fails.

God's Word: If I speak in the tongues of men or of angels, but do not have love, I am only a resounding gong or a clanging cymbal (1 Corinthians 13:1).

Prayer: Father, help me to understand that love must be demonstrated before it can be believed. Saying, "I love you," is not the same as showing it by what I do. Amen.

---

[15] President Bill Clinton, address at memorial service, Oklahoma City, Oklahoma. April 23, 1995, from CNN Specials Transcript #489.

SEPTEMBER 25

MY SHEPHERD

No psalm is more beloved than Psalm 23. Ponder this refreshing North American Plains Indian version:

> The Great Father above is a shepherd Chief. I am His and with Him, I want not. He throws out to me a rope and the name of the rope is love and He draws me to where the grass is green and the water not dangerous, and I eat and lie down and am satisfied. Sometimes my heart is very weak and falls down but He lifts me up again and draws me into a good road. His name is "wonderful." Sometime, it may be very soon, it may be a long, long time. He will draw me into a valley. It is dark there, but I'll be afraid not, for it is in between those mountains that the Shepherd Christ will meet me and the hunger that I have in my heart all through this life will be satisfied. He gives me a staff to lean upon. He spreads a table before me with all kinds of foods. He puts His hand upon my head and all the "tired" is gone. My cup, He fills till it runs over. What I tell is true. I lie not. These roads that are "away ahead" will stay with me through this life and after, and afterwards, I will go to live in the great house and sit down with the Shepherd Chief forever.[16]

God's Word: Jesus answered, "I am the way and the truth and the life. No one comes to the Father except through me" (John 14:6).

Prayer: Father, You are my Lord, Savior, and Shepherd because I have confessed my sins, repented, and asked Your forgiveness. Thank You for the assurance that You meet all my needs. Amen.

---

[16] Translation by Isabel Crawford, missionary to the Indians of the plains.

SEPTEMBER 26

FULFILLMENT

The scene in the movie is of a young man and woman leaning against the rail of an ocean liner. They have just been married, and this voyage is part of their honeymoon. Gazing into each other's eyes, the couple talks about how fulfilling their love and marriage is for them and how they look forward to the further enrichment of their love as time passes. The young man says, "If I were to die tomorrow, I would feel that my life had been full because I have known your love." His bride responds, "Yes, I feel the same way." They kiss and move away from the railing, revealing the name of the ship on a life preserver—TITANIC.

If you were to die tomorrow or today, could you say that your life has been fulfilled?

God's Word: For to me, to live is Christ and to die is gain (Philippians 1:21).

Prayer: Father, the true fulfillment of life is to love You and serve You with all my heart. Anything else related to love is a bonus. Amen.

THE TRUE MEASURE

How much does it take to arouse your anger and cause you to explode? Put another way, do you live on a short fuse? If you are constantly exploding on your family or friends for little things, you need help. Someone has said that "the true measure of a person can be determined by how little it takes to make them angry."

Solomon said, "Better a patient person than a warrior, one with self-control than one who takes a city" (Proverbs 16:32). Take note of how little it takes to "set you off" and take steps to deal with it. Get help! See your pastor or a Christian counselor before your anger destroys you.

God's Word: In your anger do not sin: Do not let the sun go down while you are still angry, and do not give the devil a foothold (Ephesians 4:26–27).

Prayer: Father, help me to deal with my anger in constructive ways so that it will not lead me into sin. Let my emotions be controlled by Your Holy Spirit. Amen.

SEPTEMBER 28

CHILDLIKE CONFIDENCE

Nothing is more impressive than the confidence of a child, and nothing touches the heart of God more than childlike faith. God is not impressed with our intelligence or wit. He is not moved by our ability to manipulate others or even to disguise our true motives. God is not awed by our craftiness or skill or "do it myself" attitude.

God is touched when we come to Him humbly and with a broken heart, a dependent faith, and an attitude of submissiveness. When we approach God in childlike faith, we can ask him for little things that many people are afraid to request. A childlike confidence will ask God for anything and then trust Him to do what is best.

Don't worry about how your prayers may sound. It is not eloquent words that catch God's attention. Pray with childlike faith and believe that God will hear you.

God's Word: And he said, "Truly I tell you, unless you change and become like little children, you will never enter the Kingdom of Heaven" (Matthew 18:3).

Prayer: Father, as a little child trusts and believes without reservation, help me to respond to You with that same confidence. Amen.

SEPTEMBER 29

THE CHRISTIAN LIFE

If you have ever wondered what a Christian is supposed to be or do, you can find the answer in chapters 5–7 of the Gospel of Matthew. This collection of sermons preached by Jesus over time is the most concise description in the Bible of what God expects of us.

No one reading the Sermon on the Mount can conclude that it is easy to live a Christian life. The truth is that it is impossible without the help of God's presence and power. People fail in living the Christian life because they lack dependency upon God's indwelling power. It is most encouraging to know that God does not ask us to do something that He does not equip or empower us to do. We have all the help we need in the Holy Spirit, who is our teacher and guide.

God's Word: But the Advocate, the Holy Spirit, whom the Father will send in my name, will teach you all things and will remind you of everything I have said to you (John 14:26).

Prayer: Father, thank You that I am not alone in living the Christian life. Help me to daily look for the guidance of the Holy Spirit and help me to faithfully obey. Amen.

SEPTEMBER 30

SURVIVAL RESOURCE

If you were lost in a jungle, taken hostage, or trapped in an isolated situation, what would you consider to be the most powerful survival resource that you could have?

David Jacobsen, who was an American hostage in Lebanon for eighteen months, blindfolded, chained, and beaten, credits his belief in God as his most powerful resource for survival.

How many souls are hostage to drugs, alcohol, sex, greed, disease, abuse, and fear? No matter the nature of our bondage, there is a God who is our refuge and help in times of trouble. If you feel trapped, imprisoned, or hostage to anyone or anything, remember that God is your best survival resource.

God's Word: Now the Lord is the Spirit, and where the Spirit of the Lord is, there is freedom (2 Corinthians 3:17).

Prayer: Father, there are so many ways that I can be held prisoner. Help me to know the freedom that is mine in Jesus Christ. Amen.

OCTOBER 1

CRITICISM

Are you a person who is prone to criticizing others? Be honest with yourself in answering the question. It is challenging, if not impossible, to avoid criticizing our fellow man. The temptation to "tear down" a fellow human being is all too prevalent.

The next time you find yourself geared up to criticize someone, stop and think:

> It is easy to sit in your recliner and criticize
> the man who is mowing your lawn.
> It is easy to sit in the bleachers of a football
> stadium and criticize the quarterback.
> It is easy to sit in the pew and criticize the
> choir, music director, or preacher.
> It is easier to think that someone should serve
> on a church committee when you refuse.

There is an old Indian saying that you should not criticize another person until you have walked in their moccasins for two weeks. And as a wise man has said, "You'll never know the weight of the load until the pack is on your back."

God's Word: You, therefore, have no excuse, you who pass judgment on someone else, for at whatever point you judge another, you are condemning yourself, because you who pass judgment do the same things (Romans 2:1).

Prayer: Father, free me from a critical spirit. Help me work on the flaws in my own life. Amen.

OCTOBER 2

APPRECIATION NEEDED

The Seafood Festival in Morehead City, North Carolina, is an annual attraction for thousands of people who come from near and far to the Crystal Coast. It is billed as a tribute to fishermen and to those who make a living from the sea.

Seafood lovers who flock to the festival provide a tremendous economic boost to the local economy and get to enjoy the delicious food, crafts, fun, and entertainment that the event offers.

The next time you attend a seafood festival or dine at a seafood restaurant, pause and give thanks to God for those who labor so hard to provide the edible delights of the sea. The harvesting of seafood is not only hard work; it is often dangerous. Don't forget to thank God, who created all the precious food resources that sustain us, and the people who labor to get our food to market.

God's Word: And do not forget to do good and to share with others, for with such sacrifices God is pleased (Hebrews 13:16).

Prayer: Father, thank You for providing all the food on land and sea that sustains us. And thank You for those who labor to get food to our tables. Amen.

OCTOBER 3

THE FUTURE IS UP TO YOU

Former President and Mrs. Jimmy Carter have distinguished themselves in their post presidential days as faithful servants of mankind. Most notable is their work with Habitat for Humanity and the Carter Center, which has helped improve life in more than eighty countries.

In their book *Everything to Gain—Making the Most of the Rest of Your Life*, the Carters challenge us to get on with our dreams or find new ones. The truth is we have only so much time. Those who are successful keep their eye on their goals.

If you want to accomplish something worthy in life, start working on it now, and don't delay. Procrastination is your worst enemy. It is the devil's number one tool to keep you from doing something significant. With whatever time you have, the future is up to you. Ponder God's Word for today.

God's Word: As long as it is day, we must do the works of him who sent me. Night is coming, when no one can work (John 9:4).

Prayer: Father, as long as You give me health and strength, help me be useful and productive, seizing the moment knowing that my time is short. Amen.

OCTOBER 4

THE BOOMERANG OF GOODNESS

I will never forget the church member who told me that she was tired of doing good for others because she got slapped in the face every time she did. She didn't mean that she literally got slapped for doing good but rather that her good deeds always produced negative results. Life is not always fair, and the best of us sometimes see evil returned for the good we do.

If you have had that experience, perhaps you have a better understanding of how God must feel. He constantly pours out his grace, mercy, love, forgiveness, and compassion upon us only to watch us disobey, rebel, and even ignore Him. Yet, God never gives up on us.

Jesus lived a sinless life, giving Himself for others, but in the end, was crucified by those who would not accept His love. Yet, He still holds out his arms to embrace us and receive us when we repent of our sins. Jesus knows better than we do about the boomerang of goodness. But He keeps on loving and giving because, in the end, truth and goodness will prevail. The cross and resurrection assure it.

God's Word: Do not be overcome by evil, but overcome evil with good (Romans 12:21).

Prayer: Father, help me not be discouraged when the good that I do results in an evil return. But instead help me to do good because it is the right thing to do. Amen.

SHARPEN YOUR SKILLS

It is exceedingly difficult to cut wood with a dull ax or saw. Those who have tried know that it takes more energy, and the results are often unsatisfactory. The best craftsmen always work with sharp tools. Michelangelo, the great sculptor/artist, spent considerable time sharpening his tools.

You and I are wonderfully made by God, but if we are not properly sharpened, what we produce will be unsatisfactory. Those who accomplish the most for God are those who are in the best spiritual condition.

Sharpen your life with prayer, Bible study, worship, and serving others. Unless we stay very close to God, our labor will be most disappointing.

God's Word: If the ax is dull and its edge unsharpened, more strength is needed, but skill will bring success (Ecclesiastes 10:10).

Prayer: Father, as tools must be sharpened to do their best work, help me to be sharp and prepared for the work You want me to do. Amen.

OCTOBER 6

LISTENING

How is your listening ability? Are you so busy talking that you fail to listen to what is important to others? Listening to what others are saying could be the best thing that we do for them. I was taught in a pastoral care seminar that when entering a patient's room in the hospital, it is important to allow them to set the agenda for the conversation. In other words, listen.

There are lonely, hurting people who need someone to listen. Instead of talking so much today, determine to be more attentive to what others are saying. The most encouraging thing that you can do for another person is to listen. And while you are developing the ability to listen to others, don't forget to listen to God when you pray.

God's Word: Therefore everyone who hears these words of mine and puts them into practice is like a wise man who built his house on the rock (Matthew 7:24).

Prayer: Father, I am guilty of talking too much when I pray, always telling You about myself or asking for something. Help me to practice being quiet, still, and attentive so that I can listen to You. Amen.

OCTOBER 7

EMERGENCY GOD

Do you treat God as if he is a 911 emergency responder? All too often, we find ourselves neglecting our relationship with God but calling upon him when we have an immediate need. It is not calling on God in times of emergency, trauma, sickness, or death that gives us security, but rather it is an intimate relationship with Him. A close relationship with God gives us the freedom to address Him in our time of need.

If you are in the habit of only calling upon God when there is an emergency, you should be embarrassed. When you don't get an immediate answer to your prayer, it might be that God is busy taking care of his regular followers. It's not knowing that God exists that counts; it's walking daily in a personal relationship with Him.

If you only see God as an emergency responder, you might want to rethink your relationship with Him.

God's Word: Not everyone who says to me, "Lord, Lord," will enter the Kingdom of heaven; but only the one who does the will of my Father who is in heaven (Matthew 7:21).

Prayer: Father, help my relationship with You be so strong that I will not be embarrassed to call upon You in an emergency. Amen.

OCTOBER 8

GAME

It was Monday, October 8, 1956. The New York Yankees and the Brooklyn Dodgers were in the fifth game of the World Series at Yankee Stadium. Yankee pitcher Don Larson pitched the first perfect game in the history of the World Series. It was better than a no-hitter; Larsen didn't give up a hit. He didn't walk anyone. The Yankees made no errors. No Dodger ever got to first base.

On that same day, the most important thing in the life of Phil Hoose, a cousin of Don Larson, was getting his education. Phil's mother thought it was far more important for her son to be in school than to stay home because his cousin was playing in the World Series. At 3:00 p.m. that afternoon, Mr. Northcott, the principal, interrupted Phil's class with the announcement that Phil's cousin had done something no other pitcher had ever done in a World Series game—pitched a perfect game. The class erupted in applause and congratulations to Phil.[17]

Take note that the class congratulated Phil. The point is this—Phil didn't pitch a perfect game, but he was related to the one who did. You and I may never have a perfect day, let alone a perfect life, but we can be related to one who is perfect—Jesus Christ. We may never receive the accolades of our fellow man, but on a far greater scale, we benefit from the special accomplishment of Jesus Christ, who died at Calvary for our sins.

God's Word: God made him who had no sin to be sin for us, so that in him we might become the righteousness of God (2 Corinthians 5:21).

Prayer: Father, I thank You for Jesus Christ, Your Son, who had no sin, and was the perfect one to take my sins upon himself so that I might have life eternal. Amen.

---

[17] *Reader's Digest*, April 1990.

OCTOBER 9

FIGHTING BATTLES

You don't have to be a wizard to know that most people are fighting a hard battle. Our battles may be economic, physical, emotional, or spiritual. They may be family-related or business-related, but all of us have battles to fight. A friend of mine calls battles alligators. Battles or alligators, it all boils down to the conflicts we face.

In our battles, we need words of encouragement and hope. We need sound advice, not platitudes. We need direction, not criticism. We need assurance and comfort. For all our battles, for guidance, for comfort, there is one who can meet our deepest needs. His name is Jesus.

The hymn writer put it this way: "No one ever cared for me like Jesus." Don't attempt to fight your battles alone; turn to Jesus. Read His Word, the Bible, and draw encouragement and strength for your life. Do not forsake prayer and worship. Do not try to fight your battle alone. God will help you if you let him.

God's Word: We are hard pressed on every side, but not crushed; perplexed, but not in despair; persecuted, but not abandoned; struck down, but not destroyed (2 Corinthians 4:8–9).

Prayer: Father, I do not pray that You take the battle away from me but that You give me strength in the fight. Amen.

OCTOBER 10

GUILT

Guilt is a powerful force in our lives. Whenever it is present, it robs us of peace and joy. Guilt causes us to avoid other people, to run and hide rather than face the music. Guilt, if prolonged, can even have damaging physical effects.

King David knew the damage of guilt. He said, "There is no soundness in my bones because of my sin" (Psalm 38:3). Guilt is a destructive force in our lives that can only be cured with confession and repentance. That is why King David said, "My guilt has overwhelmed me like a burden too heavy to bear" (Psalm 38:4). That is why we must also confess and repent as did David, "I confess my iniquity; I am troubled by my sin" (Psalm 38:18). "Come quickly to help me, my Lord and my Savior" (Psalm 38:22).

Confess your guilt today. Seek God's forgiveness and ask forgiveness of those you have wronged. The soul that is freed from the power of sin by confession and repentance is the soul that is truly liberated.

God's Word: "Come now, let us settle the matter," says the Lord. "Though your sins are like scarlet, they shall be as white as snow; though they are red as crimson, they shall be like wool" (Isaiah 1:18).

Prayer: Father, hear my prayer. I confess my sins; I repent and ask You to remove this terrible weight of guilt and be at peace. Amen.

OCTOBER 11

OBEYING GOD

Scripture is clear about the relationship between obedience and experiencing God. It is impossible to know God unless there is in us an obedient spirit. Abraham would never have been called "the friend of God" if he had not obeyed. Moses would not have had the insight or power to deliver the children of Israel from bondage without obeying God. Elijah could not have stood against the prophets of Baal on Mount Carmel without obedience to God.

The Bible says: "Whoever believes in the Son has eternal life, but whoever rejects the Son will not see life, for God's wrath remains on them" (John 3:36). If you are serious about experiencing God, then you must do what He says.

God's Word: If you love me, keep my commands ... The one who loves me will be loved by my Father, and I too will love them and show myself to them (John 14:15, 21).

Prayer: Father, help me to express my love to You by living in obedience to Your Word. Amen.

OCTOBER 12

WORRY AND ANXIETY

Worry and anxiety will beat you down, rob you of joy, and greatly limit your productivity. Did you know that worry and anxiety can be defeated? The secret is to concentrate on experiencing God and doing His Will.

Don't focus on your circumstances because you don't have enough knowledge to know everything that is going on around you. Don't focus on your needs because no individual knows all his or her needs. Don't focus on your wisdom because you are not smart enough. Don't rely on the opinion of others who are in the same situation you find yourself. Rather, focus on God. Nothing in your life is more important than keeping your focus on God.

You will never defeat worry and anxiety alone. Someone has said, "This is the first day of the rest of your life." So, why not begin by taking all your concerns to God?

God's Word: Turn to me and be saved, all you ends of the earth; for I am God and there is no other (Isaiah 45:22).

Prayer: Father, help me to cast my burden of worry and anxiety upon You so that I lean completely on your wisdom and guidance. Amen.

OCTOBER 13

TOO BUSY

Is this one of those days in which you are meeting yourself coming and going? You find yourself not only hurried but anxious, frustrated, and bewildered. As it has been said, "Everything you thought was nailed down is coming loose." The demands and responsibilities that are upon you require you to stop for a moment and take a break. Find a quiet place. Take a deep breath—take five or six deep breaths. Call upon God.

Martin Luther once said that he had so much pressing business that he had to spend an extra hour in prayer. Good thinking! Good advice! What a difference it will make in your life if you turn to God rather than continue dealing with your problems in a frenzy.

God's Word: You will keep in perfect peace those whose minds are steadfast, because they trust in you (Isaiah 26:3).

Prayer: Father, give me the wisdom to pull away from the pressures of the day. Help me to pause long enough to catch my breath and talk with You. Calm my nerves, help me to refocus, and get my directions from you. Amen.

OCTOBER 14

SCRIPTURE

Have you ever wondered just what scripture you ought to read? While it is always good to read consistently and consecutively and to deal with one book at a time, I find it helpful to read according to my moods and my needs for the moment. To do this, a good Bible concordance or dictionary is helpful. The book of James is helpful for the practical issues of life such as temptation, the tongue, doing for others, listening, suffering, etc. Reading about Paul will increase your faith and courage. The psalms will lift your spirit while the book of John explains the love of God. For a glimpse of glory and victory, read Revelation.

There is something helpful and uplifting in God's Word for every need and every person. Time spent reading and studying scripture is well spent. Try it!

God's Word: All scripture is God-breathed and is useful for teaching, rebuking, correcting and training in righteousness, so that the servant of God may be thoroughly equipped for every good work (2 Timothy 3:16–17).

Prayer: Father, Your Word speaks truth to my deepest needs and guides me in responding to the challenges of life. Keep me immersed in it. Amen.

OCTOBER 15

FALSE TEACHING

False teaching, known today as misinformation or conspiracy theories, is strongly confronted and rebuked by apostle Paul in the first century. It was being taught that it is all right to increase your sins because God's grace was sufficient to cover them all. Paul considered it absurd to teach that the more sin one committed, the more grace it took for God to forgive.

Misinformation, conspiracy theories, and lies are a travesty and insult to God. No one claiming to be a Christian can honor God by supporting anything that God hates. The world today, like the world of the first century, abounds in false teaching. The Bible teaches that God will severely judge those who call Him "Lord" and disregard what he tells us to do. Any doctoring, teaching, philosophy, or way of life that disregards the judgment of God is flawed.

The grace of God is offered to us not because God is tolerant of our sins but because God is love. God's forgiveness is given to us not as a license to sin but because without it, we are hopelessly doomed.

God's Word: Watch out for false prophets. They come to you in sheep's clothing, but inwardly they are ferocious wolves. By their fruit you will recognize them (Matthew 7:15–16).

Prayer: Father, keep me alert to false teaching, and if I hear anything that does not comply with Your Word, give me the wisdom to avoid it. Amen.

OCTOBER 16

COMMON SENSE VS. FAITH

Perhaps you have been told all your life to use common sense. But common sense is only good up to a point. Common sense can keep you out of trouble and save you a lot of worries, but common sense is not faith. From a common-sense standpoint, Moses would not have attempted to cross the Red Sea with thousands of weary Hebrews. Common sense would tell you that Elijah could not call down fire from heaven, nor could one dying on a cross save you from your sins. But faith says that the sea can part, that fire can come down from heaven, and that Christ dying on the cross can save you from your sins.

Serving God is not a matter of common sense but rather a matter of faith. Common sense can cause you to disobey God, while faith allows you to walk in obedience.

God's Word: Now faith is confidence in what we hope for and assurance about what we do not see (Hebrews 11:1).

Prayer: Father, help me to understand that common sense relies on the wisdom of man, which at best is vulnerable to serious error, while faith is trusting in one who will keep me on the right path. Amen.

OCTOBER 17

BEGINNING AGAIN

Louise Fletcher Tarkington wrote a poem wishing that there was a land of beginning again. How many people in the world, so messed up with bad choices, drugs, and crime, would give anything to be able to begin again?

The good news is that there is a land of beginning again. Your life can be made over again through the transforming power of Jesus Christ. Receive Christ into your life by repenting of your sins and surrendering to His will. Through Him, you can be born again. Through Him, you can begin again.

God's Word: Jesus replied, "Very truly I tell you, no one can see the kingdom of God unless they are born again (John 3:3).

Prayer: Father, thank You for making provisions for me to begin again through the power of Jesus dying on the cross to save me from my sins. Amen.

OCTOBER 18

HIDE AND SEEK

Do you remember, as a child, playing hide and seek? It was so much fun hiding and having someone try to find you. It was also fun being the seeker of those who were hiding. We could play the game for hours, and it was best played right before dark.

Somehow the game of hide and seek never seems to end. There are always those hiding from God, and there is always God seeking those who think they are hiding.

Hide and Seek started with Adam and Eve in the Garden of Eden just after they had disobeyed God and had taken the forbidden fruit. It was then, realizing their nakedness, that they hid from God. At least, in shame, they thought that they had hidden from God.

Hebrews 4:13 says, "Nothing in all creation is hidden from God's sight. Everything is uncovered and laid bare before the eyes of him to whom we must give an account." David, who tried to cover up his adultery with Bathsheba and the murder of Uriah, asked, "Where can I go from your Spirit? Where can I flee from your presence? (Psalm 139:7).

No matter what you do, no matter where you go, you cannot hide from God. So, confess your sins. Repent, receive forgiveness, and know the joy of your salvation.

God's Word: "Who can hide in secret places so that I cannot see them?" declares the Lord. "Do not I fill heaven and earth?" declares the Lord (Jeremiah 23:24).

Prayer: Father, help me to never be so foolish as to think that You do not know where I am, what I am doing, and what I am thinking. Thank You that even when I sin and try to cover it up, You are seeking me, waiting for my confession and repentance, and offering me forgiveness and a closer relationship with You. Amen.

DISCIPLINE

A teenager came to his pastor for advice. "I left home," said the boy, "and did something that will make my dad furious when he finds out. What should I do?" The pastor thought for a moment and replied, "Go home and confess your sin to your father, and he'll probably forgive you and treat you like the prodigal son."

Sometime later, the boy reported to his pastor: "Well, I told Dad what I did." "And did he kill the fatted calf for you?" the pastor asked. "No," said the boy, "but he nearly killed the prodigal son!"

It is no fun to be disciplined, but it is necessary for our good and the good of society. The Bible says, "No discipline seems pleasant at the time, but painful. Later on, however, it produces a harvest of righteousness and peace for those who have been trained by it" (Hebrews 12:11).

God's Word: Whoever heeds discipline shows the way of life, but whoever ignores correction leads others astray (Proverbs 10:17).

Prayer: Father, Help me to accept your discipline. Correct my behavior so that I can be a more effective disciple for You. Amen.

OCTOBER 20

BIBLICAL FAITH

What kind of faith do you have? Some people are content with "salvation faith"—believing that Jesus Christ is the Son of God, that He died on the cross to save us from sin, and that He is coming again to receive us unto himself. Such faith is commendable and is necessary for eternal life. But for spiritual growth and maturity, there is another kind of faith emphasized in scripture—"walking faith." "Walking faith is listening to God speak by the Holy Spirit through prayer, Bible study, circumstances, and the church, and then following wherever God leads.

"Walking faith" is trusting God to do what you cannot do. It is stepping out on thin ice. It is taking a risk. "Walking faith" requires self-abandonment and a total dependence upon God. It is through "salvation faith" that our souls are saved for eternity. It is through "walking faith" that we experience God by obedience. "Walking faith" gives us the joy of being in fellowship with God.

God's Word: Show me your faith without deeds, and I will show you my faith by my deeds (James 2:18).

Prayer: Father, let the work that I do reflect the faith that I profess. Let my deeds point others to faith in Jesus Christ. Amen.

OCTOBER 21

PRIDE

Pride may be the chief of all sins. In one way or another, it touches every life. We carry pride in our hearts yet despise it when we see it in someone else's life. Pride blinds us to truth, causes us to turn a deaf ear to reason, renders us unconscious of our faults, and causes us to depend upon ourselves rather than God. Pride keeps us from sharing our deepest hurts with friends. Pride keeps us from seeking professional help when we need it most. Pride keeps us from confessing our sins, repenting, and asking God for forgiveness.

The Bible says: "Pride brings a person low, but the lowly in spirit gain honor" (Proverbs 29:23). Never are we in deeper trouble than when we think we know it all or think that we are always right or when we set common sense aside and follow our own instincts.

Let us ask God to expose our pride, convict us of it, and forgive us.

God's Word: Pride goes before destruction, a haughty spirit before a fall (Proverbs 16:18).

Prayer: Father, guard me against the sin of pride, which blinds me and hinders me from being submissive to You. Amen.

OCTOBER 22

LITTLE THINGS

We never know when something we do will last a lifetime. A teacher at wit's end in getting her students to understand a concept she was trying to teach made an interesting request. She asked each student to take out a sheet of paper and write down the names of every student in the class. She then asked that they write something nice about each classmate.

The teacher compiled the comments and then gave each class member the summary of what had been said about them. One student was overheard saying, "I never knew that I meant anything to anyone!" Years later, at a class reunion, the students gathered around their former teacher and produced copies of the good things classmates had said about them—things they had treasured for years. The teacher was overwhelmed.

Little things we do can last a lifetime and make a powerful difference in someone's life. Jesus taught that the kingdom of God is like seeds scattered on the ground. Never underestimate the power of little things you do.

God's Word: Gracious words are a honeycomb, sweet to the soul and healing to the bones (Proverbs 16:24).

Prayer: Father, help me to take care of the little things in life, knowing that in so doing, big things will be accomplished. Amen.

OCTOBER 23

INVESTMENTS

Books and magazines giving advice on how to play the stock market, get rich, and build wealth for retirement abound. They go into great detail on how to protect your paycheck, where to get the best credit card offers, and which stocks are most promising. These publications sell because people are interested in their well-being on earth. But what about eternity? Let's face it. We only live on this earth for less than a hundred years, with a few exceptions. Why are we so eager to give this brief existence on earth more importance than eternity? To live for the "here and now" and disregard eternity is the height of foolishness. How we live on this earth is important, but it pales in significance when compared to where we will spend eternity.

The Bible cautions us about laying up treasures on earth where they can be taken away and urges us to lay up treasures in heaven where they are eternally secure. The question that Jesus asked cannot be ignored without eternal consequences, "What good is it for someone to gain the whole world, yet forfeit their soul" (Mark 8:36)? Today might be a good day to ponder this profound question and find the answer that will give you eternal peace and security.

God's Word: So we fix our eyes not on what is seen, but on what is unseen, since what is seen is temporary, but what is unseen is eternal (2 Corinthians 4:18).

Prayer: Father, trusting You for the things I need in this life helps me to focus on eternal things. Amen.

OCTOBER 24

PERSPECTIVE

It is a serious and dangerous situation when a ship loses power and is adrift in the ocean. Drifting ships have been known to run aground either on land or on treacherous rocks. Ships adrift have been compared to a drifting life. Some people find themselves hopelessly wandering here and there with no purpose or destination in mind.

There is a saying that "if you don't know where you are going, any road will do." The Bible tells us that there is a broad road that leads to destruction and a narrow road that leads to life.

Jesus Christ said, "I am the way and the truth and the life. No one comes to the Father except through me" (John 14:6). Jesus is the one in whom we find meaning, purpose, peace, joy, happiness, and eternal salvation. If you are drifting, wake up before it is too late. Turn your life over to Jesus. He is the anchor your soul needs.

God's Word: For this reason, we must pay the most careful attention, therefore to what we have heard, so that we do not drift away from it. For if the word spoken through angels proved unalterable, and every transgression and disobedience received a just penalty, how will we escape if we neglect so great a salvation (Hebrews 2:1–2)?

Prayer: Father, the pull of the world's attractions is powerful and can so easily cause me to drift away from You. Please help me to be steadfast in my faith and walk. Amen.

OCTOBER 25

KNOWING ONE THING

What do you know about yourself? What do you consider the most important thing about life that you need to know? Ponder the response to those questions given by John Wesley, who wrote, "I am a creature of a day, passing through life, as an arrow through the air. I am a spirit come from God, and returning to God; just hovering over the great gulf; until a few months hence, I am no more seen! I will drop into an unchangeable eternity. I want to know one thing, the way to Heaven; how to land safely on that happy shore."[18]

People who know who they are and where they will spend eternity are people in touch with reality. God did not intend for life to be sad, but he certainly meant it to be serious. Know yourself and know where you will spend eternity, and things of lesser importance will take care of themselves.

God's Word: Therefore, since we are surrounded by such a great cloud of witnesses, let us throw off everything that hinders and the sin that so easily entangles. And let us run with perseverance the race marked out for us, fixing our eyes on Jesus, the pioneer and perfecter of faith (Hebrews 12:1).

Prayer: Father, help me to join the faithful in carrying out Your purpose for my life. Above all else, help me to keep my eyes on Jesus. Amen.

---

[18] John Wesley, preface to his two volumes of sermons.

OCTOBER 26

READING THE BIBLE

It is good to read the Bible for pleasure. Some of the most intriguing stories of mankind and history are to be found within its pages. But we should read the Bible for instruction and guidance. It is God's love letter to us explaining in detail how we are made, how much He loves us, what He has done to save us from our sins, how we can have eternal life, and how we should live. The Bible tells us what God expects of us and how we can love and serve Him and know joy and peace. The Bible helps us to understand how we can experience God in our daily lives.

Reading the Bible through from Genesis to Revelation is a noble goal and achievement. There are those who, with pride, can tell you how many times they have done it. According to the book of Acts, a young preacher named Philip encountered an Ethiopian eunuch reading the scriptures. He asked him if he understood what he was reading. Keep in mind that the most important thing is not just reading the Bible or how many times you have read the Bible from cover to cover. What matters is our understanding of what we read and how we are applying what we read to our lives. Reading the Bible in part or whole is not the same as obeying God's Word and living its message.

God's Word: Let the message of Christ dwell among you richly as you teach and admonish one another with all wisdom through psalms, hymns, and songs from the Spirit, singing to God with gratitude in your hearts (Colossians 3:16).

Prayer: Father, give me understanding and a hunger and thirst for Your Word and a desire to live a life that is pleasing to You. Amen.

OCTOBER 27

POWER OF ETERNITY

I was amused by the story of a prospective house buyer who saw a "For Sale" sign in the front yard of an attractive home. Taking down the phone number, the interested party called the homeowner. A lady answered the phone and explained that the house belonged to her brother. She said, "He lives in another state, but he gave me the power of eternity."

Here on earth, we can only give others a "power of attorney," which enables them to legally function on our behalf. But when it comes to heavenly matters, only Jesus can give us the power of eternity. The life he offers comes with a guarantee that never ends. First Peter 1:3–4 explains it this way: "Praise be to the God and Father of our Lord Jesus Christ! In his great mercy, he has given us new birth into a living hope through the resurrection of Jesus Christ from the dead, and into an inheritance that can never perish, spoil or fade. This inheritance is kept in heaven for you, who through faith are shielded by God's power until the coming of the salvation that is ready to be revealed in the last time."

Have you received the power of eternity that only Christ provides?

God's Word: I give them eternal life, and they shall never perish; no one will snatch them out of my hand. My Father, who has given them to me, is greater than all; no one can snatch them out of my Father's hand. I and the Father are one (John 10:28–30).

Prayer: Father, thank you for the security that is mine through Jesus Christ who died for my sins, rose again, and who gives me eternal life. Amen.

OCTOBER 28

DON'T WORRY, BE HAPPY!

Bobby McFerrin's song, "Don't Worry, Be Happy!" evolved from a time of stress and tension in the singer's life. In an exceedingly difficult time, it dawned upon Bobby that unhappiness, anxiety, and worry were counterproductive. Using his creativity, he wrote a song that became popular and offers wisdom and good common sense.

Face the facts, as Bobby McFerrin did. Worry drains your energy, robs you of joy, reduces your effectiveness, and can even give you ulcers or heart disease. Singing "Don't Worry, Be Happy" always helps in difficult times. Bobby's song will put a smile on your face, and putting it into practice will make your day. The words "don't worry, be happy" are not found in the Bible, but the message is clear.

With the Christians at Philippi facing persecution, division, and uncertainty, apostle Paul wrote words of encouragement: "Rejoice in the Lord always, I will say it again: Rejoice! Let your gentleness be evident to all. The Lord is near. Do not be anxious about anything, but in every situation, by prayer and petition with thanksgiving, present your requests to God. And the peace of God, which transcends all understanding, will guard your hearts and your minds in Christ Jesus" (Philippians 4:4–7).

God's Word: Who of you by worrying can add a single hour to your life? Since you cannot do this very little thing, why do you worry about the rest? (Luke 12:25–26).

Prayer: Father, help me not to succumb to the foolishness of worry but rather fill me with faith so that I can rejoice in the Lord. Amen.

OCTOBER 29

THE ROAD LESS TRAVELED

Robert Frost wrote a poetic masterpiece entitled "The Road Not Taken." The poem describes a traveler who comes to a fork in the road requiring him to decide which way he will go. After evaluating his options, the traveler makes his choice. As he begins his journey on the road less traveled, he discovers the significant difference it makes in his life.

The Bible says there are two roads in life—the broad road that leads to destruction and the narrow road that leads to life. Sadly, the Bible says that there are more people on the road to destruction than on the road to life. The road to destruction leads to eternal separation from God, while the road to life leads to eternity with God. One is called hell, and the other is called heaven. Which road have you chosen?

God's Word: Enter through the narrow gate. For wide is the gate and broad is the road that leads to destruction, and many enter through it. But small is the gate and narrow the road that leads to life, and only a few find it (Matthew 7:13–14).

Prayer: Father, you have told us to take the road less traveled. Give me the wisdom to listen and obey. Amen.

OCTOBER 30

A JOB OR A CALLING

Read Proverbs 22:13, and put your imagination to work. You might find help in discovering whether what you do is a calling or just a job. Imagine the lazy man who wakes up one morning and sees a lion outside. He tells his wife about it. She looks out the window and sees no lion at all. By this time the children, in excitement and fear, are also looking out the window, but they don't see a lion either. The lazy man doesn't want to get out of the house, and he certainly has no drive to go to work. So, he reasons that with the lion in the street he would probably be killed. Therefore, he goes back to bed.

If you have an occasional morning when you get up and don't want to go to work, that may be normal. But if that same feeling hits you every morning you wake up, there is a problem. The heart of the matter could be that you have a job, not a calling.

If your daily work is just a job, you are in no hurry to get there, and when you are on the job you are in a hurry to get home. But if what you do is a calling, there is joy in doing it. There is fulfillment in doing something important, useful, and beneficial to others. If what you are doing is a calling, you can no more help doing it than you can help breathing. When you are called to the thing you do, you never consider it work. It is sheer pleasure. It is not even a sacrifice. It is a labor of love.

God's Word: So I saw that there is nothing better for a person than to enjoy their work, because that is their lot (Ecclesiastes 3:22).

Prayer: Father, help me to see what I do as a calling and not as a job. May my work be pleasing to You, fulfilling to me, and beneficial to others. Amen.

OCTOBER 31

HIDDEN

Working with computers can sometimes be frustrating and intimidating. When a computer is working well it is a fantastic tool. When it is down, crashes, or seems to lose your material, it can be devastating. Having experienced the negative side of computers, my secretary put a sign above her desk that said, "Do what I tell you!"

After hours of working on a special project, I accidentally hit the wrong key and all my hard work vanished from sight. Not being computer savvy, I panicked. "My time has been wasted; my work is lost," I thought. Fortunately, with a guidebook for dummies, I recovered my project. My computer experience helped me to understand how God must feel when, for all practical purposes, we just vanish from our usefulness to Him. It's not that God doesn't know where to find us. Remember His walk in the Garden of Eden when Adam and Eve had sinned and were trying to hide? God knew where they were. God was not only grieved by their disobedience; He was grieved because Adam and Eve didn't want to be found. Can you identify with them? Can you feel God reaching out to you?

God's Word: The Lord is not slow in keeping his promise, as some understand slowness. Instead he is patient with you, not wanting anyone to perish, but everyone to come to repentance (2 Peter 3:9).

Prayer: Father, forgive me when I sin and try to hide from your presence. Help me to know that it is not Your will for me to ever be separated from You. Help me to quickly confess my sins and seek Your forgiveness. Amen.

NOVEMBER 1

WHO IS SERVANT TO WHOM?

Are you guilty of making plans and then asking God to bless you? Shouldn't you ask for God's guidance before you make plans? Likewise, do you find yourself getting into difficulty and then asking God to get you out? We make a major mistake in life when we fail to consult God before we make our plans. God does not exist to please, serve, or bless us. Rather, we exist to serve God, whether we recognize it or not.

We get into trouble by ignoring God, by shutting Him out of our lives, by not consulting Him before we plow ahead fulfilling our own desires. Because we shut God out of our decision-making, we plan things and do things that are often contrary to His will.

Until we understand that God is God, and we are His servants, we will continue to make bad decisions. Don't expect God's blessings on things you plan and do if you have not consulted Him. Acknowledge Him as Lord of Lords and King of Kings and seek His permission and guidance before you move ahead.

God's Word: Submit yourselves, then, to God. Resist the devil, and he will flee from you. Come near to God and he will come near to you. Wash your hands, you sinners, and purify your hearts, you double-minded. Grieve, mourn and wail. Change your laughter to mourning and your joy to gloom. Humble yourselves before the Lord, and he will lift you up (James 4:7–10).

Prayer: Father, forgive my presumption when I make decisions without consulting You. Help me to understand that Your blessings are available when I am doing Your will and not my own. Amen.

NOVEMBER 2

NEVER GIVE UP

Larry King tells the story of baseball great, Ty Cobb, who at the age of seventy was asked by a reporter, "What do you think you'd hit if you were playing these days?" Cobb's lifetime batting average was .367. He responded to the reporter by saying "About .290, maybe .300." The reporter inquired, "That's because of travel, the night games, the artificial turf, and all the new pitches like the slider, right?" "No," said Cobb, "it's because I'm seventy."

At seventy or eighty you may not be able to match the achievements of younger years, but you don't have to give up. The most inspiring senior citizens I know are those who still have the heart to be in the game—to give life the best they can.

A strong personal relationship with God makes life worthwhile at any age. Some of the most significant achievements made in life have occurred in senior years. Knowing God's constant care, don't quit life before it's over. My mother-in-law, Alma Little, got it right in her senior years. She said, "I'm going to live until I die!" She did! Amen.

God's Word: The righteous will flourish like a palm tree, they will grow like a cedar of Lebanon; planted in the house of the Lord, they will flourish in the courts of our God. They will still bear fruit in old age, they will stay fresh and green, proclaiming, "The Lord is upright; he is my Rock, and there is no wickedness in him" (Psalm 92:12–14).

Prayer: Father, thank you that our usefulness to you lasts even into our golden years. When we can no longer do what we were able to do in our younger years, we can find ways to serve and honor you as long as we live. Amen.

NOVEMBER 3

GOD'S WAY

Numbers 20:8 tells of God instructing Moses to "speak to that rock ... and it will pour out its water." But instead of speaking to the rock, "Moses raised his arm and struck the rock twice with his staff" (v. 11). Water gushed from the rock, but God rebuked Moses for his disobedience. "The Lord said to Moses and Aaron, 'Because you did not trust in me enough to honor me as holy in the sight of the Israelites, you will not bring this community into the land I give them." (v. 12). God's punishment was quick and decisive.

Why do we not realize that it is always best to do things God's way? "I'll do it my way!" is the downfall of many. How many times have you "done things your way," and suffered greatly because you did not follow God's instructions?

A young girl confessed to her pastor that she had experienced a great deal of trouble, and most of it she had brought upon herself. Have you experienced the same thing? What will it take for you to begin to do things God's way? The Bible is God's Word of instruction to us. Ignore it and you will bring much grief into your life. Follow His Word, and whatever the outcome, God will be honored, and you will receive the blessing.

God's Word: Walk in obedience to all that the Lord your God has commanded you, so that you may live and prosper and prolong your days in the land that you will possess (Deuteronomy 5:33).

Prayer: Father, remind me every day that obedience to your Word brings blessings whereas doing things my way gets me into trouble. Amen.

NOVEMBER 4

BE PREPARED

Students sometimes feel that they will be in school forever and will never be able to get on with their lives. Abraham Lincoln is reported to have said, "I will study and get ready, and my day will come." He did, and he was right. To this day Lincoln is revered and considered one of the greatest presidents the United States has ever had. Do not neglect preparation, whether in your school studies or the requirements of your job. Preparation is a lifelong challenge and requirement. "Be Prepared," is more than a Boy Scout motto; it is essential to success.

When God called Saul to be his spokesman to the Gentiles, He did more than change his name to Paul. He required that he spend three years in preparation for the assignment. Jesus, the Son of God, was sent by the heavenly Father to be the Savior of the world, but do not forget that he spent thirty years in preparation for his three years of ministry. Do your best today, prepare, get ready, and you won't have to worry about success tomorrow.

God's Word: Go to the ant, you sluggard; consider its ways and be wise (Proverbs 6:6)!

Prayer: Father, teach me the discipline of preparation so that when the right opportunity comes my way, I'll be able to meet the challenge. Amen.

NOVEMBER 5

UTTERLY SINCERE

Most people shy away from perfection, and those who try to achieve it usually end up frustrated. "What's the use," we say. "We can never be perfect." Perfection is the one quality that keeps people from having a close relationship with God or even attempting a relationship with Him.

The English translation of the Bible may be at fault here. We read scripture that says, "Be perfect, therefore, as your heavenly Father is perfect," (Matthew 5:48) or "Blessed are the pure in heart" (Matthew 5:8). It's our modern understanding of "perfect" and "pure," that throws us. Substitute the words "complete," and "utterly sincere," for "perfect," and "pure," and you get a clearer picture of what Jesus requires of us. God does not require of us the impossible. And what He requires of us, He equips and enables us to achieve.

God does not require us to live flawlessly. It is not our ability that impresses Him but rather our availability. When we allow God to take control of our lives, then, and only then, can He achieve the impossible through us. We're not perfect, just forgiven. In God's hands, incredible possibilities exist.

God's Word: "Can I not do with you Israel, as this potter does?" declares the Lord, "Like clay in the hand of the potter, so are you in my hand, Israel" (Jeremiah 18:6).

Prayer: Father, help me to understand that the experiences in my life are molding me and shaping me to be the person You want me to be. You are the Potter; I am the clay, and don't let me forget it. Amen.

NOVEMBER 6

GRACE GIVING

How acceptable are you to change? For example, when you come face-to-face with a Bible truth, are you willing to change your way of doing things for God's way? Stubbornness and a rebellious spirit rob us of the blessings that God wants us to have. Obedience, on the other hand, brings joy, peace, and fulfillment.

One of our stubborn areas of resistance to God's Word is in our giving. The Old Testament taught that we are to give a tenth of our income to God. The New Testament teaches that we are to give in proportion to what we have received. In other words, more than a tenth. Giving to God can be categorized in three ways: a contribution, a tithe, or an offering. A contribution is usually a token gift that doesn't come near the tithe. A tithe, of course, means 10 percent of our income. An offering is above and beyond the tithe. As Christians, we should be showing our love and appreciation to God by giving an offering. Giving beyond a contribution or tithe is grace giving. Better yet, try increasing the percentage of your giving each year.

Remember that God is a God of grace. Therefore, those who commit to "grace giving" usually don't have difficulty obeying in other areas of their lives.

God's Word: "Bring the whole tithe into the storehouse, that there may be food in my house. Test me in this," says the Lord Almighty, "and see if I will not throw open the floodgates of heaven and pour out so much blessing that there will not be room enough to store it" (Malachi 3:10).

Prayer: Father, to obey You is to allow Your truth to be lived out in my life. Help me to grow in my faithfulness. Amen.

NOVEMBER 7

PRAYER DIFFERENCE

There is a startling contrast between the way Christians today pray and how Christians of the New Testament prayed. Christians today pray for their burdens to be lifted, their problems to be removed, and relief from pain. New Testament Christians prayed for strength to bear their burdens, confront their problems, and endure their pain.

The Bible never teaches that life will be free from suffering, problems, or pain. Jesus was clear: "In this world you will have trouble" (John 16:33). Dr. Frank Means, our supervisor when we were missionaries in Brazil, said in a devotional message, "There is strength in struggle." First-century Christians knew that truth and lived it. They never prayed to be relieved of trials and tribulations but rather that through their troubles they would bring glory to God.

Suffering gives us an identity with Christ. Those who pay the price know, as apostle Paul, that God's grace is sufficient, and the reward for faithfulness has no comparison on earth.

God's Word: I was given a thorn in my flesh, a messenger of Satan, to torment me. Three times I pleaded with the Lord to take it away from me. But he said to me, "My grace is sufficient for you, for my power is made perfect in weakness" (2 Corinthians 12:7–9).

Prayer: Father, when my requests for relief are denied, help me to know your grace and to let others see Jesus in me through my suffering. Amen.

NOVEMBER 8

GENUINE OR COUNTERFEIT

Canadian-born Henry Blackaby, whose "Experiencing God" studies are known around the world, tells how the Royal Canadian Mounted Police are trained in identifying counterfeit money. A trainee never sees a counterfeit bill. They study the genuine bill so thoroughly that anything that does not measure up to that which is genuine is counterfeit.

Christians should apply the same principle in following Jesus Christ. We must be able to identify false teachings, twisted doctrines, human opinions, modified Christian teachings, and any conduct or action that does not measure up to biblical standards. Sadly, many who call themselves Christians find themselves agreeing to and promoting the very things that Christ condemns. One who focuses on Jesus should not have a problem quickly identifying evil or compromising with the devil. The Bible says: "By their fruit you will recognize them" (Matthew 7:16). Any teaching, belief, lifestyle, or conduct that does not hate the things that God hates and love the things that God loves is counterfeit and should be avoided at all costs.

God's Word: For the time will come when people will not put up with sound doctrine. Instead, to suit their own desires, they will gather around them a great number of teachers to say what their itching ears want to hear. They will turn their ears away from the truth and turn aside to myths. But you, keep your head in all situations (2 Timothy 4:3–4).

Prayer: Father, help me to live so close to you and Your Word that I quickly identify anything that is counterfeit and contrary to Your teaching. Amen.

PERSEVERANCE

On a Florida track race, a fine athlete came within one second of breaking the state record in the mile run. The workers started to set up the hurdles for the next race when a judge spotted a runner coming toward the finish line. The runner staggered across the finish line and fell in exhaustion. The judge asked him why he was in the race. He explained that their top athlete was sick, and the coach promised to have someone in the race. "But why didn't you just drop out?" the judge asked. To which the last runner replied, "They sent me here to finish the mile race, and I did."

If you are prone to give up before you finish the task, remember—to be successful, you don't have to win; you just must finish the race. Perseverance is the key to success.

God's Word: I know your deeds, your love and faith, your service and perseverance, and that you are now doing more than you did at first (Revelation 2:19).

Prayer: Father, in serving You, help me to understand that it is not important for me to win or lose, to succeed or fail but rather to be faithful to Your call—to persevere to the finish line. Amen.

WORKING TOGETHER

Two men working for a moving company were struggling with a big crate in a doorway. They pushed and tugged until they were both exhausted, but the crate wouldn't move. Finally, the man on the outside said, "We'd better give up, we'll never get this crate inside." His coworker on the inside said, "What do you mean get it inside, I thought you were trying to get it out."

In working with others, it is important that you understand what you are doing and to assure your fellow worker that you are working with, not against, him or her. Little is accomplished when people fail to work together. Miracles happen when people pull together for a common cause.

Happy are those who are part of the solution and not part of the problem. Happy are those who make the work of others easier when people see a need and work together to meet it, when people see a wound and join to heal it. Are you a stepping-stone or a stumbling block? Are you working for the team or against it?

God's Word: Woe to the world because of the things that cause people to stumble! Such things must come, but woe to the person through whom they come *(*Matthew 18:7)!

Prayer: Father, help me to work for the good of others, to help rather than hinder, to make the burden of my fellowman lighter rather than heavier, to be a solution to solving problems rather than an obstacle. Amen.

NOVEMBER 11

NEGATIVE THINKING

If you are a negative thinking person you have either been programed by your environment or you have chosen to be that way. As a pastor, I have watched negative and positive powers at work in the lives of numerous individuals. I once spent two hours in the home of the most bitter man I ever knew. There was no good he could see in anyone. In the course of time, his negative attitude had turned his life into a raging fire of hatred, prejudice, and jealousy destroying friendships and even the love and devotion of his wife and children. I was so drained from that visit, I found a quiet place and stayed there for hours talking to God. I prayed for the man with the negative spirit and those whose lives had been damaged by it.

On the positive side, I have seen individuals whose family situation was deeply stained by drugs, crime, immorality, dishonesty, divorce, and trauma. Yet, they maintained a positive attitude and strong faith in God. By their demeanor and warm smile, you would never know the burden of their heart.

A negative attitude can play havoc on your mind and on the lives of those closest to you. We can choose to be positive or negative. So, choose to be positive. Think positively. Think with gratitude.

God's Word: All the days of the oppressed are wretched, but the cheerful heart has a continual feast (Proverbs 15:15).

Prayer: Father, knowing how destructive negative thinking is and how distasteful it is to others, help me to choose to think positively as I face the challenges of life. Amen.

CHASING THINGS

Have you ever desired something so badly that you could not get it out of your mind? If so, you find yourself sacrificing everything you have to fulfill your desire. I read of a dog who liked to chase cars. Try as he would, his owner could not break him of the habit. One day, the dog took on an antique 1938 Chevy. He caught it, held on to it, and then didn't know what to do with it. Before he could decide to turn loose, the car had critically injured him.

Sometimes our pursuit of material things is so strong that once we have the desire of our heart in hand, we discover that what we longed for, wanted so badly, and sacrificed to obtain is not what we thought it would be. We discover too late that what we wished for so desperately doesn't satisfy at all. In fact, once obtained, we wish that we didn't have it.

Be careful what you chase. It might disappoint you, critically injure you, or fatally wound you.

God's Word: If you do what is right, will you not be accepted? But if you do not do what is right, sin is crouching at your door: it desires to have you, but you must rule over it (Genesis 4:7).

Prayer: Father give me the wisdom to make wise choices so that I pursue things that are good for me and not harmful or destructive. Amen.

NOVEMBER 13

EXCLUDING GOD

According to a 1993, *US News and World Report*, six thousand world religious leaders from 125 faith traditions met in Chicago the week of September 6 and reduced the Ten Commandments to four. The deliberations of Buddhists, Roman Catholics, Zoroastrians, and even devotees of witchcraft resulted in the signing of a Declaration of Global Ethics two years in the making and involving more than one hundred theologians. The resulting commandments are:

> Thou shall not kill
> Thou shall not steal
> Thou shall not lie
> Thou shall not commit sexual immorality

In greater detail, violence, environmental destruction, poverty, hunger, sexual discrimination, aggression, and hatred in the name of religion are condemned. But there is one glaring omission to these four commandments—God is left out![19]

Whether it is God's Ten Commandments or the four commandments of religious leaders, if God is not included, the effort to incorporate them into daily living is useless. Without God, not even six thousand or ten thousand religious leaders can make it work.

God's Word: Woe to the obstinate children, declares the Lord, to those who carry out plans that are not mine, forming an alliance, but not by my spirit, heaping sin upon sin ... without consulting me (Isaiah 30:1–2).

---

[19] *US News & World Report*, September 13, 1993, 14.

Prayer: Father, You warn us in scripture not to add or take away from Your Word. When we fail to include You in our thinking and our conclusions, we miserably fail. Help us Lord to see the evil in ignoring You and the futility to work out a better plan. Amen.

NOVEMBER 14

ON DIETING

Have you noticed the inconsistencies in all the talk about dieting? While waiting in a doctor's office, I picked up a woman's magazine and discovered that half of the magazine talked about dieting while the other half gave recipes that work against dieting. The subject of dieting in America is almost a joke. As one man put it, "I went on a diet of polyunsaturated oils for two months. I didn't lose any weight," he said, "but I don't squeak anymore."

Eating in moderation allows you to enjoy more foods with less stress and still keep your weight down. Discipline yourself to eat smaller portions, cut fat, and walk two to three miles four or five times a week. Taking care of our bodies is essential to better health. The Bible teaches that our bodies are the temple of God. Take extra care of God's temple.

God's Word: Don't you know that you yourselves are God's temple and that God's Spirit dwells in your midst? If anyone destroys God's temple, God will destroy that person; for God's temple is sacred, and you together are that temple (1 Corinthians 3:16–17).

Prayer: Father, help me to recognize the sacredness of my body and keep it holy. Amen.

NOVEMBER 15

GOOD NEWS FOR BAD NEWS

Doctors, nurses, pharmacists, policemen, counselors, lawyers, and ministers probably hear more about human affliction than many other professions. We can be grateful that God calls and gifts individuals who find fulfillment in meeting human needs.

Bad news abounds, but we do not have to be bound by it. Trials, tribulations, and sins flourish, but there is a God who has an answer for man's greatest difficulties. There is a great need for Christians to serve in professions that make a difference in people's lives. Christians can point others to a loving God and provide "good news" for those with "bad news." To those with "bad news," Christians are messengers of Christ, like the angels who appeared to the shepherds on a hillside saying, "I bring you good news that will cause great joy for all the people" (Luke 2:10).

God's Word: For we are to God the pleasing aroma of Christ among those who are being saved and those who are perishing (2 Corinthians 2:15).

Prayer: Father, in a world of bad news, help me to faithfully proclaim the good news of Jesus Christ and his power to save us from our sins and to give us a purpose for living. Amen.

NOVEMBER 16

PERSPECTIVE

Two special pictures hang on my study wall proving that two people can see the same picture differently and both can be right. In reality, there are two pictures in each one, and only those who are willing to spend the extra time can see them.

Taking a glance, one picture looks like a page of ink dots. A closer look reveals an artist's painting of the face of Jesus. The second picture, upon first glance, is that of a skull. Looking deeper, one can clearly see a woman sitting in front of her dresser. The difference in what each picture reveals is in the eye of the viewer.

The lesson we need to learn is that things are not always as they seem. The obvious that we see at first glance becomes entirely different with a deeper look. Never judge on first impressions. Look deeper before you come to a conclusion. Life is more than what appears on the surface, more than we can see or touch. The most important things in life cannot be handled, only felt and experienced—like love, joy, and peace.

God's Word: People look at the outward appearance, but the Lord looks at the heart (1 Samuel 16:7).

Prayer: Father, my perceptions are often inaccurate and lead me to the wrong conclusions. Open my eyes to see the truth and guard me against the deception of first impressions. Amen.

SIGNIFICANT PEOPLE

In every life there are significant people who influence us, encourage us, and push us to be better. These angels, often unawares, make the difference in our success or failure. They are people who share their lives with us, listen to our troubles, counsel us when we need guidance, encourage us when we are depressed, and correct us when we are wrong. Significant people in our lives challenge us when we are weak, visit us when we are sick, comfort us when we are sad, and instill within us courage when we are afraid.

Take time today to think of those significant individuals who have made a difference in your life. Give them a call, write them a letter, email, or text them expressing your appreciation for the impact they have made on your life. And when you pray, thank God for putting these significant people in your path.

God's Word: I thank my God every time I remember you. In all my prayers for all of you, I always pray with joy (Philippians 1:3).

Prayer: Father, thank You for those You have placed in my life in a significant way. I am a better person because of their influence. Thank You for who they are and for the difference they have made in my life. Amen.

NOVEMBER 18

VISION

On this date in 1620, 120 Saints, as they called themselves, landed on the northeastern shore of what is now America. They came seeking relief from religious oppression in England and with a desire to build a church. The first year they established a townsite. The second year, they elected a government. The third year, the town government began to build a road five miles into the wilderness. In the fourth year, the citizens impeached the town officials for wasting public funds on a road into the wilderness.

Think about the irony of such impeachment. Here was a people who had the vision to see new life three thousand miles across the Atlantic Ocean, but in four years were unable to see five miles out of town. They had lost their pioneering vision.

Without vision, people wander in darkness and accomplish little. Whatever your vision, hold on to it. Don't give up. Don't stop even when you achieve your goal as did those early pilgrims. Those who lose sight of new opportunities shrivel up and die as God's Word illustrates.

God's Word: Commit to the Lord whatever you do, and he will establish your plans (Proverbs 16:3).

Prayer: Father, open my eyes that I might see the possibilities of the future under Your leadership. Give me faith and vision to see that with You nothing is impossible. Amen.

COUNT YOUR BLESSINGS

Traditionally, we think of Thanksgiving in November. But we should have "thanksgiving" on our minds every month and every day of the year. When I was in the sixth grade, our class presented a play in which we sang:

> "Count your many blessings, name them one by one.
> Count your many blessings, see what God has done.
> Count your blessings, name them one by one,
> and it will surprise you what the Lord has done."

It is hard to count your blessings and complain at the same time. Counting blessings focuses our mind on positive things that are happening in our lives. Counting blessings will put a smile on your face, joy in your heart, and a prayer of praise on your lips to God, who is the giver of every good and perfect gift.

Why not pause right now and focus on the blessings you have received. Then breathe a prayer of thanks to God.

God's Word: Rejoice always, pray continually, give thanks in all circumstances; for this is God's will for you in Christ Jesus (1 Thessalonians 5:16).

Prayer: Father, I am so blessed to have You in my life and to have salvation through Jesus Christ who died on the cross to save me from my sins. Give me a grateful heart, and let my life sing alleluia in everything I do. Amen.

NOVEMBER 20

TODAY

There are two days of the week for which we should never worry—yesterday and tomorrow! Yesterday has passed forever. It cannot be recalled. Tomorrow may be filled with possibilities or disappointments, but you do not have it yet. Tomorrow may never come.

The only day left to us is today. It is called "the present" because it is a gift from God. So, take advantage of today. Live today to its fullest. Do what is right. Do what is good. Be faithful to your task today and make the best of it. Fulfill your responsibility today. Think noble thoughts; do noble deeds. Appreciate what you have. Be grateful for your blessings. Today, God will help you in your work. He will help carry your burden. He will guide your path. As for yesterday and tomorrow, leave that to God. Embrace God's help. Make the best of today. Today is all you have!

God's Word: Let us rejoice today and be glad (Psalm 118:24).

Prayer: Father, help me to take full advantage of today, leaving yesterday and tomorrow in your hands. Amen.

NOVEMBER 21

ON GIVING

A New England couple found themselves in a divorce court where the husband told the judge that he wanted a divorce because all his wife ever wanted from him was money. The aggravated spouse told the judge, "My wife hounds me for money morning, noon and night, and I'm sick and tired of listening to her." The judge was feeling some sympathy for the distraught husband when he asked, "And what does your wife do with the money?" To which the husband replied, "I don't rightly know judge; I ain't given her none yet!"

Some folk get pretty upset when their church asks them for money when in reality they have given nothing or very little. Sometimes those who give the least want the largest say in how the church spends money. They know nothing of the joy of giving and certainly receive none of the blessings. Tithes and offerings are part of worshipping God. How can we expect His daily blessings and feel no obligation to return a portion to Him?

God's Word: Give and it will be given to you. A good measure, pressed down, shaken together and running over, will be poured into your lap. For the measure you use, it will be measured to you (Luke 6:38).

Prayer: Father, let me experience the joy of giving back to You a portion of the blessings You have bestowed upon me. There is no way that I can outgive You, and there is no end to the joy that giving brings to my heart. Amen.

IS CHURCH MEMBERSHIP NECESSARY?

You may have asked, "Can I be a Christian without being a member of the church? The answer is simple: yes! Church membership does not save you nor does it guarantee you a place in heaven. The thief on the cross who asked Jesus to remember Him never belonged to a church. Yet, Jesus guaranteed Him a place in heaven.

While church membership is not essential to salvation, it is critical to our spiritual growth and development. A Christian separated from the body of Christ is like a football player without a team, a salesman without customers, a seaman without a ship, a businessman on a deserted island, a bee without a hive, or a musician without an instrument.

Your witness will be more effective, your service to God will be more enjoyable, your spiritual growth will be greater and your life, in general, will be more blessed by being a full part of the church. Being a member of a church provides identity, fellowship, support, a sense of belonging, and the enrichment of life. An arm or leg doesn't function well apart from the body.

God's Word: And let us consider how we may spur one another on toward love and good deeds, not giving up meeting together, as some are in the habit of doing, but encouraging one another—and all the more as you see the Day approaching (Hebrews 10:24–25).

Prayer: Father, help me to know the joy and enrichment of fellowship with fellow believers in a church family and the effectiveness of working together for Your glory. Amen.

NOVEMBER 23

WHAT EVERY CHRISTIAN NEEDS

It was in the middle of the night, and the day before I had been asking God to give me a message for my congregation. The message came in the form of a dream and in such clarity that I thought I was preaching it. I woke up, got out of bed, and immediately went to my study to write down the points, fearing I would get up the next morning and not remember what I had just experienced.

The title of the message was in the form of a declaration—"What Every Person Needs." There were five points to the message:

1. Every person needs Jesus (John 14:6).
2. Every person needs peace in their heart (John 14:27).
3. Every person needs boldness in the Word (1 Thessalonians 2:2).
4. Every person needs wisdom in the work (James 3:17).
5. Every person needs purpose in the kingdom. (Philippians 3:10).

After writing down the points, I went back to bed and slept soundly. The next morning as I searched the scriptures, the key Bible verses listed above came to my attention.

The following Sunday, I delivered the fully developed message that God gave me through a dream that was an answer to prayer.

God's Word: As he spoke, the Spirit came into me and raised me to my feet, and I heard him speaking to me (Ezekiel 2:2).

Prayer: Father, help me to hear what You say. Give me faith and boldness to obey. Amen.

NOVEMBER 24

KNOW THYSELF

"Know thyself," is the response that Socrates gave Phaedrus in answer to why he had no time to rationally explain mythology or other far-flung topics. Socrates said, "But I have no leisure for them at all; and the reason, my friend, is this: I am not yet able, as the Delphic inscription has it, to know myself; so it seems to me ridiculous, when I do not yet know that, to investigate irrelevant things."

Knowing who you are could be one of the most difficult studies you ever undertake. A good starting point is the Bible. God's Word explains that we are made in the image of God and that we were made to have fellowship with Him. We were made to worship God and to serve Him. Saint Augustine, after a reckless, godless life, discovered the truth that everyone must acknowledge before they can truly know themselves. He said, "Thou hast made us for Thyself and our souls are restless till they find their rest in thee." Once we understand how we relate to God and how God relates to us, we can more easily figure out the rest.

God's Word: So God created mankind in his own image, in the image of God he created them; male and female he created them (Genesis 1:27).

Prayer: Father, it is logical and reasonable to understand that if You made me in Your image, I can never be true to the purpose for which I have been made apart from You. Help me to acknowledge that truth and devote my life to living for You. Amen.

NOVEMBER 25

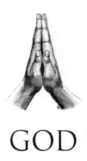

GOD

We fool ourselves if we try to take God out of our lives. Whether we acknowledge Him or not, we are dependent upon the blessings that He provides. How could we live without oxygen, water, food, shelter, sunshine, gravity, or a multitude of things provided by God that we take for granted?

In Psalm 14:1, we read: "The fool says in his heart, "There is no God." That same psalm goes on to ask, "Do all these evildoers know nothing?" (Psalm 14:4). Then comes the inescapable truth in verse 6: "You evildoers frustrate the plans of the poor, but the Lord is their refuge."

When the Constitutional Convention bogged down, Benjamin Franklin spoke about the "imperfections of human understanding," and that he was convinced of the importance of including God in their decisions. He said, "if a sparrow cannot fall to the ground without His notice, it is probable that an empire cannot rise without His aid."

God's Word: For since the creation of the world God's invisible qualities—his eternal power and divine nature—have been clearly seen, being understood from what has been made, so that people are without excuse (Romans 1:20).

Prayer: Father, all Your creation testifies to Your existence. Help me to open my eyes and behold Your majesty and be in awe of what You have created. Help me to acknowledge You as Lord of Lords and King of Kings and to serve You with all my being. Amen.

NOVEMBER 26

SUCCESS

Most people want to be successful. Successful people are not lazy. They do not waste time. Study the lives of successful people, and you will discover one common thread that ties their stories together—hard work. Your dreams will never be realized if you continue to sing in the shower or lounge on the couch. You must act, take risks, sweat, and labor long hours to achieve your goals. As the old saying goes, "Life doesn't come on a silver platter."

There is a difference between the world's view of success and God's view. The world views success in terms of possessions and wealth. God's view of success requires putting Him first, walking in faith and obedience, serving others, and storing up treasures in heaven. Everything associated with worldly success is temporary and can be taken away from you. Everything that is associated with God's view of success is eternal.

There is nothing wrong with being successful in this life. But we must be careful not to allow earthly success to become a priority over our relationship with God and desire to honor him with all our being.

God's Word: For everything in the world—the lust of the flesh, the lust of the eyes, and the pride of life—comes not from the Father but from the world. The world and its desires pass away, but whoever does the will of God lives forever (1 John 2:16–17).

Prayer: Father, keep my eyes focused on your view of success rather than the world's view. Amen.

LISTS

How many mailing lists are you on? Do you ever wonder how you get so much "junk mail"? If you ever respond to a questionnaire about products you use or give an opinion through a mail survey, you have exposed yourself to hundreds of special interests that pounce on you with "junk mail." When you subscribe to magazines or periodicals, your name and address are sometimes sold or shared with businesses without your permission or knowledge.

If "junk mail" is your thing, you might even pride yourself on being on so many lists. But the question comes to mind: "Are you on God's list?" Amid all the attention-grabbers, has God gotten your attention? God's plea for your attention is not "junk." Rather, it is a matter of eternal life or eternal separation from Him.

The message cries out to you through the Bible, through the circumstances of your life, through people you encounter, and through the life, death, and resurrection of His Son, Jesus Christ. While you may pride yourself on the number of mailing lists you are on, if you ignore being on God's list, you are in serious trouble.

God's Word: Anyone whose name was not found written in the book of life was thrown into the lake of fire (Revelation 20:15).

Prayer: Father, you have taken the initiative to reach out to all mankind with Your love and forgiveness. Help those who have ignored Your invitation to wake up before it is too late. Having our name on your book of life is the most important list of all. Amen.

NOVEMBER 28

YOUR TREASURE

During a children's sermon in one of our worship services, the leader showed the children a world globe. He asked if anyone knew where Saudi Arabia was. One bright five-year-old raised his hand and then to the astonishment of the leader and congregation pointed to the exact spot on the globe. The child had a special interest in Saudi Arabia because, you see, his daddy was there.

In like manner, God cares about each one of us and knows exactly where we are. We are his treasure—His special creation. There is little doubt that God would leave us in our trespasses and sins without attempting a rescue. The unique characteristic of God is that He always takes the initiative to reach out to us.

Remember the story that Jesus told about the shepherd who left the ninety and nine to search for one lost sheep? Jesus is the shepherd looking for sheep outside of His fold. Just as our heart is with those we love no matter where they may be, so God's heart is with us. Have you ever thought about the great treasure you are to God?

God's Word: Your Father in heaven is not willing that any of these little ones should perish (Matthew 18:14).

Prayer: Father, I stand amazed and humbled to know that I am treasured by You. My heart is filled with gratitude that You love me so much that You sent Your Son to die for my sins. Help my life to reflect my gratitude in thought, word, and deed. Amen.

NOVEMBER 29

ADVERSITY

Stress, conflict, adversity—we hear these words every day, but more dramatically we experience them. The holiday season from Thanksgiving to Christmas is an especially stressful time, in part because we make it that way. We tend to add on parties, get-togethers, and events that often have little or no focus on the real meaning of Christmas. Too much of what we plan is about ourselves rather than about Jesus.

It is also true that we tend to treat stress, adversity, and conflict as an enemy rather than a teacher. There are important lessons to be learned. Pearls are not made by ease and comfort but rather by irritation within the oyster. Most problems that we face are of our own doing and our own choices. On the surface, what we feel or experience can be overwhelming. But there is a God who is willing and ready to help us.

God gives us intelligence, faith, and friends to help and support in adversity. But most importantly, we have the Holy Spirit to walk with us through the storm. We are only overcome and defeated when we try to deal with stress, conflict, and adversity on our own instead of calling upon God to see us through.

God's Word: Do not be anxious about anything, but in every situation, by prayer and petition, with thanksgiving, present your requests to God. And the peace of God, which transcends all understanding, will guard your hearts and your minds in Christ Jesus (Philippians 4:6–7).

Prayer: Father, in this holiday season, help me to keep my priorities on bringing glory and honor to Your name. Help me reduce my stress and anxiety by allowing You to guide my decisions and activities so that I will experience your peace. Amen.

NOVEMBER 30

HELP YOUR PASTOR

Pastors qualify as firefighters, mechanics, referees, counselors, and advocates. Pastors spend a significant amount of time putting out fires, oiling squeaky wheels, keeping people out of each other's hair, keeping order, and negotiating conflicts, not counting their role as preachers and teachers.

Christians do not always conduct themselves in a Christlike manner. Personal opinions often take precedence over God's Word, and the devil likes nothing better than to stir up discord within the church. Pastors have a unique role in shepherding the sheep and keeping the flock together and safe.

Rather than criticize your pastor, pray for him. Rather than try to win him over to your side, pray that he will seek God's leadership in his personal life and church matters. When you hear people criticize your church or pastor, put in a positive word for him and the church and don't permit others to get by with half-truths or complete lies. Your pastor, like you, is called by God to uphold the faith, proclaim the gospel, and be a good and faithful ambassador of Christ. As Aaron held up the hands of Moses, take it upon yourself to help your pastor be the best spiritual leader he can be. Be incredibly careful how you treat God's anointed.

God's Word: Now we ask you, brothers and sisters, to acknowledge those who work hard among you, who care for you in the Lord and who admonish you. Hold them in the highest regard in love because of their work (1 Thessalonians 5:12–13).

Prayer: Father, as Aaron gave support to Moses, help me to be supportive and helpful to my pastor, recognizing that he has been called by You to be a spiritual leader. Amen.

DECEMBER 1

INCREDIBLE FACTS

My children gave me a fascinating book entitled *Incredible Facts*. The book is filled with architectural wonders, astonishing feats, botanical marvels, daredevils, extraordinary people, fascinating creatures, human oddities, incredible athletes, strange achievements, and wonders of nature.

Of all the incredible facts I have encountered in this fact-filled book, no fact is more incredible than the one we find in the Bible—the fact of God's amazing grace and love for sinners like you and me. It is absolutely beyond our imagination to understand how a God who made this vast universe could be personally interested in sinful creatures. Yet, He is. The psalmist must have had the same thoughts when he wrote, "What is mankind that you are mindful of them, human beings that you care for them?" (Psalm 8:3–4).

December is a good time to reflect upon God's amazing grace and love as we celebrate the birth of Jesus.

God's Word: I will give thanks to you, Lord, with all my heart; I will tell of all your wonderful deeds. I will be glad and rejoice in you; I will sing the praises of your name, O Most High (Psalm 9:1–2).

Prayer: Father, my feeble mind cannot grasp Your majesty, grace, and love. Thank You for loving me, a sinner, and for sending Your Son, Jesus, into the world to die for my sins. Amen.

DECEMBER 2

GOODNESS IS NOT SEASONAL

You may recall Willie in Eugene Field's classic poem, "Just Before Christmas." Willie admits to less than good behavior during the year but declares how good he is just before Christmas.

Parents, friends, a spouse, our children, and especially God deserve more from us than play-acting or pretending. Genuine goodness comes from the heart and from a proper relationship with God, not from selfish motivation to receive something we don't deserve.

The true spirit of Christmas, genuine goodness, is not seasonal—it is a lifestyle. If you are good only for a reward and not because of who you really are, your goodness is false and deceptive. You may fool other people sometimes, but you cannot fool God anytime.

God's Word: Do not be deceived: God cannot be mocked. A man reaps what he sows. Whoever sows to please their flesh, from the flesh will reap destruction; whoever sows to please the Spirit, will reap eternal life (Galatians 6:7–8).

Prayer: Father, help me to be genuine and be guided by Your Holy Spirit so that my love for You is reflected in my life. Guard me against selfishness and deception and help my desires and actions to be genuine. Amen.

DECEMBER 3

THE JERICHO ROAD

Jesus told the story of a man who was attacked and beaten on the Jericho Road and left for dead. A priest and a Levite passed by but offered no help. It was a despised Samaritan who saved the wounded man's life and paid for his care. We are all travelers on the Jericho Road. Life is filled with dangers. We never know when we might be wounded, disabled, or killed. Innocent people are often victims of violence. On the other hand, we never know when we might be able to assist a victim in distress.

Each of us must decide, and sometimes in an unexpected moment, whether we are going to be selfish or useful when a need arises. On the road we travel, we are either the victim, priest, Levite, or the Good Samaritan. On your Jericho Road, which one do you hope to be?

God's Word: Do nothing out of selfish ambition or vain conceit. Rather, in humility value others above yourselves, not looking to your own interests but each of you to the interests of others. In your relationships with one another, have the same mindset as Christ Jesus (Philippians 2:3–5).

Prayer: Father, as I travel the road of life, help me to be alert to the needs of others. Help me to be a Good Samaritan to those who may need my help. Amen.

DECEMBER 4

PRAY FOR CHILDREN

The Night of the Hunter is a compelling and frightening 1955 movie about a cruel stepfather, a murderous self-ordained preacher who has "L-O-V-E" tattooed on the knuckles of one hand and "H-A-T-E" tattooed on the knuckles of his other hand. Floating down a river in a skiff, to get away from him, the brother and sister reach the home of an old woman who was known to take in orphans. In the end, she kills the self-appointed preacher and says, "My soul is humbled when I see the way little ones accept their lot. Lord save the little children," she prays. "The winds blow and the rains are cold, yet they abide."

It's a dangerous world out there for little children. Millions are physically or verbally abused every year, abducted, kicked, beaten, stabbed, kidnapped, and killed. Millions of children around the world live on the streets and get caught up in gangs and prostitution, not to mention those caught in the horrors of war and famine. Additional millions a year are the victims of divorced parents. Pray for children and help them all you can.

God's Word: Let the little children come to me, and do not hinder them for the kingdom of heaven belongs to such as these (Matthew 19:14).

Prayer: Father, so many children in the world are mistreated and abused. Help me to be loving, kind, considerate, encouraging, and helpful to the children in my world. Amen.

DECEMBER 5

SNAKES AND SIN

It was just a small clipping in the *News and Observer* on August 23, 1992, and in a column one would hardly notice. Yet, it was the most profound article on the page. In Vancouver, Canada, Larry Moor, a snake handler, who founded a group to dispel the fear and misunderstanding of snakes, was bitten by his Egyptian cobra and died within minutes. In hundreds of lectures to children, Moor had pointed out that only a very small percentage of snakes are deadly. Ironically, the snake that bit him was in that small percentage.

Snakes are snakes, and they will do what snakes do. One who handles snakes must be willing to take the consequences of their actions. Likewise, those who entertain sin and play with sin must be prepared to take the consequences of sin. Sin is deadly. The Bible names seven deadly sins: lust, gluttony, greed, sloth or excessive laziness, wrath, envy, and pride. Jesus died on the cross to save us from sin's death, which is eternal separation from God. We should fear and avoid sin as much or more than we might fear a snake.

God's Word: But each person is tempted when they are dragged away by their own evil desire and enticed. Then, after desire has conceived, it gives birth to sin; and sin, when it is full-grown, gives birth to death (James 1:14–15).

Prayer: Father, help me to understand how deceptive and deadly sin is and why Jesus died on the cross to keep me from eternal separation from You. Amen.

DECEMBER 6

A HARDENED HEART

A hardened heart has been compared to ice that forms on a pond during a winter freeze. The thickening of the ice doesn't happen overnight. It is a hardening process that takes place over time.

We aren't born with hard hearts. There is not a more tender heart on earth than that of a baby or a little child. A hard heart is a spiritual condition, a sickness of the soul that only God can heal. In Matthew 13:15, Jesus described the calloused heart as coming from a mind closed to God and closed to the truth.

David, king of Israel, went through a period when his heart was hardened toward God because of his own personal sins. Fortunately, he recognized the spiritual vacuum that had developed, and he cried out to God for forgiveness. If you find your heart hardening toward your fellow man and God, it is not too late to repent.

God's Word: Have mercy on me, O God, according to your unfailing love; according to your great compassion blot out my transgressions. Wash away all my iniquity and cleanse me from my sin. For I know my transgressions, and my sin is always before me. Against you, you only, have I sinned and done what is evil in your sight (Psalm 51:1–4).

Prayer: Father, I can only echo David's prayer as I recognize my sins, confess them, and repent. Take away any hardness of my heart and restore me to a right relationship with You. Amen.

DECEMBER 7

GOD ANSWERS PRAYER

There is a portion of Psalm 61 in which David asks God to save his life. But his prayer wasn't just to save his life. He prayed for God to extend his life and restore him to his throne. But it wasn't just to extend his life and restore him to his throne. David asked God to enthrone him forever and protect him with love and faithfulness. David, of course, knew that he would not live on earth forever. He is asking God to let the royal line of David go on forever. It is a bold prayer.

Fast-forward a thousand years when the angel Gabriel told Mary that she had found favor with God and would give birth to a son that she would call Jesus, "He will be great and will be called the Son of the Most High. The Lord God will give him the throne of his father David (Luke 1:32).

The birth of Jesus is proof that God answers prayer even if it takes a thousand years. The one who prays may never see the answer to his prayer. But the one who prays can rest assured that God will answer prayer in His own time and in His own way.

God's Word: And if we know that He hears us—whatever we ask—we know that we have what we asked from Him (1 John 5:15).

Prayer: Father, thank You for hearing my prayers. Thank You for answering them according to Your plan and in Your time. Amen.

DECEMBER 8

GOD OF THE IMPOSSIBLE

God is God of the impossible. There are four powerful biblical examples of God doing the impossible in childbirth: Abraham and Sarah were well past the childbearing age when God gave them Isaac (Genesis 18). Hannah was barren, but God answered her prayer, and Samuel was born (1 Samuel 1). Zachariah and Elizabeth were well past childbearing age when their son, John, was born (Luke 1). And Mary was a virgin when the angel Gabriel told her that she would have a child that she would name Jesus (Luke 1:31).

We have in four women—Sarah, Hannah, Elizabeth, and Mary—four historical, documented childbirths giving testimony to God's ability to do the impossible. We need to drill that thought into our hearts and minds. There is no aspect of life where God is limited. Therefore, we must always pray believing.

God's Word: But when you ask, you must believe and not doubt, because the one who doubts is like a wave of the sea, blown and tossed by the wind. That person should not expect to receive anything from the Lord (James 1:6).

Prayer: Father, I know in my heart that there is nothing impossible for You. Help me to pray in faith, live in faith, and wait for You to respond. Amen.

DECEMBER 9

THE VOICE

The Gospel of John describes John the Baptizer as a witness to the light who is Jesus.

In comparison to God's Son, note that John was a voice; Jesus is the Word. John was a witness; Jesus is the Christ. John bore witness of the light; Jesus is the light. John is the friend of the Bridegroom; Jesus is the Bridegroom. John was beheaded; Jesus was crucified. John died a martyr; Jesus died a Savior who rose from the dead.

The prophet Isaiah predicted the ministry of John as "A voice of one calling: ... prepare the way for the Lord" (Isaiah 40:3–5). Through Jesus, the glory of the Lord was revealed in a way that human beings could understand.

God gave John the responsibility to prepare the way for the Lord and to get out of the way of the Lord. John the Baptist faithfully fulfilled God's purpose. As witnesses of Christ, we are to do the same.

God's Word: In the same way, let your light shine before others, that they may see your good deeds and glorify your Father in heaven (Matthew 5:16).

Prayer: Father, just as John the Baptizer was called to proclaim Christ, so am I called to share his love with others. Help me to be faithful to the calling. Amen.

DECEMBER 10

DREAMING OF A RIGHT CHRISTMAS

"I'm Dreaming of a White Christmas," written by Irving Berlin and memorialized by Bing Crosby in the 1942 movie *Holiday Inn*, features a New Yorker stranded in sunny California longing to be "up North" where it snows. With a slight twist of thought, rather than dreaming of a white Christmas, I'm dreaming of a "right Christmas."

A right Christmas makes room for Jesus. After all, it is His birthday. At Christmas, we make room for relatives and friends, gifts and parties, self-gain and self-gratification, but we miss the significance of Christmas if we make no room for Jesus.

A right Christmas includes worship. Worship is praise and thanksgiving to God for His unspeakable gift.

A right Christmas includes the grace of giving. God loves us so much that He gave His Son to die for our sins. Giving to God is an expression of our love and devotion. When we give ourselves to Him, everything we have is included.

A right Christmas involves telling others the story of Jesus and His love. We are commissioned by Jesus to go into all the world making disciples for Him.

God's Word: You are worthy, our Lord and God, to receive glory and honor and power, for you created all things, and by your will they were created and have their being (Revelation 4:11).

Prayer: Father, help me to have a right Christmas giving You the praise and glory for who You are and for what You have done to save us from our sins and give us eternal life. Amen.

DECEMBER 11

ODYSSEY

The word "Odyssey" might cause you to think about the very popular Honda van. To those of an earlier generation, "Odyssey" would call to mind the classic writing of Homer whose hero traveler spent twenty years returning home from the Trojan War. Odyssey experiences astonishing adventures in which he learns a great deal about the world and himself. Webster defines "odyssey" as "any long, complicated journey, often a quest for a goal." Odyssey may be a spiritual or psychological journey as well as an actual voyage.

Life is an odyssey, a journey with an astonishing number of adventures designed to teach us all about ourselves and the world we live in. Life is complicated, not simple, intriguing, not boring, mysterious, not easily understood The Bible helps us understand ourselves, the world in which we live, and the purpose and meaning that God put into life when he made us in His image. The Bible clearly defines us as spiritual beings who cannot be complete without a relationship with God. You can search the world over and never "find yourself" unless you understand that God made you for Himself. Until you surrender to Him, receive His forgiveness, and accept the eternal life that He offers, you will be forever lost.

God's Word: The Lord is not slow in keeping his promise, as some understand slowness. Instead he is patient with you, not wanting anyone to perish, but everyone to come to repentance (2 Peter 3:9).

Prayer: Father, when I struggle to understand the mystery of life and my purpose for being here, help me to see that only in You can I find myself. Only in You can I find peace and purpose. Amen.

DECEMBER 12

ZECHARIAH'S SONG

Remember Zechariah, the Jewish priest who lost his voice because he doubted the angel's news that he would be the father of a son who would be the forerunner of Jesus? Strangely enough, Zechariah had prayed for a son, but because he and Elizabeth were well past the childbearing age, he had given up hope.

Nevertheless, Elizabeth got pregnant and delivered a son. When Zechariah was asked what his son would be named, he said, "John." Then the miracle occurred, Zechariah was able to speak again. With his voice restored, he composed a "song of praise" recorded in Luke 1:67–79. It is a song of praise for God's faithfulness to His Word and the people. It is a song acknowledging his son John's role to "go on before the Lord to prepare the way for him" (Luke 1:76). Although Zechariah doubted that God would ever answer his prayer, his nine months as a mute and the actual birth of the promised son changed his life forever.

Do you have unanswered prayers? Remember Zechariah's song of praise and how God answered his prayer beyond his imagination.

God's Word: Therefore I tell you, whatever you ask for in prayer, believe that you have received it, and it will be yours (Mark 11:24).

Prayer: Father, help me to learn from Zechariah's experience that You are a God who answers prayer, and nothing is impossible for You. Help me to pray believing and not doubting. Amen.

JOHN THE BAPTIST

John the Baptist holds a unique place in history as the one who prepared the way for Jesus's ministry. He was without equal. Jesus said of him, "among those born of women there has not risen anyone greater than John the Baptist" (Matthew 11:11). In so many ways he was strange. He lived an isolated life in the desert and wore camel's hair for clothing, held together with a leather belt around his waist. He ate locusts and wild honey and appeared in public only when he had a message from God. He preached a message of repentance from sin and baptized people by immersion in the Jordan River and died a martyr's death, being beheaded by King Herod Antipas.

The truths that John the Baptist preached—the deity, the atonement, the kingdom, sin, repentance, baptism, confession of faith—are the foundation stones of Christian doctrine. Those truths were expanded by apostle Paul. It was John who declared the preexistence of Jesus: "He was before me" (John 1:15)! It was John who declared Jesus as "The Lamb of God" (John 1:36). It was John who called Jesus "the Son of God (John 1:34). The prophets prophesized Jesus coming, but John declared his presence.

For all his notoriety, John humbly accepted his role in God's plan for redemption. Blessed are those who know God's plan for their lives and who humbly exalt Jesus as did John the Baptist.

God's Word: He must become greater; I must become less (John 3:30).

Prayer: Father, as John the Baptist fulfilled his role in your kingdom plan, help me to be faithful to the calling you have given me. Amen.

DECEMBER 14

THE WORK OF CHRIST IN US

When I was pastor of First Baptist Church, Morehead City, North Carolina, Jim Sykes, chairman of the Pastor Search Committee that called me to that ministry, determined that I needed a hobby. Since his hobby was duck carving, he thought I ought to carve a duck. He convinced me that I could do it. So, I went over to Jim's shop where he handed me a duck he had carved. After I looked it over, he handed me a rectangular piece of wood and said, "Now your task is to shape this piece of wood into the image of this duck." Little by little he showed me how to cut away the big parts of wood and then with a sander and a special grinding tool to shape the head and body. With Jim's watchful eye and counsel, I saw my block of wood take on the image of a duck, and I found it to be quite an exciting experience.

God must find great joy in chipping away from our lives all that does not look like His Son Jesus. The more He shapes us, the closer we come to be like His Son. The more we become like His Son, the more joy we experience.

God's Word: And we all, who with unveiled faces contemplate the Lord's glory, are being transformed into his image with ever-increasing glory, which comes from the Lord, who is the Spirit (2 Corinthians 3:18).

Prayer: Father, in my struggles with life, help me to understand that you are molding and shaping me into the image of your Son, Jesus. Amen.

DECEMBER 15

CHRIST MAKES US ALIVE

In one of Charles Schulz's "Peanuts" cartoons, Lucy is philosophizing, and Charlie Brown is listening. She compares life to a deck chair where some people are looking at places they have been, and others are looking at what is around them. Charlie sighs and confesses that he can't even unfold his deck chair.

Christ has the power to unfold our chair—to bring us to life. He puts purpose and meaning into our lives. He gives us a reason to get up in the morning. He challenges us to look beyond ourselves and to be of service to others. He makes us alive so that we see the danger of sin. He makes us alive so that when we sin, we confess our sins and seek His forgiveness. He makes us alive so that we see needs and meet them in His name.

We are sinners for whom Christ shed His blood. He died and rose again to give us eternal life.

God's Word: In him was life, and that life was the light of all mankind. The light shines in the darkness, and the darkness has not overcome it (John 1:4).

Prayer: Father, You are light and life. Thank You for making me alive through Jesus Christ. Amen.

DECEMBER 16

BRINGING JOY TO JESUS

Christmas is usually too much focus on ourselves and too little focus on Jesus. We are guilty of thinking more about our joy during the holidays than bringing joy to Jesus. Today, I encourage you to think of ways that you can bring joy to Jesus.

We bring joy to Jesus when we accept the invitation to abide in Him. The word "abide" means to remain, to dwell, to last, and to endure. Jesus wants us to be with him, not just on Sunday but every day, here on earth and in eternity. We bring joy to Jesus when we bear fruit. Apostle Paul says, "But the fruit of the Spirit is love, joy, peace, forbearance, kindness, goodness, faithfulness, gentleness and self-control" (Galatians 5:22). This is the fruit the Holy Spirit produces in the life of one who abides in Christ. We bring joy to Jesus when we keep His commandments. Jesus said, "If you keep My commandments, you will remain in My love" (John 15:10). Our obedience brings joy to Jesus. We bring joy to Jesus when we serve others. James, the brother of Jesus, said, "Do not merely listen to the word and so deceive yourselves. Do what it says" (James 1:22). And Jesus said, "Truly I tell you, whatever you did for one of the least of these brothers and sister of mine, you did for me" (Matthew 25:40).

As you celebrate the coming of Jesus into the world, look for all the ways you can bring joy to Jesus.

God's Word: So we make it our goal to please him, whether we are at home in the body or away from it (2 Corinthians 5:9).

Prayer: Father, help me to bring joy to You, showing my love and gratitude for all that You have done for me. Amen.

DECEMBER 17

SIMPLE THINGS

Human beings have a way of complicating life when, in essence, God has made things simple. Over two thousand years ago, people looked for a Messiah to be born to royalty. Little wonder they missed Him who was born in a manger. Some looked for a military leader with the power to overthrow the Roman Empire. Little wonder they missed Him when He announced that His kingdom was not of this world.

Some people complicate the salvation process by trying to earn their way into heaven with good works. Jesus offers salvation freely through grace and by faith. Some people look for God in the spectacular and miss Him when He comes in a still small voice. God is majestic and awesome, but He comes to us in ways a little child can understand.

If you want to experience God, look for Him in simple ways and simple things.

God's Word: But God chose the foolish things of the world to shame the wise; God chose the weak things of the world to shame the strong. God chose the lowly things of this world and the despised things—and the things that are not—to nullify the things that are, so that no one may boast before Him (1 Corinthians 1:27–29).

Prayer: Father, thank You for revealing Yourself in simple ways. Amen.

DECEMBER 18

WHAT YOU GIVE COUNTS

Wheeling Gaunt, an ex-slave, was born in 1812. Just before he died in 1894, Wheeling deeded nine acres of land at the south edge of town to the village of Yellow Springs, Ohio, with instructions that the proceeds from the sale were to buy perpetual Christmas gifts for poor widows.

Little wonder that the widows of Yellow Springs hold a special place in their hearts for Wheeling Gaunt, a man they never knew personally. Each year at Christmas, just in time for holiday baking, every widow in Yellow Springs receives a present from Wheeling—ten pounds of flour and ten pounds of sugar.

As a slave, Wheeling Gaunt knew great hardship and personal abuse, but his suffering did not leave him bitter. On his gravestone are written the words, "Not What You Get, But What You Give."

God's Word: Remember this: Whoever sows sparingly will also reap sparingly, and whoever sows generously will also reap generously. Each of you should give what you have decided in your heart to give, not reluctantly or under compulsion, for God loves a cheerful giver (2 Corinthians 9:6–8).

Prayer: Father, help me to be a cheerful giver like Wheeling Gaunt and like You. Amen.

DECEMBER 19

HONESTY IN WORSHIP

Worship is as vital to our spiritual lives as food is to our physical well-being. How honest are you in your worship of God? "Let's take an inventory!

> We sing, "Sweet Hour of Prayer," but go for days without a serious prayer escaping our lips. We sing, "Onward Christian Soldiers," and then refuse to serve. We sing, "O For a Thousand Tongues to Sing," and don't use the one we have. We sing, "Throw Out the Lifeline," but spend our time throwing out the fishing line. We sing, "Cast Thy Burden Upon the Lord," but worry ourselves to death. We sing, "I'll Go Where You Want Me to Go," but sit at home. We sing, "Serve the Lord With Gladness," and then complain when we are asked to do something. We sing, "Bless Be the Tie That Binds," and then let the least little offense divide us. We sing, "I Love to Tell the Story," but never share our faith. We sing, "Trust and Obey," and fuss and delay.[20]

Let these thoughts help you reevaluate your worship of God!

God's Word: Come, let us bow down in worship, let us kneel before the Lord our Maker; for he is our God and we are the people of his pasture, the flock under his care (Psalm 95:6).

Prayer: Father, help me to worship You honestly with all my heart, mind, and soul. Amen.

---

[20] *Illustration Digest*, January-February 1992.

DECEMBER 20

LIVING IN A WHIRLWIND

In this Christmas Season, you may feel like you are living in a whirlwind. With decorations to put up, presents to buy, parties, errands to run, engagements, rehearsals, family responsibilities, Christmas programs, and worship services to attend, you find yourself overworked, overstressed, and exhausted with no time to relax.

Caught up in the whirlwind of life, we not only face the danger of having no time for ourselves but the greater danger of having no time for God. Being caught up in our celebrations and busyness can easily cause us to miss the real meaning of Christmas.

In a time of desperation, fear, and confusion, the prophet Elijah discovered that God was not in the whirlwind, earthquake, or fire but a still small voice. We are admonished to be still if we want to experience God. Without a quiet time, our holidays can quickly turn into trauma days. We must carve out time to worship God, to praise Him, and to find peace in Him while the storms of life rage around us.

Right now might be a good time to take a break and remind yourself that you will not find God in the whirlwind of life but rather in a quiet place where you can hear his gentle whisper.

God's Word: Be still, and know that I am God. (Psalm 46:10).

Prayer: Father, help me to step out of my whirlwind today by finding a place of solitude and quiet so that I can regain my perspective and experience the peace and calm that only you can give. Amen.

DECEMBER 21

MARY'S SONG

Never in a lifetime would a young girl from an obscure village in Nazareth expect to be visited by an angel and told that she was going to be the mother of God's Son, the Savior of the world. But that is exactly what happened to Mary. Mary's experience not only changed her life forever, but it changed the world. The song that came from her heart is recorded in the Gospel of Luke 1:46–55, and speaks of God's revolutionary, transforming power. It is called "The Magnificat."

Mary's song is filled with anticipation, excitement, joy, awe, and gratitude to God. She sang, "Holy is His name. His mercy extends to those who fear him, from generation to generation." Take time today to meditate on Mary's song and rejoice with her as she exclaims, "My soul glorifies the Lord and my spirit rejoices in God my Savior" (Luke 1:46–47).

God's Word: For the Mighty One has done great things for me—holy is his name (Luke 1:49).

Prayer: Father, let Mary's song remind me of the great things that You have done for me and for all who believe in Your name. Amen.

DECEMBER 22

SHEPHERDS

The role of shepherd was one of the most important occupations in ancient times. Yet, the task was often given to those considered the least important in the family. Was God trying to send a profound message about unconditional love when He commissioned angels to bring the good news of Jesus's birth to lowly shepherds? I think so.

On a hillside, outside of Bethlehem that glorious night, shepherds received the message from the angel. First, they were overcome with fear and awe. Who wouldn't be? But to their credit, the shepherds believed an almost unbelievable message. Their belief immediately turned into action as they went with haste to the manger where the Christ Child lay.

Acceptance of the Word, belief in the Word, and verifying the Word with their presence overwhelmed them with joy. "The shepherds returned, glorifying and praising God for all the things they had heard and seen, which were just as they had been told" (Luke 2:20).

There is always immense joy and reason to praise God when we are obedient to His Word. The joy grows when we share what we have experienced with others. Let the shepherds be your role model in hearing, believing, and putting your faith into action. In following their example, you will find great joy and fulfillment.

God's Word: When the angels had left them and gone into heaven, the shepherds said to one another, "Let's go to Bethlehem and see this thing that has happened which the Lord has told us about" (Luke 2:15).

Prayer: Father, help me to put my faith into action as did the shepherds so that I too can experience great joy and fulfillment in my life. Amen.

DECEMBER 23

A GOD WHO UNDERSTANDS

A store owner was putting a sign in his window that read "Puppies For Sale." A little boy, attracted by the sign, came in and asked the owner, "How much are you asking for the puppies?" The owner said, "anywhere from thirty to fifty dollars." The little boy reached in his pocket and pulled out some change. "I have $2.37," he said. "Can I please look at them?"

The owner smiled, whistled, and out of the kennel came Lady followed by five tiny balls of fur. One puppy was lagging way behind. Immediately the little boy singled out the limping puppy and asked, "What's wrong with this little dog?" The owner explained, "He doesn't have a hip socket, and he will always limp." The little boy excitedly exclaimed, "That's the puppy I want to buy!" "Son," the owner responded, "You don't want to buy that little dog. But if you really want him, I'll give him to you.

The little boy got upset. He looked the owner straight in the eye, pointed his finger, and said, "I don't want you to give him to me. That little dog is worth every bit as much as all the other dogs, and I'll pay full price. In fact, I'll give you $2.37 now and fifty cents a month until I have him paid for." The store owner countered. "You really don't want to buy this little dog. He's never going to be able to run and jump and play with you like the other puppies." To the owner's surprise, the little boy reached down and rolled up his pant leg to reveal a badly twisted, crippled leg supported by a metal brace. He looked at the owner and softly replied, "Well, I don't run so well myself, and this little puppy will need someone who understands."

You and I need someone who can understand us, and that is why God sent His Son into the world.

God's Word: You discern my going out and my lying down; you are familiar with all my ways (Psalm 139:3).

Prayer: Father, thank You for sending Your Son, Jesus, into the world because through Him, I am comforted and encouraged in knowing that You understand completely what it means to be human. Amen.

DECEMBER 24

A FULFILLED PROMISE

It's Christmas Eve, and tomorrow we celebrate the arrival of the long-awaited Jesus. Reflect upon the amazing way in which God fulfilled His promise. The first promise of a Savior was given to Satan, who had deceived Adam and Eve in the Garden of Eden. The promise came in God's pronouncement of judgment and defeat upon His archenemy. "I will put enmity between you and the woman, and between your offspring and hers; he will crush your head, and you will strike his heel" (Genesis 3:15).

It was God's way of letting us know that Jesus would suffer, but that Satan would be utterly defeated.

The promise continued to Abraham, who was told that he would be the father of the nation through whom the Savior would come. Jesus was born in Bethlehem through the royal line of David, king of Israel. The place of His birth was foretold by the prophet Micah. The time of His coming was revealed to Daniel, and His name was revealed to Mary, His mother.

From the moment that Adam and Eve rebelled, disobeyed, and sinned against God, our loving heavenly Father was at work to redeem them and restore humankind's relationship. Through the centuries His revelation was made known to those who responded to Him by faith. God is always faithful to His promises. Miraculously, He continues to reveal Himself and to fulfill His promises to those who believe.

God's Word: For the Word of the Lord is right and true; he is faithful in all he does (Psalm 33:4).

Prayer: Father, the words of a hymn come to mind as I ponder how you have fulfilled Your promises: "Only believe, only believe. All things are possible if you only believe." Amen.

DECEMBER 25

HOW JESUS CAME

Happy birthday, Jesus! As we celebrate the birth of Jesus today, ponder the amazing way in which He came into the world.

Jesus came into the world by means of a virgin birth. Mary's conception was by the Holy Spirit and not by an earthly father, making Jesus fully God and fully man. His birth was the fulfillment of the prophecy of Isaiah: "Therefore the Lord himself will give you a sign: The virgin will conceive and give birth to a son and will call him Immanuel" (Isaiah 7:14).

He came as a servant. In all aspects of His life, Jesus served others and modeled servanthood. In His entire life, he never did one selfish thing for Himself. Jesus came as Savior. He came to seek and to save those who were spiritually lost. He who knew no sin came to take our sins upon Himself and to receive the punishment that we deserve.

Jesus came as Sovereign Lord. The angel revealed to Mary that there would be no end to his reign. Kingdoms would rise and fall, kings would live, reign, and die, but He would reign forever. And those who abide in Him will have eternal life. Apostle Paul said, "He is before all things, and in him all things hold together. And he is the head of the body, the church; he is the beginning and the firstborn from among the dead, so that in everything he might have the supremacy" (Colossians 1:17–18).

God's Word: For God was pleased to have all his fullness dwell in him, and through him to reconcile to himself all things, whether things on earth or things in heaven, by making peace through his blood, shed on the cross (Colossians 1:19).

Prayer: Father, we acknowledge you as Lord of Lords, and King of Kings. Yet, you have reached out to us in ways that even a little child can understand. Because of Jesus, we know of your love and desire for everyone to believe and be saved. Thank you for doing for us what we are unable to do for ourselves. Amen.

DECEMBER 26

NO EQUAL

Jesus, the Son of God, the Savior of the world, has no equal. Ponder the words of the apostle in Colossians 1:15–17:

> The Son is the image of the invisible God, the firstborn over all creation. For in him all things were created: things in heaven and on earth, visible and invisible, whether thrones or powers or rulers or authorities; all things have been created through him and for him. He is before all things, and in him all things hold together.

In his own words, Jesus declared himself to be the Messiah (John 4:25–26). In his famous prayer, he said, "Righteous Father, though the world does not know you, I know you, and they know that you have sent me (John 17:25). He called himself "The bread of life" (John 6:35) and "the light of the world" (John 8:12). He said, "I am the way and the truth and the life. No one comes to the Father except through me" (John 14:6), "I am the gate for the sheep" (John 10:7), "I am the good shepherd" (John 10:11), "I am the resurrection and the life" (John 11:25), "I am the true vine" (John 15:1).

Time devoted to exploring all that Jesus said about Himself will not only increase your understanding and appreciation of our Lord; it will also enrich your life and enhance your relationship with Him. No one cares more for you than Jesus.

God's Word: Hallelujah! Salvation and glory and power belong to our God, for true and just are his judgments (Revelation 19:1).

Prayer: Father, I stand amazed at the very thought of Jesus—who He was, what He did, and how much He loves me. Amen.

DECEMBER 27

LATE MAIL

A magazine to which I subscribe arrived in the mail on December 14. Inside was a note from the editor stating that I should be receiving this issue during the first week of November. He went on to complain of mail that took eleven days to go eighteen miles. Another mailing took three weeks to arrive. You may be experiencing some of the same problems.

If inefficient Postal Service and late mail disturb you, think how God must feel when over two thousand years ago he wrote a love letter to the world, and there are still those who have not received it.

God has called us to be His messengers and ambassadors to deliver His message of love to a lost world. Are you delivering the message? Why not? Someone is waiting to hear the good news, and you may be responsible for the late mail.

God's Word: Therefore go and make disciples of all nations, baptizing them in the name of the Father and of the Son and of the Holy Spirit, and teaching them to obey everything I have commanded you. And surely I am with you always, to the very end of the age (Matthew 28:19–20).

Prayer: Father, help me to spread the good news of Your love and salvation to those who are lost. Help me to deliver Your message without delay. Amen.

THE WISE MEN

We know little about the wise men who visited Jesus when He was about two years old. What we do know is worthy of our attention. We know that they were ancient-day astrologers. They were intelligent gentiles, foreigners, and were frowned upon by the Jews. They recognized Jesus as the promised Messiah while most of God's chosen people in Israel did not. Their response to the birth of Jesus was an act of faith. Their faith was so strong that they made a very long journey to worship Him.

The wise men represent those who are far away yet believe. Ironically, many who were physically close to Jesus, like the scribes, Pharisees, Jesus's brothers and sisters, the chief priests, and even Herod, refused to believe that Jesus was the Messiah.

When the wise men reached Jesus, they were filled with joy. They fell down and worshipped Him and presented their best gifts—gold, frankincense, and myrrh: gold, a gift offered to kings; frankincense, a perfume for priests; and myrrh, a bitter fragrance associated with sorrow and suffering, used for embalming the dead.

I like the bumper sticker that reads, "Wise Men Still follow the Star." Wise men embrace Jesus by faith. Wise men worship Him and serve Him. Wise men acknowledge Him as promised Messiah, King of Kings, High Priest, and Savior.

God's Word: Let the wise listen and add to their learning, and let the discerning get guidance" (Proverbs 1:5).

Prayer: Father, as the wise men of old found great joy in worshipping Jesus, help me to experience joy in my worship and in serving You. Amen.

DECEMBER 29

YOU ARE AN ORIGINAL

In his book *The Religion of a Mature Person*, Lofton Hudson writes: "Did you ever think of the fact that, of all the people in the world, of all those who have lived and of those who now live and even those who will live, there never has been or never will be another person just like you?"[21]

God has made you for your particular place in the world. Yet you may be burning up a great deal of energy trying to be like someone else. If you were born an original, why in the world would you want to be a copy of someone else?

The happiest people I know are those who are striving to be just what God intended them to be. The Bible says that you are made in the image of God. That makes you very special. In fact, you are unique! Be yourself. Don't waste time trying to be someone else.

God's Word: For we are God's handiwork, created in Christ Jesus to do good works, which God prepared in advance for us to do (Ephesians 2:10).

Prayer: Father, help me to use my uniqueness for your glory and honor. Amen.

---

[21] R. Lofton Hudson, *The Religion of a Mature Person*, Broadman Press, Nashville, TN, 1952, 43.

OUR CALLING

Karl Barth, the renowned theologian, said, "Christianity is not one of the world's great religions." He is right. Christianity is a movement of the Spirit of God in the heart of believers. Christianity is God taking the initiative to seek out humans while religion is humans seeking God.

When we become a Christian, we do not get the Christian religion. We get a personal relationship with the living Christ. Jesus does not call us to believe a certain doctrine or agree to a new ethical system. He calls us to follow Him, to be with Him, and to become like Him. You can be religious without being Christian, but you cannot go to heaven when you die unless you have a personal relationship with Jesus Christ who died to save you from your sins. Our calling is to come to Jesus.

God's Word: He has saved us and called us to a holy life—not because of anything we have done but because of his own purpose and grace (2 Timothy 1:9).

Prayer: Father, thank You for calling me into a personal relationship with You. Help me, I pray, to be faithful to my calling. Amen.

DECEMBER 31

THE MINISTRY OF ENCOURAGEMENT

Barnabas is one of the more significant personalities in the New Testament. His real name was Joseph, but the apostles affectionately nicknamed him Barnabas, which means "son of encouragement." We can call him the minister of encouragement.

Barnabas introduced the converted terrorist Saul to the Jerusalem church. Barnabas asked Paul to assist him in the work at Antioch where believers were first called Christians. Barnabas encouraged Paul to help him settle a dispute in the Jerusalem church and took famine relief to that Christian body. Barnabas sold his property and gave the proceeds to the Jerusalem church. Barnabas saved the ministry of John Mark, who gave up on the first missionary journey when Paul would have nothing more to do with him. Because of the encouragement of Barnabas, John Mark was not only reconciled to Paul but ministered to him when he was a prisoner in Rome. John Mark went on to write the Gospel of Mark. Tertullian, a prolific Christian author of early Christianity, refers to Mark as the author of Hebrews. In every aspect of his life, Barnabas was a minister of encouragement.

I know of no greater need in our world today than for Christians to be ministers of encouragement. I challenge you to be a Barnabas. Who can you encourage today?

God's Word: And let us consider how we may spur one another on toward love and good deeds, not giving up meeting together, as some are in the habit of doing, but encouraging one another—and all the more as you see the Day approaching. (Hebrews 10:24–25).

Prayer: Father, as Barnabas was a minister of encouragement to the church, help me to be an encourager in word and deed. Amen.

CELEBRATING ADVENT AT HOME

The four weeks before Christmas are traditionally called "Advent" or "Coming." Since the fourth century, Christians have set aside these weeks in December as a time for celebrating the coming of Jesus Christ, God's only Son, into the world. It is a time to focus on the wonder of the incarnation and God's love.

Traditionally, many churches provide a special time during the worship hour to focus on Advent. Church members are usually involved in explaining the meaning of the Advent wreath, reading scripture, and lighting the candles. Let me encourage you to also observe Advent in your home by purchasing or making an Advent Wreath with real or artificial greenery. On the outer circle, you will need three purple and one pink candle. Place one large white candle in the middle of the wreath to represent Christ.

A simple Advent service is provided in this devotional guide to help you in your family or personal worship. If you live alone, consider inviting a friend or neighbor to join you. Encourage everyone present to participate in the readings, scripture, and prayer.

Advent is a period of spiritual preparation as we celebrate Jesus's birth. Our preparation includes prayer, scripture, and reflecting on the significance of Jesus becoming flesh and dwelling among us. Use this time for prayer, confession of sins, and repentance.

The Advent wreath is filled with symbolism expressing our faith in Jesus, the King of Kings and Lord of Lords. The evergreen wreath signifies continuous life. The circle of the wreath with no beginning and no end symbolizes the eternity of God, the immortality of the soul, and the everlasting life we find in Christ.

The four candles around the wreath's circle represent the four weeks of Advent.

The first purple candle represents hope. The second purple candle represents peace. The pink candle represents joy, and the third purple candle represents love.

The Christ candle is white, and represents Christ, who is the center of our faith, the chief cornerstone, the Prince of Peace.

Chose a day and time that best fits your schedule and spend time meditating upon the significance of Jesus coming.

FIRST WEEK OF ADVENT

LIGHTING THE CANDLE OF HOPE
(PURPLE CANDLE)

This is the first week of Advent. We join Christians around the world in celebrating the coming of Jesus to save us from our sins. In the Gospel of John, we read the joyful news:

"The Word became flesh and made his dwelling among us. We have seen his glory,
The glory of the one and only Son, who came from
the Father, full of grace and truth.
(John 1:14)

Light the Candle

Today, we light the candle of hope, sometimes referred to as the prophet's candle. One of the unique features of Christianity is that the birth of Jesus was proclaimed by the prophets of the Old Testament many years before Jesus was born.

The psalmist said, "Blessed are those whose help is the God of Jacob, whose hope is in the Lord their God." (Psalm 146:5). Apostle Paul prayed for the Christians in Rome saying, "May the God of hope fill you with all joy and peace as you trust in Him, so that you may overflow with hope by the power of the Holy Spirit" (Romans 15:13). Justin Martyr, a second-century apologist, speaking about Jesus's birth said, "To declare a thing shall come to pass long before it is in being, and to bring it to pass, this or nothing is the work of God."

The prophets of the Old Testament proclaimed the preexistence, ancestry, birth, character, ministry, dual nature, death, and resurrection of Jesus centuries before he was born in a Bethlehem manger. No other faith tradition in the world can claim such a marvelous truth.

God's Word: The people walking in darkness have seen a great light; on those living in the land of deep darkness a light has dawned (Isaiah 9:2).

Prayer: Father, in this first week of Advent, we thank You for the hope that You brought into the world through your Son, Jesus Christ. Lighting the candle of hope today reminds us that Jesus is the Light of the World and that He also commissioned us to be the Light of the World. Let our light shine so that others can see Jesus through us. Amen.

SECOND WEEK OF ADVENT
LIGHTING THE CANDLE OF PEACE
(PURPLE CANDLE)

This is the second week of Advent. The Gospel of Luke records that amazing night when the angel visited the shepherds while they watched over their sheep by night. Their message to the startled shepherds was, "Do not be afraid, I bring you good news that will cause great joy for all the people. Today in the town of David a Savior has been born to you; he is the Messiah, the Lord" (Luke 2:10–11). The shepherds were told how they could find the baby and suddenly a host of angels appeared and began to sing:

> Glory to God in the highest heaven,
> And on earth peace to those on whom his favor rests.
> (Luke 2:14)

Today we light the Candle of peace, sometimes referred to as the angel's candle, because the heavenly hosts brought the good news of Jesus's birth to the humble shepherds.

Light the Candle

Trouble and fear abound in our world today. The reason is found in the sinful, rebellious nature of man. The only solution is Jesus Christ, the Son of God, the Savior of the world, and the personal Savior of all who will surrender to His Will.

God's Word: Peace I leave with you; my peace I give you. I do not give to you as the world gives. Do not let your hearts be troubled and do not be afraid (John 14:27).

May Jesus, who is peace, abide in our hearts in this season and forevermore.

Prayer: Father, as we light the candle of peace, we are reminded that only Jesus can give us the peace that passes understanding. Only Jesus, who is peace Himself, can guide us through the landmine of troubles that we face here on earth. Only Jesus can calm our fears, dry our tears, give us a purpose for living, and prepare a home for us in heaven. Thank You, Father, for the peace we have in Jesus. Amen.

THIRD WEEK OF ADVENT

LIGHTING THE CANDLE OF JOY
(PINK CANDLE)

This is the third week of Advent. As we ponder the significance of God sending His Son into the world, our hearts are filled with joy. We join the hymn writer Henry Van Dyke in praising God and singing:

> All Thy works with joy surround Thee,
> Earth and heaven reflect Thy rays,
> Stars and angels sing around Thee,
> Center of unbroken praise.
> Field and forest, vale and mountain,
> Flow'ry meadow, flashing sea,
> Singing bird and flowing fountain
> Call us to rejoice in Thee.

The prophet Isaiah said, "Shout aloud and sing for joy, people of Zion, for great is the Holy One of Israel among you" (Isaiah 12:6).

We light the candle of joy, sometimes known as the shepherd's candle, because joy filled the hearts of these humble herdsmen when they heard that the long-expected Messiah had been born in Bethlehem.

Light the Candle

God's Word: Trust in the Lord and do good ... take delight in the Lord ... commit your way to the Lord ... be still before the Lord and wait patiently for Him (Psalm 37:3–4, 5, 7).

Let us give thanks to God for the joy that Jesus brings to the lives of all who open their heart to Him.

Prayer: Father as we celebrate the coming of your Son into the world, we take delight in the joy that He brings to our lives. Without Him, we live in darkness and despair. Without him, we have no hope, no peace or joy. Thank you, heavenly Father, for lifting us out of the pit of sin and setting our feet upon the rock of salvation, and for putting the song of joy in our hearts. Amen.

FOURTH WEEK OF ADVENT
LIGHTING THE CANDLE OF LOVE
(PURPLE CANDLE)

This is the fourth week of Advent. John 3:16 is the central scripture of the Bible both in print and in truth:

> For God so loved the world, that he gave his one and only Son,
> that whoever believes in him shall not perish but have eternal life.

But that is not the end of the message. Verses 17 and 18 are equally important:

> For God did not send his Son into the world to condemn the world, but to save the world through him. Whoever believes in him is not condemned, but whoever does not believe stands condemned already because they have not believed in the name of God's one and only Son.

During the past three weeks of Advent, we lit the candles of hope, peace, and joy. Today, we light the candle of love.

Light the Candle

Jesus, the Son of God, was sent into the world to die for our sins. We cannot celebrate Christmas without thinking of Easter when we celebrate the death, burial, and resurrection of Jesus. He came to earth and laid down his life to save us from our sins.

We show our love for Jesus by surrendering our lives to Him, receiving His love into our hearts, accepting His forgiveness for our sins, and committing ourselves to serve Him without shame. We are commissioned by Jesus to take His gospel of love to all the world, teaching others what Jesus taught us, preaching the good news of His salvation, and baptizing those who repent of their sins.

In doing so, we have Jesus's promise that He will be with us always, even to the end of time. With the hope, peace, joy, and love that Jesus brings to us, let us be faithful in living for Him and proclaiming His message to a lost world.

God's Word: Greater love has no one than this: to lay down one's life for one's friends. You are my friends if you do what I command (John 15:13–14).

Prayer: Father, thank You for the love that You have given to us through Jesus Christ Your Son. Help us to show our gratitude and love to You by living for Jesus and helping others to know Him as their personal Savior. In Jesus's name we pray. Amen.

ADVENT ON CHRISTMAS DAY
LIGHTING THE CHRIST CANDLE
(WHITE CANDLE)

Over the past four weeks, we have lit the candles of hope, peace, joy, and love in celebration of the coming of Jesus Christ, the Son of God into the world.

We have been preparing our hearts for the greatest event in history. Our spiritual preparation has included prayer, reflection on the significance of Jesus becoming flesh and dwelling among us, confession of our sins, and repentance.

Apostle Paul described Jesus in this way:

> The Son is the image of the invisible God, the firstborn over all creation ... He is before all things, and in him all things hold together ... For God was pleased to have all his fullness dwell in him, and through him to reconcile to himself all things, whether things on earth or things in heaven, by making peace through his blood, shed on the cross." (Colossians 1:15, 17, 19–20)

Being pure and sinless, Jesus took upon Himself the punishment that we deserve for our sins. "God made him who had no sin to be sin for us, so that in him we might become the righteousness of God" (2 Corinthians 5:21).

Light the Candle

Today, we light the Christ candle. The Christ candle is white and represents Christ, who is the center of our faith, the chief cornerstone, the Prince of Peace. White signifies purity because Christ was without sin. The prophet John, exiled on the Isle of Patmos for preaching the gospel, had a vision. Ponder what he said:

God's Word: Then I heard every creature in heaven and on earth and under the earth and on the sea and all that is in them, saying

To him who sits on the throne and to the Lamb be praise and honor and glory and power forever and ever (Revelation 5:13).

Prayer: Father, as we celebrate Christmas, we thank You for sending Your son, Jesus, to save us from our sins. We thank You for the hope, peace, joy, and love that we have in Christ. Help us to walk in obedience to Christ. Help us to share our faith with boldness and to give Him honor and praise in all that we do. In Jesus's name we pray. Amen.

ABOUT THE AUTHOR

Charles Allard, a native of Wilmington, North Carolina, graduate of New Hanover High School, Mars Hill College, Furman University, and Southeastern Baptist Theological Seminary. has served as a pastor of six churches in North Carolina and as a missionary to Brazil for sixty-one years. He led mission teams to Brazil, Peru, and Spain for evangelism and church construction. Charles and his wife Gloria live in Apex, NC and have three children and four grandchildren.

CPSIA information can be obtained
at www.ICGtesting.com
Printed in the USA
BVHW042002010522
635848BV00017B/73

9 781664 262287